ersey, 1772) cf. *afterbirth, posthumous* **abscond** [...] n hiding, bu

]. (James Murray et al., 1888–1928) ✦"The poor [...] *ling* himself

[...]s, tasteless, foolish, [and] *surdus*, deaf, inaudible, [...] es Murray e

[...]ghthood, anciently consisting in an embrace, afte[...] w upon the

*collum*, the neck. (Edward Lloyd, 1895) **acre** In ancient times, an *acre* did not signify any dete[...]

[...]) cf. *yard* **actuary** The register or officer who compiles the minutes of the proceedings of the [...]

[...]Coxe, 1817) **adamant** A stone of such impenetrable hardness that it cannot be subdued—th[...]

[...]erring of this name to the lodestone, but it is common enough in our best English writers. (Rich[...]

[...]sed in this sense. Some of the old English writers so employed it. (James Bartlett, 1849) ✦A livel[...]

[...]y. (John Phin, 1902) ✦Licence. Shakespeare says, "Sir John, you are a gentleman of excellent br[...]

[...]e avowed another prince to be under his protection. *Merry Wives of Windsor*. (E. Cobham Brewe[...]

[...] to signify the person who adulterates or debases. In this sense, it has long been obsolete in Englan[...]

[...]onisation of new lands, or for trade with remote parts of the world. The official name which it [...]

[...]02) ✦Advice, counsel. (C. H. Herford, 1902) ✦Moral instruction. "My griefs cry louder than *adve*[...]

[...]ng." *Merchant of Venice*. (C. H. Herford, 1902) **afterbirth** Birth after a father's death or last w[...]

[...]ion of one's earthly life. (Edward Lloyd, 1895) ✦"Untutor'd minds stop here, and *after-life* leads them[...]

[...]35–36) ✦Second crop of grass mown in autumn. (Thomas Sheridan, 1789) ✦English *math*, or *mow*[...]

[...]ld French *eyme* and *estme*, is the same word with *esteem*, from Latin *æstimatio*, and should there[...]

[...]ik, 1886) **air-line** A direct line through the air; a bee-line. (James Murray et al., 1888–192[...]

[...]evel prairies lends itself admirably to those *air-lines*. Although strictly limited at first to the abo[...]

[...] to go direct by the shortest route. The origin of the expression is to be found in the straight lin[...]

[...]lines of railway are called *air line roads*, or "straight shoots." (John Farmer, 1889) **alchemy** [...]

[...]xed metal that, having the appearance of gold, was yet mainly composed of brass. Thus the notic[...]

[...]–60) cf. *chemist, medicine, multiplication* **alien** An outlandish man. (John Bullokar, 1616) cf. *ba*[...]

[...]t was not permitted to any one to alienate his property without the consent of the superior lord[...]

[...], 1895) cf. *ostracize* **amateur** One who loves, or is fond of; one who has a taste for anything[...]

[...]ds with people unable to leave their homes. (Albert Barrère, 1911)**ambidextrous** Double-d[...]

[...]inister **ambition** *Ambition*, strictly speaking, means the going from house to house, [from] th[...]

[...] different dwellings to solicit votes, and those who did so were *ambitious* of office. (E. Cobham

# Altered English
## Surprising Meanings of Familiar Words

# Altered English
## Surprising Meanings of Familiar Words

### JEFFREY KACIRK

*Pomegranate*

SAN FRANCISCO

Published by Pomegranate Communications, Inc.
Box 6099, Rohnert Park, California 94927
800 277 1428; www.pomegranate.com

Pomegranate Europe Ltd.
Fullbridge House, Fullbridge
Maldon, Essex CM9 4LE, England

Engravings by George Cruikshank (1792–1878) and his contemporaries, reproduced from three
London publications of William Hone: *The Every-day Book, or Everlasting Calendar* (1826–7), *The
Table Book of Daily Recreation and Information* (1827), and *The Year Book of Daily Recreation and
Information* (1832).

**Library of Congress Cataloging-in-Publication Data**
Kacirk, Jeffrey.
  Altered English : surprising meanings of familiar words / Jeffrey Kacirk
    p. lcm.
  Includes bibliographical references.
  ISBN 0-7649-2019-7 (alk. paper)
    1. English language—Archaisms—Dictionaries. 2. English language—Glossaries,
  vocabularies, etc. I. Title.

PE1667 .K325 2002
422'.03—dc21                                                      2001051155


Pomegranate Catalog No. A623

Cover and book design by Laura Lind Design

Printed in China

10  09  08  07  06  05  04  03  02      10 9 8 7 6 5 4 3 2 1

# Introduction

"When I use a word," Humpty Dumpty said in
rather a scornful tone, "it means just what I choose
it to mean—neither more nor less."

"The question is," said Alice, "whether you can
make words mean so many different things."

—Lewis Carroll, *Through the Looking-Glass*

Our language may be "the immediate gift of God," as pious lexicographer Noah Webster declared in the preface to his 1828 dictionary, but a significant number of the words we utter today have wandered a long and often mysterious path, affected by countless unobserved influences. In this regard, the eminent nineteenth-century language historian Max Müller even suggested that "there is background to almost every word we are using." Although many English words now mean essentially what they did five hundred years ago, much of what we assume to be an immutable bedrock of English has in fact been recycled, resurrected, or renovated in various ways. It was not uncommon for words like *gossip*, originally a baptismal sponsor, to broaden in scope to accommodate additional meanings, while some of their earlier meanings fell by the wayside. Other expressions, formerly more liberal in application, were later confined to increasingly specific tasks; examples include *autograph*, once to write anything by one's own hand, and *luggage*, first penned by Shakespeare in about 1596 to denote a heavy burden of any sort.

The well-documented impermanence of the meanings associated with English words—and those of other languages, for that matter—is certainly not a recent trend. The father of English poetry, Geoffrey Chaucer, confirmed this when he wrote in *Troilus and Criseyde* the Middle English equivalent of "You know well that, for a thousand years, the form of speech has changed, and words that then had certain meanings now seem wondrously foolish and odd to us. And yet people really spoke like that, and they succeeded as well in love as men do now." This comment seems as true today as it probably was when written, over six centuries ago.

# ANTIQUINYMS

The selections in *Altered English* offer terms with their earlier meanings that have gently faded or disappeared over time, often after helping to form successors. Surprisingly, we have no name for these bygone definitions, but I sometimes think of them as "antiquinyms." My goal in assembling these archaisms is to leave readers with a sense of where some modern expressions have come from, or in some cases have strayed, whether we think of the changes as corruptions or improvements. Many of these curious definitions contrast sharply with their modern counterparts; for example, the now-prestigious *penthouse* once referred to a lowly slope-roofed add-on to a building. Others diverged more subtly; the verb *abscond*, for instance, at one time meant to be in hiding, rather than to actively sneak away, as it does now.

A few arcane meanings presented here, such as that for *beef-eater*, may be familiar to a minority of readers, particularly those from the British Isles, but are included for the benefit of others. I have also included some formerly prominent usages that are still found in modern dictionaries yet for practical purposes are all but obsolete, even when not indicated as such by many dictionaries. Although these older meanings are occasionally employed by modern writers, teachers, and others in a historical context, they enjoyed their heydays in times past. Consider whether a word like *decimate* still refers to a brutal punishment of one soldier in ten, as it did during the Roman Empire. It seems that dictionaries must apply as much art as science to designating a meaning as defunct, in their quest to satisfy the technical and even legal needs of a very diverse readership. But I prefer to appreciate these linguistic fossils for their own sake, regardless of whether they persist in limited ways during their decline.

Today, the word *cockpit* most commonly denotes a portion of an aircraft or boat where control is maintained by navigators, but the traditional meaning of a purposely constructed place for the cruel and widely outlawed sport of cockfighting has not completely disappeared. This earlier meaning is slowly heading toward extinction from everyday English, along with many others of its kind, and may soon become a linguistic relic, embalmed in museums, dictionaries, and historical texts. As a footnote, *cockpit's* meaning was extended in Shakespeare's time to include the central portion of a theater—a building used then for animal-baiting. This area is still known as the orchestra *pit*.

# How Words Change

A distinctive pattern is often seen when a word's meaning changes significantly over time. First, the word acquires an additional, sometimes barely related, sense. Then, typically, the newer meaning coexists with the original —for a short time or for centuries. Finally, the elder usage recedes and disappears, leaving the newcomer as the sole reason for the word's existence. At the end of the tenth century, *cheap* indicated a marketplace in general, or the price or value of something; two hundred years later, it came to mean the act of buying or selling; then over time it represented something for sale that was inexpensive but worthwhile; and now it describes goods or services that are either inexpensive or of inferior quality or both. These "steps" are, in fact, a mostly seamless process analogous to the muscle-tendon-bone continuum of our body "parts."

As long ago as 1854, linguist Richard Chenevix Trench, whose insightful etymological comments highlight the following pages, described this transition in detail in a lecture at London's King's College:

> No word would illustrate this process better than that old example, familiar probably to us all, of *villain*. The villain is, first, the serf or peasant, [Latin] *villanus*, because attached to the *villa* or farm. He is secondly the peasant who, it is further taken for granted, will be churlish, selfish, dishonest, and generally of untoward moral conditions, these having come to be assumed as always belonging to him, and to be associated with his name by those of higher classes of society . . . who in the main commanded the language. At the third step, nothing of the meaning which the etymology suggests, nothing of *villa*, survives any longer.

A few more "textbook" cases may help us appreciate the organic nature of languages, particularly our own. A *waif* was once any kind of property found without an owner, which later included a man's woman, and eventually referred to a downtrodden person of either sex, or even an animal. Another progression involved the *stationer*, who was at first a nonitinerant merchant with a "station," then one who sold books and writing supplies, still in a shop or stall, and finally a person or company that sold these items—even exclusively on the Internet. Likewise, the Dutch word *ezel* referred to a donkey four centuries ago, but at one point artists discovered that these animals were useful for holding up their canvases. *Easel* was eventually imported by the English in the early 1600s, but only to describe the wooden frame used to support artistic works in progress.

## MEDIA INFLUENCE

Audiences have long relished and readily adopted mannerisms, new words, and variant meanings of traditional ones found in literature, song, stage shows, and now motion pictures. Eighteenth-century actor, director, and impresario David Garrick demonstrated this by breathing legitimacy into certain patterns of English pronunciation, such as the affected *ah* sound once commonly heard in words like *rather*, particularly among English aristocrats. After people witnessed Garrick's popular productions, life seemed to imitate art, and well-to-do English theatergoers adopted and maintained this theatrical peculiarity well into modern times. As a result of the phenomenon of media amplification, artists successfully fashioned a host of durable, media-sanctified terms. Those that have remained in our language include Shakespeare's inventions *launder*, *flawed*, and *outbreak*.

## WHAT I LOOK FOR

Expressions with multiple meanings—what an academic wordsmith might call polysemous words—initially piqued my interest because of their potential to show not only how words have evolved but also how the institutions or concepts they designate have developed. Thomas Blount's description of the term *veterinarian*, for instance, in his 1656 *Glossographia*, does this well: "He that lets horses or mules to hire; a muletor, a horse-courser, a hackney-man. Also, an horse-leach or farrier." With minimal explanation, Blount was able to convey to both contemporary and subsequent readers a foreshadowing of the modern veterinary profession, from a person who trained, sold, or rented out horses, to a blacksmith who shod, bled, medicated, and otherwise looked after an animal's health.

## ABOUT THE DEFINITIONS

In the interest of improving readability, I have lightly edited the most distracting archaic spellings, punctuation, and grammar, while attempting to represent the passages as faithfully as possible. Where an entry contained an obscure word or reference, I inserted brief bracketed comments, but only where their absence would give rise to unnecessary confusion. At the end of some entries, other entries with common characteristics are cross-referenced (marked cf.).

The dates of usage I have supplied point to the existence of literary evidence of a word's chronological whereabouts. They tell us that a specific meaning was used within a certain time period, but in fact this usage may have begun before, or echoed beyond those parameters, especially in oral context. These dates, which I drew from secondary sources such as the *New English Dictionary*, should be thought of as approximations, since correspondence, manuscripts, and other unpublished literary sources have been regularly lost.

A number of definitions include etymologies, which sometimes present an array of differing interpretations. For example, *nepos*, the Latin forerunner of *nepotism*, was translated by mid-nineteenth-century American dictionarian Joseph Worcester as a "nephew," while his younger contemporary Hensleigh Wedgwood opted to describe the same root more generally in 1878 as a "descendant," and Edward Lloyd chose "a grandson" as the meaning two decades later.

## ECCENTRIC ENTRIES

As I collected and prepared this manuscript, I noticed that my dictionaries and glossaries, especially the older ones, contained scattered examples of off-beat material. I included a few of these, along with a number of in-print malapropisms, which were not rare from the 1600s to the 1800s in written context and undoubtedly more common in speech. Shakespeare created characters, such as the comically self-important watchman Dogberry in *Much Ado about Nothing*, to demonstrate and parody the malapropism and its perpetrator, putting into his mouth such laughable sentences as, "Our watch, sir, hath indeed *comprehended* two *aspicious* persons." I also include a few spicy idioms, some specimens of slang and dialect, a dash of figurative terms, and samples of strangely worded oddities as they appeared in early dictionaries. For a bit of welcome counterpoint, I offer these semiprecious gems, such as Henry Cockeram's amusing stab at *anarchy*, "a kingdom without a king."

My fondest hope in presenting these weird and wonderful old meanings is that the reader will not only look at the particular words more closely but also marvel, as I often do, at the diverse and unforeseen word histories of the ocean of English that surrounds us.

# Acknowledgments

As I hinted in the introduction, I am deeply indebted to Richard Trench, considered by some to be the "godfather" of the *Oxford English Dictionary*, for his valuable contributions to the study of English. James Murray and his many colleagues and assistants from the *New English Dictionary* project, which gave rise to the *OED*, made my locating of these remarkable vignettes immeasurably easier and more enjoyable. The other mostly nineteenth-century philological professionals and amateurs who were the sources of my entries also deserve recognition, since without their love of this subject the roots of English might have remained partially obscured much longer.

Although I consider myself personally responsible for all lapses of judgment, I would like to heartily thank each member of my team of living assistants, beginning with my wife, Karen, and including (in alphabetical order) Zipporah Collins, Virginia McRae, Bruce Newling, Vincent P. O'Hara, and David Williams, for bringing their literary knowledge and editorial skills to bear on this undertaking. Thanks also to my agent Bonnie Solow, without whom I might still be sharing this material around my kitchen table, instead of seeing it distilled into the present form.

**abandon** This word, in Shakespeare's time, signified to banish, to drive away. "Therefore you, Clown, *abandon*—which is, in the vulgar—leave." *Taming of the Shrew.* (John Phin, 1902)

❖From French *à bandon*, at liberty . . . and Low Latin *bandum* a feudal term signifying an order, decree. *Abandon* means properly to go away from your general's ensign, to fly from your colours; [from] Latin *a*, away from, *bandum*, the general's banner. (E. Cobham Brewer, 1887)

cf. *transportation*

**abortion** The birth of a child before due time. (John Bullokar, 1616)

❖Miscarriage in women. (John Kersey, 1772)

cf. *afterbirth, posthumous*

**abscond** Abscond means properly to be in hiding, but we generally use the word in the sense of stealing off secretly. (E. Cobham Brewer, 1887)

❖To hide away; to conceal anything [1600s–early 1700s]. (James Murray et al., 1888–1928)

❖"The poor man fled from place to place, *absconding* himself." (John Strype, *Ecclesiastical Memorials*, 1721)

**absurd** Musically, inharmonious, jarring, out-of-tune; adaptation of Latin *surdus*, inharmonious, tasteless, foolish, [and] *surdus*, deaf, inaudible, insufferable to the ear [1600s]. (James Murray et al., 1888–1928)

❖"A harpe maketh not an *absurd* sound." (*Janua Linguarum*, 1617)

cf. *tune up*

**accolade** A ceremony used in conferring knighthood, anciently consisting in an embrace, afterward in giving the candidate a blow upon the shoulder with the flat of a sword, the latter being the present method; hence, the blow itself. (William Whitney, 1889)

❖From Latin *ad*, to, and *collum*, the neck. (Edward Lloyd, 1895)

**acre** In ancient times, an *acre* did not signify any determinate quantity, and when at length it came to mean a specific part, the measure still varied, until it was fixed by statute. (John Brockett, 1825)
cf. *yard*

**actuary** The register or officer who compiles the minutes of the proceedings of the court. (Thomas Sheridan, 1789)

**acupuncture** The Eastern method of bleeding, by striking needles into any pained part. (John Redman Coxe, 1817)

**adamant** A stone of such impenetrable hardness that it cannot be subdued—the diamond. Still used in this sense, but chiefly in poetry. (Edward Lloyd, 1895)
❖It is difficult to trace the exact motives which induced the transferring of this name to the lodestone, but it is common enough in our best English writers. (Richard Chenevix Trench, 1859–60)

**admire** To wonder at; to be affected with slight surprise. In New England, particularly in Maine, this word is used in this sense. Some of the old English writers so employed it. (James Bartlett, 1849)
❖A lively, eager wish. "I should *admire* to see the president." (M. Schele De Vere, 1872)

**admittance** Of high fashion; admitted into the best company. (John Phin, 1902)
❖Licence. Shakespeare says, "Sir John, you are a gentleman of excellent breeding, of great *admittance,*" that is, to whom great freedom is allowed. The allusion is to an obsolete custom called *admission*, by which a prince avowed another prince to be under his protection. *Merry Wives of Windsor.* (E. Cobham Brewer, 1887)

**adulterer** This word is, in the United States, not solely applied to a violator of the marriage vows. It is also used, instead of *adulterator*, to signify the person who adulterates or debases. In this sense, it has long been obsolete in England. (John Farmer, 1889)
cf. *sophistication*

**adventurer** Originally all who belonged to a company of merchants united for the discovery and colonisation of new lands, or for trade with remote parts of the world. The official name which it ultimately bore in this country [England] was the *Merchant Adventurers*. (Edward Lloyd, 1895)

**advertisement** Information. (John Phin, 1902)
❖Advice, counsel. (C. H. Herford, 1902)
❖Moral instruction. "My griefs cry louder than *advertisement*." *Much Ado about Nothing*. (Alexander Dyce, 1902)

**advice** Reflection. "My Lord Bassanio, upon more *advice*, hath sent you this ring." *Merchant of Venice*. (C. H. Herford, 1902)

**afterbirth** Birth after a father's death or last will; posthumous birth. Later birth, late-born children. (James Murray et al., 1888–1928)
cf. *abortion, posthumous*

**after-life** The subsequent portion of one's earthly life. (Edward Lloyd, 1895)
❖"Untutor'd minds stop here, and *after-life* leads them no further." (William Wordsworth, *Notebook Y in Prelude*, c. 1805)

**aftermath** That which comes and grows after mowing. (Samuel Pegge, 1735–36)
❖Second crop of grass mown in autumn. (Thomas Sheridan, 1789)
❖English *math*, or *mowth*, a mowing. (Edward Lloyd, 1895)

**age** A space of time containing one hundred years. (John Kersey, 1772)
cf. *century, world*

**aim** Aim, in Old French *eyme* and *estme,* is the same word with *esteem*, from Latin *æstimatio*, and should therefore signify properly a judgement, or conjecture of the mind, which is very nearly its meaning [in] "I have some *aim*." *Julius Caesar*. (George Craik, 1886)

**air-line** A direct line through the air; a bee-line. (James Murray et al., 1888–1928)
❖A railroad built in a straight line, avoiding all curves and windings. The term originated in the [American] West, where the surface of the level prairies lends itself admirably to those *air-lines*. Although strictly limited at first to the above sense, an air-line is now often extended to mean the most direct road from one point to another. (Sylva Clapin, 1902)
❖*To take the air line*, to go direct by the shortest route. The origin of the expression is to be found in the straight lines of railroad, without expensive detours and grades that in the New World are rendered possible by the vast

expanse of unbroken level. These lines of railway are called *air line roads*, or "straight shoots." (John Farmer, 1889)

**alchemy** By this word we always understand now the pretended art of transmuting other metals into gold, but it was often used to express itself a certain mixed metal that, having the appearance of gold, was yet mainly composed of brass. Thus the notion of falseness, of show and semblance not borne out by reality, frequently underlay the earlier uses of the word. (Richard Chenevix Trench, 1859–60)
cf. *chemist, medicine, multiplication*

**alien** An outlandish man. (John Bullokar, 1616)
cf. *barbaric, far-fetched, outlandish, uncouth*

**alienate** To transfer one's title of property to another. . . . Whilst the feudal law existed in full force, it was not permitted to any one to alienate his property without the consent of the superior lord. . . . Anciently, a person *alienating* lands and tenements to another contrary to law, as a punishment, forfeited them altogether. (Edward Lloyd, 1895)
cf. *ostracize*

**amateur** One who loves, or is fond of; one who has a taste for anything; adopted from French *amateur*, adaptation of Latin *amare*, to love. (James Murray et al., 1888–1928)
❖A man who makes a living by playing cards with people unable to leave their homes. (Albert Barrère, 1911)

**ambidextrous** Double-dealing. (Samuel Johnson, 1755)
❖Pretending agreement with each of two antagonistic parties. (Edward Lloyd, 1895)
cf. *dexterity, left-handed, sinister*

**ambition** *Ambition*, strictly speaking, means the going from house to house, [from] the Latin *ambitio*, going about canvassing. In Rome, it was customary some time before an election came on for the candidates to go round to the different dwellings to solicit votes, and those who did so were *ambitious* of office. (E. Cobham Brewer, 1887)
❖Oddly, and perhaps ignorantly, used instead of *grudge* or *spite*, is limited to Virginia and North Carolina, and those parts of the West to which it has

been carried thence. "He brought an action against me for *ambition*."
(M. Schele De Vere, 1872)
cf. *candid*

**amnesty** Forgetfulness, oblivion [1500s–1800s] (James Murray et al., 1888–1928)
cf. *oblivion*

**amphibious** Creatures of a doubtful kind, or of a doubtful element, as a bat, between a bird and a beast, [and] an otter, between a beast and a fish. (B. E., Gent, c. 1690)
cf. *antelope, caterpillar, reptile, snail*

**anarchy** A kingdom without a king. (Henry Cockeram, 1623)

**anatomy** An incision or cutting. (John Bullokar, 1616)
❖Now the act of dissection, but it was often used by our elder writers for the thing or object dissected, and then, as this was stripped of its flesh, for what we now call a *skeleton*. *Skeleton* had then another meaning . . . in stricter agreement with its etymology, the dried mummy. (Richard Chenevix Trench, 1859–60)

**ancient** Of children, precocious; of animals, cunning, clever. A well-trained dog would be called an *ancient* dog. A fox is a very *ancient* animal. (Michael Traynor, 1953)

**animosity** Courage. (John Bullokar, 1616)
❖Animation, spirit, as the fire of a horse, called in Latin *equi animositas*. (E. Cobham Brewer, 1887)
❖Spirit, boldness, without implying the presence of the malignant element. (Edward Lloyd, 1895)

**annoy** Injury, molestation. (Samuel Johnson, 1755)
❖Now rather to vex and disquiet than seriously to hurt and harm. But until a comparatively late day, it was true to its etymology, and admitted no such mitigation of meaning. (Richard Chenevix Trench, 1859–60)
cf. *worry*

**anointed** It is clear that to *anoint* a man was to give him a sound drubbing, and that the word was so used in the fifteenth century. An *anointed* *rogue* means either one who has been well thrashed, or deserves to be. In the North, they say humourously, "to *anoint* with the sap of a hazel rod." (Walter Skeat, 1896)

**antelope** A certain mongrel beast begotten of an hart and a goat. (Edward Phillips, 1706)
cf. *amphibious, caterpillar, reptile, snail*

**anthropomorphose** One would expect this verb to mean to change into the form of a man, but Davies shows an example from Howell's *Parley of Beasts* [1660] in which it evidently means to change from the form of a man into that of a beast: "I humbly desire to see some of those human creatures that you have *anthropomorphos'd* and transform'd to brute animals." [From] Greek *anthropos*, a man, and *morpho*, to form, to give shape to. (Edward Lloyd, 1895)

**antichrist** Any one who denies the Father and the Son, or who will not confess that Jesus Christ is come in the flesh. (Edward Lloyd, 1895)
cf. *Christian*

**antics** Strange gestures now, but the makers of these strange gestures once. (Richard Chenevix Trench, 1859–60)
❖Clowns, jesters. *Troilus and Cressida*. (C. H. Herford, 1902)
cf. *cosmetic, pantomime, zany*

**aplomb** True to the plumb line. (E. Cobham Brewer, 1887)
cf. *plumber*

**apology** The act of making a defence against an accusation; also the defence made, [from] Greek *apologia*, a speech in defence. (Edward Lloyd, 1895)
❖When Bishop Watson, in defending Christianity and the Bible from the attacks of Gibbon and Thomas Paine, entitled his books *An Apology for Christianity*, and *An Apology for the Bible*, he used the word *apology* in its primitive sense of a defence. (William Mathews, 1884)

**apostrophe** A figure of speech by which . . . a speaker turns from his audience to one person, and addresses him singly. Now, however, the signification is wider, and is made to include cases in which an impassioned orator addresses the absent, the dead, or even things inanimate, as if they were present and able to hear and understand his words [1500s–1800s]. (Edward Lloyd, 1895)

**apparel** The furniture of a ship, as sails, rigging, anchor, &c. [From] French *appareil*, preparation, dressing, apparatus. (Edward Lloyd, 1895)
❖The furniture and appendages of a house, fortress, gun, etc. [1300s–1500s]. (James Murray et al., 1888–1928)
cf. *furniture*

**applicant** One who applies himself closely to his studies. (James Bartlett, 1849)
❖A diligent student. (John Pickering, 1816)
cf. *undertaker*

**aquarium** Latin for, "a watering place for cattle." (Edward Lloyd, 1895)

**ark** The large chest in farmhouses used for keeping meal or flour. The arks are usually made of strong oaken planks, which are sometimes elaborately carved. They resemble the chests found in churches which are never . . . called *arks*. Many of the arks are of high antiquity. The making of them must have constituted a distinct trade, as we have the surname, Arkwright. As the Welsh have *arkh* in the sense of 'coffin,' it is not impossible that the ark may be a relic of the Celtic. (Joseph Hunter, 1829)

**artificial** Cunning, well contrived, skillful. (John Bullokar, 1616)
❖That was *artificial* once which wrought, or which was wrought, according to the principles of art. The word has descended into quite a lower sphere of meaning. (Richard Chenevix Trench, 1859–60)

**aspersion** Sprinkling, as of dew. *The Tempest*. (C. H. Herford, 1902)
❖The original [biblical] sense of the word [to cast *aspersions*, or false accusations] is now not in use. (James Halliwell, 1855)
cf. *mildew*

**assassinate** A robbing, spoiling, or murthering in the highway. (John Bullokar, 1616)
cf. *bribery*

**ass-hole** A place for receiving ashes; [from] Saxon asce, ashes. (John Brockett, 1825)
❖*Asse-hole*, or ash-pit, is supposed by some philologists to be derivable from the Gaelic *aisir*, a receptacle; *ais*, the back part of anything. (Charles Mackay, 1888)

**asterisk** A little star. (Elisha Coles, 1713)
cf. *disaster*

**astrology** Originally, the word *astrology*, as yet unspecialized, included both the true science of *astronomy* and the pseudo-science. (Edward Lloyd, 1895)
❖As *chemist* only little by little disengaged itself from *alchemist* . . . so *astronomer* from *astrologer*. . . . It was long before the broad distinction between the lying art and the true science was recognized and fixed in words. (Richard Chenevix Trench, 1859–60)

**asylum** *Asylum* is a word often used in America when the idea intended to be conveyed is that which an Englishman attaches to the word *almshouse*. (Sylva Clapin, 1902)
❖*Asylum* means, literally, a place where pillage is forbidden, [from] Greek *a sylaö*, not to pillage. (E. Cobham Brewer, 1887)

**attire** *Attire* originally meant a head-dress; [from] French *atour*, a *tour de tête*. (E. Cobham Brewer, 1887)

**attorney** Such a person as, by consent, commandment, or request, takes heed, fees, and takes upon him the charge of other men's business in their absence. It was anciently used for those who did any business for another; now only law. (Samuel Johnson, 1755)
❖Shakespeare makes a verb of it in *Measure for Measure*. (James Halliwell, 1855)
cf. *vicarious*

**aunt** A woman of bad character; a procuress or a bawd. This sense is common in the early plays, although *aunt* and *uncle* were the usual appellations given by a jester or fool to all elderly persons, without implying any improper meaning, a custom, according to Pegge, generally pursued in Cornwall. (James Halliwell, 1855)

❖"One of my *aunts*" is, in Newcastle, a designation for a lady of more complaisance than virtue. (John Brockett, 1825)
❖A grandmother. (Joseph Wright, 1896–1905)
cf. *brother-in-law, father-in-law, foster-child, nephew, niece*

**autograph** Anything written with one's own hand, as a letter; an original manuscript, as distinguished from a copy. (Edward Lloyd, 1895)
cf. *character*

**avalanche** *Avalanche* means properly a gulp, something swallowed, [from] French *avaler*, to swallow. (E. Cobham Brewer, 1887)

**average** The first part of the word corresponds to the French *avoir*, to have; or, if we put an *h* to it, and turn the *v* back to the original *b*, we shall see the original Latin *habere*, to have. The "havings" or possessions of a farmer were his cattle—oxen, mules, and horses—and he was obliged, when called upon to do so, to place them at the disposal of his lord's retainers for carrying their armour and provisions in any warlike expedition. It was incumbent upon him to carry a stipulated quantity—say twenty or a hundred loads—and this was the "average" laid upon his cattle, but the number of cattle he might use was optional. An ox or an ass cannot carry what a horse can, [so] he might have many yoke of oxen and few horses, or the reverse, but the *average* remained the same. (Basil Hargrave, 1925)

**avid** Greedy, covetous. (Edward Lloyd, 1895)

**awesome** Frightful, horrible. (Adam and Charles Black, 1851)
cf. *tremendous*

**awful** *Awe*-inspiring. *King John*. (C. H. Herford, 1902)
❖Sublime; majestic in a high degree. Fitted to inspire veneration, or actually inspiring it. Respectful in a high degree; done or performed with great reverence. (Edward Lloyd, 1895)

**awkward** Turned to the left; [from] English *awk*, the left hand. (Edward Lloyd, 1895)
❖Morally or physically perverse; contrary, sinister, unlucky. (Richard Chenevix Trench, 1859–60)
❖Backward. Shakespeare, Marlowe, and Drayton have *awkward* for 'adverse,' [regarding] winds. (James Halliwell, 1855)
cf. *sinister*

**awning** A sail or tarpawling hung over any part of a ship; [from] *awn*, the scale or hulk of any thing; the spire or beard of barley, or any bearded grain. (Nathaniel Bailey, 1749)

**bachelor** A person who, though a knight, had not a sufficient number of vassals to have his banner carried before him in battle. One who was not old enough to display a banner of his own and therefore had to follow that of another. One who, on the first occasion that he took part in a tournament, overcame his enemy. (Edward Lloyd, 1895)
❖From Low Latin *baccalaria*, a cowherd, or man attached to a *baccalaria*, or grazing farm, so named from Low Latin *bacca*, a cow. (Walter Skeat, 1923)

**backlog** A large log, used in fireplaces to support the other fuel. (Sylva Clapin, 1902)

**backward** A privy, so called from its position at the back of the house. (Sylva Clapin, 1902)

**bad egg** A Californianism for a worthless speculation. (John Farmer, 1889)

**baffle** To treat ignominiously. (Alexander Dyce, 1902)
❖To use contemptuously; to unknight. It was originally a punishment of infamy, inflicted on recreant [cowardly or unfaithful] knights, one part of which was hanging them up by the heels. . . . The word appears in Shakespeare's *Richard II*, in the more general sense, but in the following passage [from 1 *Henry IV*] . . . something of the same kind is implied, where Falstaff says, "If thou do it half so gravely, so majestically, both in word and matter, hang me up by the heels." (Robert Nares, 1859)
❖Baffled, disgraced, dishonoured. (James Murray et al., 1888–1928)
cf. *ordeal, treadmill, whirligig*

**baker's dozen** Sometimes fourteen. (Joseph Wright, 1896–1905)
cf. *forty*

**bald** Rotund, full of habit, corpulent. (James Murray et al., 1888–1928)

❖Mean, base, without dignity or value. (Noah Webster, 1828)
cf. *crummy, morbid*

**ballad** *Ballad* means, strictly, a song to dance-music, or a song sung while dancing; [from] Italian ballare, to dance, our ballet. (E. Cobham Brewer, 1887)
❖A proverbial saying, usually in form of a couplet. (James Murray, 1888–1928)
❖"Spend, and God shall send . . . saith th'olde *ballet*." (John Heywood, *Epigrammes*, 1562)
cf. *burden, carol*

**ballot** The *ballot* is properly a mode of voting in which little balls are used. (Sidney Low and F. S. Pulling, 1904)
❖A small ball used for secret voting; adaptation of Italian *ballotta*, 'a rounde bullet' [late 1500s–1700s]. (James Murray et al., 1888–1928)

**bamboozle** A Chinese and Gypsie word meaning to dress a man in bamboos to teach him swimming. Like the bladders used for the same purpose by little wanton boys, the apparatus is dangerous and deceitful. (E. Cobham Brewer, 1887)

**banister** A hamper in which charcoal used to be carried to the furnace. (Joseph Wright, 1896–1905)

**banquet** What we now call a *dessert*, a slight refection, consisting of cakes, sweetmeats, and fruit, and generally served in a room to which the guests removed after dinner. (Alexander Dyce, 1902)
❖Evelyn used *banquet* in the sense of a dessert as late as 1685, though the modern signification had already come into partial use. (Edward Lloyd, 1895)
❖The common place of *banqueting*, or eating the dessert, was the garden-house or arbour, with which almost every dwelling was furnished. . . . It was not uncommon to have the performance of a play, or some other amusement, between the dinner and the *banquet*. (Robert Nares, 1859)
cf. *junkets, symposium*

**barbaric** Foreign; far-fetched. (Samuel Johnson, 1755)
cf. *alien, far-fetched, outlandish, uncouth*

**barbarize** To *barbarize* is a word fortunately confined to barbers, whose occupation it is intended to express. (M. Schele De Vere, 1872)
❖For gentlemen, instead of "barbourising" themselves, to use the expression

of the day, they were dependent on their servants or their wig-makers to shave their heads. (H. G. Graham, 1899)

**barge** A state or pleasure boat, built with a room capable of containing several persons. (Daniel Fenning, 1775)
❖A sea-commander's boat. (William Grimshaw, 1854)

**barnacles** Spectacles, or rather reading-glasses, so called because in shape they resemble the twitchers used by farriers to keep under restraint unruly horses during the process of bleeding, dressing, or shoeing. This instrument, formerly called a *barnacle*, consisting of two branches joined at one end by a hinge, was fixed on the horse's nose. Dr. Latham considers the word a corruption of *binocles*, double-eyes. (E. Cobham Brewer, 1887)

**baseness** Deepness of sound. (Edward Lloyd, 1895)

**bashful** In a bad sense, of cunning, or any similar quality. *The Tempest*. (Edward Lloyd, 1895)

**bastard** An artificially-sweetened Spanish wine. *1 Henry IV*. (C. H. Herford, 1902)

**bastardize** To convict of being a bastard. (Stephen Jones, 1818)
❖To render one a bastard by legislation. To beget a bastard. *King Lear*. (Edward Lloyd, 1895)

**bauble** Originally, a stick with a lump of lead hanging from its summit, used to beat dogs with. Later, a short stick or wand with a head with asses' ears carved at one end of it. (Edward Lloyd, 1895)
❖Primarily, a sort of scepter or staff of office, the attribute of Folly personified, carried by the jesters of kings and great lords in the middle ages, and down to the seventeenth century. It is generally represented as crowned with the head of a fool or zany, wearing a party-colored hood with asses' ears, and with a ring of little bells, like sleigh-bells. At the other end, there was sometimes a ball or bladder inflated with air, with which to belabor people. (William Whitney, 1889)
cf. *zany*

**bawd** Figuratively of things, whatever renders anything else more attractive than it otherwise would be, with the view of gaining the favour of spectators. (Edward Lloyd, 1895)

❖Once not confined to one sex only, but could have been applied to pandar and pandaress alike. (Richard Chenevix Trench, 1859–60)

**beauty-sleep** The sleep taken before midnight, popularly regarded as the most refreshing portion of the night's rest. (William Whitney, 1889)

**bed and board** Of a wife, full connubial relations, as wife and mistress of the household. (James Murray et al., 1888–1928)

**beef-eater** The French *buffitier*, a man who waits at the *buffet*, which was a table near the door of the dining-hall for poor people, travellers, and pilgrims, to help themselves to what was not wanted at the high table, has been changed in English into *beef-eater*, and it is no doubt a vulgar error that these tall, stalwart fellows are chiefly fed on beef. (Max Müller, 1863)
❖So called because they used to watch the *buffet*, and hence were called *boufitiers*, in Norman-French, "waiters at the side-board." (E. Cobham Brewer, 1887)

**belch** In early use . . . having no offensive meaning, but in later use confined, by association with other senses, to the utterance of things foul or offensive. (James Murray et al., 1888–1928)

**belfry** A military tower pushed by besiegers against the wall of a besieged city, that missiles may be thrown more easily against the defenders; [from] Greek *belos*, a missile, and *phreo*, to dart forth. Probably a church steeple is called a *belfry* from its resemblance to these towers, and not because bells are hung within it. (E. Cobham Brewer, 1887)
❖Sentinels were placed on it to watch the avenues, and to prevent surprise, or to give notice of fires by ringing a bell. (Edward Lloyd, 1895)

**benefit of clergy** Exemption of the clerical order from civil punishment, based on the text, "Touch not mine anointed, and do my prophets no harm," (1 Chronicles 16:22). In time, it comprehended not only the ordained clergy but all who, being able to write and read, were capable of entering into Holy Orders. This law was abolished in [1827]. (E. Cobham Brewer, 1887)

**beverage** The third sense of this term, as given by Johnson, is "A treat upon wearing a new suit of clothes." In Scotland, it suggests another idea. The *beverage* of a new piece of dress is a salute given by the person who appears in it for the first time, more commonly by a male to a favourite female. One is said to *give the beverage*, or to *get the beverage*, as "She got the *beverage* of his brand new coat." One or two generations ago, when the use of the razor was more sparing, it was very common for a man to give the *beverage of his beard*. (John Jamieson, 1879)
❖A treat at first coming into a prison, called also *garnish*. (Samuel Johnson, 1755)
cf. *footing, garnish*

**bible** A book of any kind [in] Scotland [1300s–1600s]. (Joseph Wright, 1896–1905)

**bicker** To pelt with stones; to indulge in rough or indelicate horseplay. (Alexander Warrack, 1911)
❖To skirmish, exchange blows; to fight. Said of archers and slingers before battle was joined. (James Murray et al., 1888–1928)
❖*Bickering*, a fight carried on with stones. (John Jamieson, 1879)

**bigamy** The marriage of [a man to] two wives, not both together but [a second] after the death of the first. (John Bullokar, 1616)
❖An impediment that hinders a man from being a clerk, because he has been married twice. (Nathaniel Bailey, 1749)

**billion** A million of millions [1,000,000,000,000]. (James Donald, 1877)
cf. *century, myriad, trillion*

**binge** To soak, especially to swell a leaky wooden vessel by filling it with, or plunging it into, water. Figuratively, of persons, to soak, to drink deeply. (Joseph Wright, 1896–1905)

**birth-right** Of the privileges thus acquired by a first-born. (Edward Lloyd, 1895)

**biscuit** Literally, 'bread twice cooked or baked'; so prepared by Roman soldiers. From French *bis,* twice, *cuit,* baked. (Daniel Lyons, 1897)

**bisexual** Having the organs of both sexes in one individual. (William Whitney, 1889)
cf. *testicle, womb*

**bisque** A fault at tennis. (Elisha Coles, 1713)
❖A stroke allowed to the weaker player. (Nathaniel Bailey, 1749)

**bitch** A term of contempt applied to a man. (William Grant, 1941)
❖To spoil, destroy, disfigure. If several people were making an arrangement, and one by a blunder spoilt it, he would have *bitched* the whole thing. (Michael Traynor, 1953)
❖*Bitching,* a cant term denoting a species of low buffoonery much admired and practised in some of our Paisley clubs. Still heard, meaning "pulling one's leg," trying to belittle one. (William Grant, 1941)

**bitter end** Originally a nautical expression applied to the end of a ship's cable. Admiral Smyth's *Sailor's Word-book* explains it as, "that part of the cable which is abaft the bitts," the two pieces of timber to which a cable is fastened when a ship rides at anchor. When a chain or rope is paid out to the *bitter end,* no more remains to be let go. It seems, therefore, that the phrase "to the bitter end," was originally used as equivalent to the extreme end, but the non-nautical mind, misinterpreting the word *bitter,* gradually made it synonymous with "to the bitter *dregs,*" to the death, in a severe or pitiless manner, from a fancied analogy to such expressions as "a bitter foe." (William Walsh, 1900)

**blackballing** Stealing or pilfering; a sailor's word. It originated amongst the employees of the old Black Ball line of steamers between New York and Liverpool. The cruelty and scandalous conduct of officers to men, and sailors to each other, became so proverbial that the line of vessels in question became known all over the world for the . . . thieving propensities of its sailors. (John Farmer, 1889)

**black-list** A name popularly given in England and the United States to printed lists privately circulated among subscribers . . . of insolvents and bankrupts, protested bills, judgments for debt, and other matters affecting the credit of firms and individuals, and intended for the guidance of merchants, and others in the trade. (A. Colange, 1871)

**blame** To attribute to, give credit to, where no fault is implied. (Michael Traynor, 1953)

**bland** Whey, mixed with water, a drink used in the Shetland Islands. . . . *Soor blannd* is a delicious and quenching drink, and used to be in every cottage for common use. It is what fashionable doctors recommend for consumptives under the name of the "sour whey cure." (William Grant, 1941)

**blink** To exercise the powers of the "evil eye." If a cow shows symptoms of illness, moans, gives little milk, she has been *blinked* by someone; also said of milk if it fails to make butter. A remedy, which is still seen, is to tie a red ribbon on the horns of the animal. Hence *blinker*, one who has the powers of the evil eye. (Michael Traynor, 1953)

**blizzard** This word at first meant a smart blow, and was so used by Col. Crockett['s] *Tour Down East* in 1834. During the hard winter of 1880–1, it came into general use . . . to signify an intolerable snowstorm. (Richard Thornton, 1912)
❖Some authorities derive it from the German *blitz*, lightning. . . . The word [perhaps imported by Pennsylvanians] was always used to include the idea of violence, spitefulness, or vindictiveness. If one dealt another a hostile blow, he gave him a *blizzard* on the nose. If a man's wife scolded him, she gave him a *blizzard*. When it is remembered that Pennsylvania is the state in which the Dutch or German element most largely predominates, it does not seem so farfetched to attribute its origin to a Teutonic source. (John Farmer, 1889)

**blockhead** A wooden head; a wooden block for hats or wigs. (James Murray et al., 1888–1928)

**blood money** Money paid to the next of kin [to compensate] for the slaughter of a relative. (James Murray et al., 1888–1928)

**bloody** Allied by blood; of good blood; well descended. (James Murray et al., 1888–1928)
❖"He comes from a *bloody* stock." (Edward Peacock, 1877)

**blunderbuss** Primarily a man who *blunders* in his work, does it in a noisy, violent way; subsequently applied to a short, wide-mouthed noisy gun [late 1600s–1700s]. (Hensleigh Wedgwood, 1878)

**blush** Resemblance. "He has a *blush* of his mother." (John Brockett, 1825) cf. *favour*

**boggle** To flinch, to start, as a horse does at a visible object. (Samuel Pegge, 1814)
❖To fumble, bungle, make a clumsy attempt. (James Murray et al., 1888–1928)
❖*To boggle,* meaning to embarrass, is often used in the state of New York. "His affairs were found to be woefully *boggled,* and his creditors have little chance to recover anything." (M. Schele De Vere, 1872)
❖To be uncertain what to do; probably from *bog,* a quagmire. (Nathaniel Bailey, 1749)
❖To play the hypocrite. (Edward Lloyd, 1895)
❖A spectre or ghost; [from] Welsh *bugal,* fear. *Boggle about the stacks*, a favourite play among young people in the villages, in which one hunts several others. (John Brockett, 1825)

**bombard** A large, leathern vessel for distributing liquor. *The Tempest.* (Alexander Dyce, 1902)

**bombast** Now inflated diction, words which, sounding lofty and big, have no real substance about them. This, which is now the sole meaning, was once only the secondary and the figurative, *bombast* being literally the cotton wadding with which garments are stuffed out and lined. (Richard Chenevix Trench, 1859–60)

✧Cotton padding used in giving an artificial rotundity to the Elizabethan doublet. "My sweet creature of *bombast*." *1 Henry IV.* (C. H. Herford, 1902)

**bonfire** If the opinion of so high an opinion as Skeat be accepted, the etymology of this word is more nearly connected with Protestantism than is generally admitted. He considers that it is formed from the English *bone* and *fire*, and that it originally had reference to the burning of ecclesiastical relics in the time of Henry VIII. Certainly the derivations *baun*, as Scandinavian for 'beacon,' and *bon*, French for 'good,' do not appear to be adequately supported. (Basil Hargrave, 1925)

**bonnet** A head-dress for men worn before the introduction of hats. It is what is now called a *cap*. (Edward Lloyd, 1895)
cf. *chaperon*

**bookworm** A reader who, always operating upon books, can appreciate little or nothing about them but the paper on which they are printed and the covers in which they are bound. (Edward Lloyd, 1895)

**borrow** To ransom, and not, as in English, to effect a loan. (Charles Mackay, 1888)

**botch** To make good or repair a defect, damaged article. (James Murray et al., 1888–1928)
✧*Botcher*, a mender of old clothes. (John Phin, 1902)

**bother** To deafen. Used mostly in Ireland. (Samuel Pegge, 1814)
✧To confuse with excessive noise, chatter; hence *bothered*, deaf. (Michael Traynor, 1953)

**boudoir** Literally, a place to sulk in; [from] French *bouder*, to sulk. Root uncertain, but perhaps from the same source as English *pout*. (Walter Skeat, 1879–82)

**boulevard** Originally, the horizontal surface of a rampart. [From] Old French *boulevert*, a bulwark. (Edward Lloyd, 1895)

**bouquet** A thicket, a clump or plantation of trees. (Edward Lloyd, 1895)
cf. *plantation*

**bourgeois** Thieves' [slang] for *bourg*, a large village. Literally, "man of the middle class." The peasants give this appellation to the townspeople; a coachman to his fare; workmen and servants to their employer; workpeople to the master of the house; soldiers to civilians. Artists and literary men use it contemptuously to denote a man with matter-of-fact, unartistic tastes; also [to denote] a man outside their profession. The anarchists apply this epithet to one who does not share their views. (Albert Barrère, 1911)
cf. *villain*

**bowling** The smooth, even motion of ordinary dancing, as distinguished from the jumps and capers of the satyrs. *Cymbeline*. (C. H. Herford, 1902)
❖*Bowling-match*, a game with stone bowls, played on the highways, from village to village, [in] Northern England. (James Halliwell, 1855)
cf. *gripe*

**box-seat** A square pew in church. (Joseph Wright, 1896–1905)
❖A seat . . . on the box of a coach. (William Whitney, 1889)
cf. *pew*

**braid** To nauseate, to desire to vomit; hence the word *upbraid*. *Braid* is an obsolete word for reproach. (John Brockett, 1825)
❖Untrustworthy, full of sly turns. "Frenchmen are so *braid*." *All's Well that Ends Well*. (C. H. Herford, 1902)

**brat** The same word as *brood*, it is now used always in contempt, but was not so once. Gascoigne's *De Profundis* [has] "O Abraham's *brats*, O brood of blessed seed, O chosen sheep that loved the lord indeed." (Richard Chenevix Trench, 1859–60)

**brave** Finely arrayed; hence showy, splendid. (C. T. Onions, 1911)
❖I do not very clearly trace by what steps it obtained the meaning of 'showy, gaudy, rich,' which once it so frequently had, in addition to that meaning which it still retains. (Richard Chenevix Trench, 1859–60)
❖*Bravery*, bravado. "Malicious *bravery*." *Othello*. (C. H. Herford, 1902)
❖*Bravery*, finery, sumptuous apparel, magnificence. "Witless *bravery*." *Measure for Measure*. (Alexander Dyce, 1902)

**brawl** The word *brawl*, in its signification of a dance, is from the French *branle*, indicating a shaking or swinging motion. . . . It was performed by several persons uniting hands in a circle, and giving each other continual shakes, the steps changing with the tune. . . . With this dance, balls were usually opened. *Love's Labour's Lost*. (Francis Douce, 1807)

**brawn**  The flesh of the boar, being muscular rather than fat, is termed *brawn*, and formerly the boar himself had the same name. (David Booth, 1835) ✤*Brawn* means distinctively the meat of a boar and, properly speaking, is applied to the thick portion of the boar, cut from the shoulders and neck. (W. L. Blackley, 1869)

**brazen**  Belonging to or made of brass [1000–1800s]. (John Kersey, 1772)

**breadwinner**  Any instrument of a profession by the use of which one earns a sustenance. (John Jamieson, 1879)

**breakfast**  Any meal which *breaks* the temporary *fast* of a man or a beast. *Two Gentlemen of Verona*. (Edward Lloyd, 1895)

**breast**  A voice "The fool has an excellent *breast*." *Twelfth Night*. (Alexander Dyce, 1902)

**breeder**  A particularly fine day, especially if out of season, is said to be a *weather-breeder*, [because] worse must be expected soon. . . . Also they call it a *breeder* if the sky looks red and angry in a morning. (Alfred Easther, 1883)

**breeze**  The ashes and cinders sold by the London dustmen for brickmaking are known by the name of *breeze*. In other parts of England, the term *briss* or *brist* is in use for dust, rubbish. [From] French *bris*, *débris*, rubbish. (Hensleigh Wedgwood, 1878)
✤Probably adopted from Old French *brese*, burning charcoal, hot embers. (James Murray et al., 1888–1928)

**bribery**  *Bribery*, in old English, meant not secret corruption but theft, rapine, open violence, and very often official extortion. The ministers of civil and ecclesiastical power needed not to conceal their rapacity, and they availed themselves of the authority belonging to their positions for the purpose of undisguised plunder. But when by the light—first of religious, and then civil liberty—men were able to see that it was of the essence of law that it should bind the governors as well as the governed . . . alike, it became necessary for official robbery to change its mode of procedure, and mantle with the cloak of secrecy the hand that clutched the spoil. But though the primitive form of this particular iniquity is gone, the thing remains, and the unlawful

gains of power, once seized with strong hand, are still *bribes*. (George P. Marsh, 1863)
cf. *jilt, rape, usury*

**brief** Plentiful, common, frequent; as, "vipers are very *brief* here." (Samuel Pegge, 1735–36)
❖*Brief* is used in the [American] South, as in some parts of England, very often for 'prevalent,' and has been regarded as a corruption of *rife*. (M. Schele De Vere, 1872)
cf. *viper*

**brink** The brim of a hat. (Joseph Wright, 1896–1905)

**broadside** Printed matter spread over an entire sheet of paper. The whole must be in one type and one measure, *i.e.* must not be divided into columns. A *folio* is when the sheet is folded, in which case a page occupies only *half* the sheet. (E. Cobham Brewer, 1887)

**broker** Them amongst us that buy and sell old *broken* apparell and household stuff. (William Rastell, 1624)
❖*Brokerage*, the pay or reward of a *broker*. William Grimshaw, 1854

**brother-in-law** A half-brother. (James Halliwell, 1855)
cf. *cousin, father-in-law*

**brunette** A woman with a brown complexion. (William Grimshaw, 1854)
❖A nut-browne girle. (Randle Cotgrave, 1611)
❖"Your fair women . . . thought of this fashion to insult the Olives and the *Brunettes*." (*London Guardian*, 1713)

**budget** In former days, the *budget* was literally a sack full of money, the various sums appropriated to specific purposes being sorted into little bags. The word *budget* is derived from the Latin *bulga*, a bag, coming to us from the French *bouge*, and its diminutive *bougette*, a pouch. (Basil Hargrave, 1925)
❖A travelling tinker's bag for holding implements of his trade; hence a tramp's bag. (Michael Traynor, 1953)

**buffet** A portable stool for sitting; also a foot-stool. Halliwell says it was in early times applied to a stool of three legs; certainly it is not so used here [Yorkshire]. A *buffet* has two ends to rest on, and no proper legs at all. (Alfred Easther, 1883)

**bugle**  A bull; a word forgotten even by the peasantry, and only to be seen, as at Lymington and elsewhere, on a few inn-signs with a picture sometimes of a cow, by way of explanation. (William H. Cope, 1883) ❖[A] hunting horn, being the horn of a bugle, or wild bull. (Thomas Percy, 1886)

**bully**  The protector of a prostitute. Dr. Murray suggests connection with Dutch *boll*, a lover of either sex. (Edward Lloyd, 1895)
❖A familiar, and in Shakespeare, always a favorite address to a comrade or boon companion. *Midsummer-Night's Dream*. (C. H. Herford, 1902)
❖Now generally used among keelmen and pitmen to designate their brothers, as *bully Jack*, *bully Bob*, &c. Probably derived from the obsolete word *boulie*, beloved. (John Brockett, 1825)
cf. *tomboy*

**bummer**  Primarily an idle, worthless fellow. . . . Used as a general term of reproach in the same way as *rascal*, *blackleg*, &c. are used in England. Thus, San Francisco has been called the "Elysium of bummers." Nowhere [else] can a worthless fellow, too lazy to work, too cowardly to steal, get on so well. The climate befriends him, for he can sleep out of doors four-fifths of the year. He can gorge himself daily for a nominal sum, and get a dinner that a king might envy for fifty cents. *Bummer* is most probably from German *bummler*. (John Farmer, 1889)
❖In California, men who profess to be journalists, and so obtain free dinners and drinks, are called "literary *bummers*." (J. C. Hotten, 1887)

**bundle**  A custom now obsolete but formerly in vogue, where bed accommodation was scarce, of men and women sleeping on the same bed together without having removed their clothes. The practice is mentioned by Wright as having been customary in Wales. . . . Whatever may have been the case in former times, it does not appear to be a habit either in the Mother Country or the New World at the present time, even [in] the districts most remote from civilization. No question of immodesty seems to have attached to the custom;

indeed, attempts were made to prove that *bundling* was very right and proper. On this point however, opinions will vary considerably. (John Farmer, 1889)

**bunny** A small swelling caused by a fall or blow, perhaps a diminutive of *bump*. The nurse in *Romeo and Juliet* tells of her getting a bump in her forehead by falling down. From her account of the size of it, a modern East Anglian nurse would certainly call it a *bunny*. . . . From the Greek *bouvos*, a hillock. (Robert Forby, 1830)

**burden** Old songs and ballads frequently had a chorus or motto to each verse, which in the language of the time was called a *burden* or *bob*. One of the most ancient and popular was "Hey troly loly lo," quoted in *Piers Plowman*, 1362, and other early songs. . . . The ballad *The Jolly Miller* has been a favorite from the 16th or 17th century, and was sent to Beethoven to harmonise on account of its merited popularity by Thomson, who inserted it in his *Scotch Songs*, 1824. In it we find the lines,
"This the *burden* of his song
  For ever us'd to be,
I care for nobody, no, not I,
  If nobody cares for me."
. . . *Burden* also means the drone or bass of a bagpipe. (George Grove, 1902) cf. *ballad, dildo*

**bush-whack** To propel a boat by laying hold of bushes and overhanging branches, and walking toward the stern. (Richard Thornton, 1912)

**busker** One who dresses another; [from] *busk*, to prepare, make ready [1560s–1800s]. (Edward Lloyd, 1895)
❖*Busking*, searching; "*busking* for trout" occurs in 1653. (Richard Thornton, 1912)

**butcher** One who kills meat, in contradistinction to "flesher," who sells. (Michael Traynor, 1953)
❖*Butch*, to do the business of a *butcher*. (William Holloway, 1838)

**buxom** Obedient, and hence meek or humble; Anglo-Saxon. (James Halli-well, 1855)

❖Civil. (Thomas Tyrwhitt, 1871)

❖The modern spelling of *buxom* has quite hidden its identity with the German *biegsam*, bendable, pliant, and so, obedient. Ignorant of the history of the word, and trusting to the feeling and impression which it conveyed to their minds, men spoke of 'buxom health' and the like, meaning by this having a cheerful comeliness. (Richard Chenevix Trench, 1859–60)

**buzzard** Properly a moth—not a butterfly. (Alfred Easther, 1883)

**by and by** At once. *2 Henry VI*. (C. H. Herford, 1902)

❖Now a future, more or less remote, but when our version of the Bible was made, the nearest possible future. The inveterate procrastination of men has put *by and by* farther and farther off. (Richard Chenevix Trench, 1859–60)

**cabbage** *Cabbage* designates in America, as well as in Europe, . . . the pieces of cloth purloined by dishonest tailors. (M. Schele De Vere, 1872)
❖ To pilfer or purloin. Termed by Johnson a cant word, but adopted by later lexicographers as a respectable term. (J. C. Hotten, 1887)

**caboose** The cook-room or kitchen of merchantmen; a diminutive substitute for the galley of a man-of-war. It is generally furnished with cast-iron apparatus for cooking. (William Smyth, 1867)
❖ Like much of the American terminology connected with various modes of land travel, has been borrowed from sea life, in this instance, a ship's *caboose*, or galley. (John Farmer, 1889)
❖ Any small deckhouse, but generally the galley. On shore it meant *prison*. (Frank C. Bowen, 1929)
❖ From German *kabuse*, a hut, probably from the root of *cabin*. (James Donald, 1877)
❖ A word probably of Dutch origin. Littré says that, in the form *cambuse*, it came into use in the merchant navy of France about 1750, meaning a ship's kitchen. (Richard Thornton, 1912)
cf. *shanty*

**cad** A non-member of the university, from Latin *cadaver*, a dead body. Men, in university slang, are sorted under two groups, those who are members of the university and those who are not. As the former are called *men*, the others must be *no men*, but as they bear the human form, they are human bodies ("cads") though not human beings. (E. Cobham Brewer, 1887)

**caddie** One who gains a livelihood by running errands or delivering messages. The term, I suspect, is originally the same with French *cadet* which . . . strictly denotes a younger son of a family. (John Jamieson, 1879)
❖ The *cadies* are a fraternity of people who run errands. Individuals must, at

their admission, find surety for their behavior. They are acquainted with the persons and places in Edinburgh, and the moment a stranger comes to town, they get notice of it. (Hugo Arnot, 1779)
cf. *lackey*

**cadence** Harmonious combination of colours. (James Murray et al., 1888–1928)

**cadger** A packman or travelling huckster. Before the formation of regular turnpike roads from Scotland to Northumberland, the chief part of the commercial intercourse between the two kingdoms was carried on through the medium of *cadgers*. Persons who bring fish from the sea to the Newcastle market are still called *cadgers*. (John Brockett, 1825)
cf. *haberdasher*

**calculation** When we think of the abstruse problems that are solved by means of mathematics . . . it is almost inconceivable how crude and apparently foolish were the methods of reckoning in barbaric times, which yet were the origin of all arithmetical and mathematical knowledge. The derivation of the word *calculation* enables us to realise this, for the Latin *calculare*, to reckon by means of small stones or pebbles, a method still in use among some uncivilised tribes as an aid in counting. In a sense, we are still dependent upon the pebble as a means of calculation, for the integral *calculus* invented by Newton, which enables mathematicians to grasp ideas formerly beyond their reach, has been appropriately called "the mathematician's pebble." (Basil Hargrave, 1925)
cf. *ballot, tariff*

**camel-hair** Fine hair from a squirrel's tail for making paint brushes. (A. H. Smith, 1946)

**camisole** A kind of sleeved jacket or jersey. A straitjacket formerly put upon lunatics. (James Murray et al., 1888–1928)
❖Waistcoat. (Albert Barrère, 1911)
❖"Columbus found . . . a multitude . . . naked, or clothed only in a species of *camisole*." (G. W. Bridges, *Annals of Jamaica*, 1828)
cf. *petticoat, polka, smock*

**camper** A foot-ball player. (Edward Lloyd, 1895)

**cancel** To fence in, to enclose, or surround with a fence or railing; from Latin *cancellus*, a grating, *cancelli*, lattice-work. (Edward Lloyd, 1895)

**candid** White; [from] Latin *candidus*, white, bright, clear. [Hence] *candor*, whiteness. (Edward Lloyd, 1895)
❖The word is now seldom used except in its figurative sense of 'fair, open, ingenuous,' but its literal meaning is 'white and shining,' from Latin *candidus*, white, and *candere*, to shine. The word *candidate* has the same derivation, from the fact that those who sought office in ancient Rome vested themselves in white togas, a symbol, presumably, of their immaculate intentions. Our common-place *candle* comes of the same origin. (Basil Hargrave, 1925)
cf. *ambition*

**canvas** *Canvas* means 'cloth made of hemp,' [from] Latin *cannabis*, hemp. (E. Cobham Brewer, 1887)

**capon** A love letter; from French. *Love's Labour's Lost*. (C. H. Herford, 1902)

**captivate** To make prisoner; to reduce to bondage. *Love's Labour's Lost*. (Alexander Dyce, 1902)
❖This is not used any longer in a literal, but always in a more or less allegorical sense. (Richard Chenevix Trench, 1859–60)
cf. *decimate, ordeal*

**carcass** The living human body [1500s–1800s]. (Joseph Wright, 1896–1905)
cf. *corpse*

**career** The course on which a race is run. From Old French *cariere*, a road for carrying, late Latin *carrus*, a car. In falconry, a flight of the bird, about 120 yards; if it mount higher, it is called a *double-career*; if less, a *demi-career*. (Edward Lloyd, 1895)

**careful** Now, full of diligence and attention, but once of anxiety. (Richard Chenevix Trench, 1859–60)

**carnal** In respect [to] relationship; connected by birth. (Edward Lloyd, 1895)
cf. *cousin, german*

**carnation** The flesh colour; in painting, such parts of the human body as are drawn naked. (John Kersey, 1772)

❖From Latin *carnatia*, fleshiness, French *carnation*, flesh-colour. (Edward Lloyd, 1895)
cf. *local color, morbid, pink*

**carob** A small weight, the 24th part of a grain. (John Kersey, 1772)

**carol** A circle. (Edward Lloyd, 1895)
❖To dance in a ring, to the accompaniment of song [1300s–1500s]. (James Murray et al., 1888–1928)
cf. *ballad*

**carousel** A great festival solemnized with a [race] of chariots, horses, &c. (John Kersey, 1772)
❖A tournament in which knights, divided into companies, distinguished by their liveries and dresses, engaged in various plays and exercises; to this were often added chariot races, and other shows and entertainments. (Émile Littré, 1863–77)

**carpet** The covering of floors only at present, but once of tables as well. (Richard Chenevix Trench, 1859–60)

**carriage** Now, that which carries, or the act of carrying, but once, that which *was* carried, and thus *baggage*. (Richard Chenevix Trench, 1859–60)
cf. *luggage, vinaigrette, vis-à-vis*

**carte blanche** A blank paper signed at the bottom with a person's name, given to another person with permission to superscribe what conditions he pleases. (John Ogilvie, 1865)
❖From French *carte*, paper, *blanche*, white. (James Stormonth, 1884)
cf. *subscribe*

**cash** Originally, *cash* (Old French *casse*) was a *case*, or box, in which money was kept, and by its particular use, the case gave its name to the contents. It may be well to point out that there is a difference between *cash* and *money*. *Money* is anything which serves as a circulating medium; *cash*, in its strict sense, is coin only. All cash is money, but all money is not cash. (Basil Hargrave, 1925)

**casket** sometimes used as the title of a selection of music or literary 'gems,' [as] *Casket of Modern and Popular Songs* (1850) . . . *Cassette*, a casket; French diminutive of *casse* or *caisse*, adaptation of Italian *cassetta* [1700s–1800]. (James Murray et al., 1888–1928) *Cask*, a casket. *2 Henry VI*. (C. H. Herford, 1902)

**catastrophe** The conclusion or end of comedie. (John Bullokar, 1616) ❖The unfolding and winding up of the plot, clearing up difficulties, and closing the play. The ancients divided a play into the *protasis, epitasis, catastasis*, and *catastrophe*, the introduction, continuance, heightening, and conclusion. (Noah Webster, 1828)

**catcall** A squeaking instrument, used in the playhouse to condemn plays. (John Walker, 1835) ❖A kind of short whistle, with a pea included in its inside, made use of at play houses to hinder an actor from proceeding in his part, and to show disapprobation of any dramatic performance. (Daniel Fenning, 1775) ❖It derives its name from one of its sounds, which greatly resembles the modulation of an intriguing boar cat. (Francis Grose, 1796)

**catchup** A liquor extracted from mushrooms, and used in sauces. (Thomas Browne, 1810) ❖A high East-India sauce. (B. E., Gent., c. 1690) ❖A poignant liquor made from boiled mushrooms. (Samuel Johnson, 1755) ❖*Catsup* is the form that was first introduced into the language, though *catchup* appears now to be the most in use. (Joseph Worcester, 1881) ❖A kind of pickle. (John Walker, 1835) ❖The Eastern *kitjap*, soy sauce. (E. Cobham Brewer, 1887) ❖To derive it from the 'Eastern *kitjap*' is ridiculous, for there is no such language as 'Eastern.' (Walter Skeat, 1896)

**caterpillar** In natural history, a reptile from whence butterflies or moths are produced. (Daniel Fenning, 1775) ❖A worm sustained by leaves and fruit. (William Grimshaw, 1854) cf. *antelope, reptile*

**cattle** This and *chattel* are only different forms of the same word. At a time when wealth mainly consisted in the number of heads of cattle, the word

which designated them easily came to signify all other kinds of property as well. (Richard Chenevix Trench, 1859–60)
cf. *chat*

**cavalcade** A ride, a march, or raid on horseback [1500s–1600s]. (James Murray et al., 1888–1928)
❖Love intrigue. *Avoir vu des cavalcades* is said of a woman who has had many lovers. (Albert Barrère, 1911)

**cavort** Few would recognize the proud old Spanish word *cavar*, which denoted the haughty, impatient pawing of a spirited horse in the half-ludicrous term *to cavort*. (M. Schele De Vere, 1872)

**ceiling** Not confined to the roof, but used for a partition, by which a portion of a room is said to be "ceiled off." (Alfred Easther, 1883)
❖*Ceil*, to cover the inner roof of a building. (William Grimshaw, 1854)

**celebrity** Due observance of rites and ceremonies; a celebration [1600s]. (James Murray et al., 1888–1928)

**celibacy** The state of unmarried persons. (Charles Buck, 1835)

**censure** It speaks ill for the charity of men's judgments that *censure*, which designated once favourable and unfavourable judgments alike, is now restricted to unfavourable; for it must be that the latter, being by far the most frequent, have in this way appropriated the word exclusively to themselves. (Richard Chenevix Trench, 1859–60)

**century** An aggregate number of a hundred things. (Edward Lloyd, 1895)
❖A company of a hundred men. (Alexander Dyce, 1902)
cf. *billion, myriad, trillion*

**chagrin** The rough skin of a fish, of which watch cases and handles of knives are made. (Edward Phillips, 1706)

**chairman** One whose trade it was to carry a sedan-chair, or wheel a bath-chair. (Edward Lloyd, 1895)

**champion** One who lives in or farms open, unenclosed land; from Latin *campus*, a field, place of battle. (Edward Lloyd, 1895)
❖The *champion of England* is an officer whose business it is to appear at the

coronation of a sovereign, and challenge all comers to deny the new ruler's title. The office is a very ancient one, and is popularly supposed to have been instituted by William the Conqueror. (Sidney Low and F. S. Pulling, 1904)

**chaperon** A hood or cap, especially one worn by knights. (Edward Lloyd, 1895)
❖Any hood, bonnet, or lettice cap. (Randle Cotgrave, 1611)
cf. *bonnet, domino*

**character** Handwriting. "Thou didst produce my very *character*." *King Lear*. (Alexander Dyce, 1902)
cf. *autograph*

**charade** A kind of riddle based upon a word of two or more syllables, the key to which is given by description of each of the component syllables. The origin is unknown, [but] Skeat suggests Spanish *charrada*, a speech or action of a clown. (Edward Lloyd, 1895)
❖A less frequent form of *charade* treated the component letters in a similar way. Here is one: "My first is a circle, my second a cross; if you meet with my whole, look out for a toss. Answer: *ox*. (William Walsh, 1900)
cf. *rigmarole*

**chard** The leaves of the artichoke plant (*Cynara scolymus*) bound in straw during the autumn and winter, till they become blanched and lose part of their bitterness. [From] Latin *carduus*, a thistle. (Edward Lloyd, 1895)

**charismatic** Of or pertaining to a *charism* . . . a free gift or favour specially vouchsafed by God [1600s]. (James Murray et al., 1888–1928)

**chat** To call a swine. (Joseph Wright, 1896–1905)
❖*Chatty*, verminous, a possible derivation of the word *chat* is that it is a cognate of *chattel*, or cattle. (Edward Fraser and John Gibbons, 1925)
cf. *cattle*

**chauvinism** French, from Nicolas Chauvin, a brave soldier of the Republic and First Empire. His name became a synonym for a passionate admirer of Napoleon, and the word *chauvinism* was formed to signify the almost idolatrous respect entertained by many for the first emperor, and generally any feeling of exaggerated devotion, especially patriotism. A vaudeville, *La Cocarde Tricolore,* in which there was a character named Chauvin, fixed the word in the French language. (Edward Lloyd, 1895)

**cheap** The place of buying and selling; hence in place-names, as Cheapside, Eastcheap; price, value [1000–1400s]. (James Murray et al., 1888–1928)
❖*Cheapen,* to ask the price of anything. (James Halliwell, 1855)
❖"I see you come to *cheap,* and not to buy." (Thomas Heywood, *Edward IV,* 1599)

**cheater** Officer appointed to look after the king's *escheats* (property which falls to the lord by forfeit or fine) who would have the opportunity of defrauding people of their estates. (C. T. Onions, 1911)
❖*Cheater* originally meant an *escheator,* or officer of the king's exchequer appointed to receive dues and taxes. The present use of the word shows how these officers were wont to fleece the people. (E. Cobham Brewer, 1887)

**cheek** *Cheek* has, in America, retained the old English meaning of a doorpost, as quoted in the *Craven Glossary:* "She threw up her hands against the *cheek* of the door and prevented me from putting her out." (M. Schele De Vere, 1872)
❖Little heard now, but for a long period this English provincialism survived in the States. (John Farmer, 1889)

**cheer** Diet, fare. (John Kersey, 1772)
cf. *diet, entertainment*

**chemist** An alchemist. (Edward Lloyd, 1895)
❖A surgeon. (Edward Fraser and John Gibbons, 1925)
cf. *alchemy, surgeon*

**cherish** To support and forward with encouragement, help, and protection; to shelter, nurse up. (Samuel Johnson, 1755)
❖To foster, tend, cultivate, plants, hair, etc. [1500s–1800s]. (James Murray et al., 1888–1928)

**chevron** A beam or rafter; especially in the plural, the rafters or couples of the roof which meet at an angle at the ridge; adaptation of French *chevron,* rafter [1300s–1800s]. (James Murray et al., 1888–1928)

**chimp** The grown-out shoot of a stored potato. (Joseph Wright, 1896–1905)

**chit-chat** Sprigs of oak worn on King Charles's Day, May 29, *Chit-chat day.* (Joseph Wright, 1896–1905)

**chop** A Chinese word signifying quality, first introduced by mariners in the China trade, but which has become common in all our seaports. Originally, the word was only applied to silks, teas, or other goods from China. Now it is applied to everything, for we hear *first chop teas, first chop tobacco,* and *first chop potatoes.* (James Bartlett, 1849)

**chris-cross** The mark or signature of those who cannot write. The alphabet was formerly called the *Christ-cross row,* probably from a superstitious custom of writing it in the form of a cross, by way of charm. (John Brockett, 1825)
♦Awry; bad-tempered. (Joseph Wright, 1896–1905)
cf. *earmark, marksman*

**Christendom** By *Christendom* we now understand that portion of the world which makes profession of the faith of Christ, as contradistinguished from all heathen and Mahomedan lands. But it was often used by our early writers as itself the profession of Christ's faith, or sometimes for baptism. . . . In Shakespeare, our present use of *Christendom* very much predominates, but once or twice he uses it in its earlier sense, as do authors much later than he. (Richard Chenevix Trench, 1859–60)

**Christian** A man, as distinguished from an animal. (Angelina Parker, 1881)
cf. *antichrist*

**chubby** Surly, angry; [from] Eastern England. (James Halliwell, 1855)
cf. *spleen, stomach*

**chump** A log of wood for burning. "A great chip," according to Urry's manuscript additions to Ray. (James Halliwell, 1855)
♦A block of wood, a tree root, or some other portion of a tree, sought for to be burnt on November 5th. The boys go *chumping* for some time before that date, and lay in a large stock of *chumps.* (Alfred Easther, 1883)
♦From Icelandic *kumpr,* a log, a block, and *kubba,* to chop. (Edward Lloyd, 1895)

**circus** A circular bandage [1800s]. (Edward Lloyd, 1895)
❖The arena for a bull-fight. (James Murray et al., 1888–1928)
❖An open place or theater for equestrian entertainment. (William Grimshaw, 1854)
cf. *cockpit, tent*

**civil** The tendency which there is in the meaning of words to run to the surface, till they lose and leave behind all their deeper significance, is well exemplified in *civil*. . . . A *civil* man now is one observant of slight external courtesies in the intercourse between man and man; a *civil* man once was one who fulfilled all the duties and obligations flowing from his position as a 'civis,' and his relations to other members of that 'civitas' to which he belonged. . . . A *civilian*, in the language of the Puritans, was one who, despising the righteousness of Christ, did yet follow after a certain *civil* righteousness. (Richard Chenevix Trench, 1859–60)
❖*Civilian*, one who professes a knowledge of old civil or Roman law, and of general equity. (William Grimshaw, 1854)
❖*Civil* war, wordy strife. (Joseph Wright, 1896–1905)

**clench** To turn a bucket over in such a manner that the edge goes under water in drawing from a well. (Joseph Wright, 1896–1905)

**clever** *Clever*, one of the most disputed words in our speech . . . varies almost infinitely with the locality in which it is used. . . . If Northern people among us, therefore, choose to employ it in the sense of good-natured and obliging, there seems to be no ground whatever for rejection. . . . Used in England, generally for good-looking, or handy and dexterous, it means in Norfolk, rather, honest, and respectable. In South Wales, it indicates a state of good health; in a few southern counties, perfect clearness and completeness, and in other parts, as with us, courtesy and affability. The American pet-word *smart* has, however, largely superseded it in our speech, and only in Virginia and some parts of the South clever is still much used in its old English meaning of 'skillful at work' and 'talented in mind.' (M. Schele De Vere, 1872)
cf. *nice*

**climate** The region of the sky immediately above us. *King John*. (C. H. Herford, 1902)
❖A terme used in cosmographie. It signifieth a portion of the world betweene North and South, conteining some notable difference in the sunne rising. (John Bullokar, 1616)

❖We have derived the word from the mathematical geographers of antiquity. They were wont to run imaginary parallel lines, or such at least as they intended should be parallel, to the equator, and the successive 'climates' of the earth were the spaces and regions between these lines. (Richard Chenevix Trench, 1859–60)

**clothier** A designation of the man who manufactures cloth. (John Farmer, 1889)
❖The master-clothier . . . employs in all the different processes through which the wool passes in the course of manufacture, distinct classes of persons, who sometimes work at their own houses, and sometimes in the factory of the master-clothier. (*Penny Cyclopœdia*, 1833–43)
cf. *haberdasher*

**clumsy** Stiff, rigid, and contracted with cold. (Richard Chenevix Trench, 1859–60)
❖Thick and short. (John Kersey, 1772)
cf. *chubby, dither, starve*

**clunk** The gurgling, confused sound of liquor in a bottle or cask when it is poured out, equivalent to the English *glug*. It is derived by Jamieson from the Danish *glunk* and the Swedish *klunka*, which have the same meaning. (Charles Mackay, 1888)
❖*Clunker*, a good big glassful; [from the] Shetland Islands. (Joseph Wright, 1896–1905)

**coal** Although this word is now limited to denoting that combustible substance which is dug out of the earth and used for fuel, its original meaning, when wood was general fuel, was thus not restricted. *Coal* then meant the residue obtained by the process of slowly burning wood under turf—what we now call *charcoal*—and the name *collier* was applied to charcoal burners as well as coalminers. The root of the word *kol* is common to all Teutonic languages, and is connected with the Swedish *kylla*, to kindle. (Basil Hargrave, 1925)

**cockpit** Properly, a small arena where cock-fighting took place. (Alexander Dyce, 1902)
❖Applied to a theater, and to the pit of a theater [late 1500s–1600s]. (James Murray et al., 1888–1928)
❖Of a ship-of-war, the apartments of the surgeon and his mates, being the place where the wounded are dressed. (William Falconer, 1769)

**cod** The organs of seed in men or beasts. (John Kersey, 1772)
❖The scrotum. (James Losh, 1783)
cf. *testicle*

**coffin** The raised crust of a pie. (Alexander Dyce, 1902)
❖Shakespeare speaks of a "custard coffin" [in] *Taming of the Shrew*. [From] Greek *kophinos*, a basket. (E. Cobham Brewer, 1887)

**cohort** A troop of soldiers in the Roman armies. In poetical language, a body of warriors. (Samuel Johnson, 1755)
❖The old English word *cahoot*, a slang word of the [American] West and South for keeping company legitimately and illegitimately, is . . . far removed from its original in French, *cohorte*. (M. Schele De Vere, 1872)

**cold blood** A phrase of older physiology, from the sensations felt in the face and head when the circulation is quickened by exertion or excitement; the blood itself was supposed to grow hot, or 'boil,' at other times to be 'cold.' Hence the phrase, *in cold blood*. (James Murray et al., 1888–1928)
❖*Cold-blooded*, having cold blood. (John Ogilvie, 1865)

**comedy** *Comedy* means a village-song (Greek *köme-öde*) referring to the village merrymakings in which comic songs still take a conspicuous place. The Greeks had certain festival processions of great licentiousness, held in honour of Dionysius, in the suburbs of their cities, and termed *komoi*, or village revels. On these occasions, an ode was generally sung, and this ode was the foundation of Greek comedy. (E. Cobham Brewer, 1887)

❖*Comedian*, a writer of comedies. (John Bullokar, 1616)

**comfort** The [Latin] verb *comfortare* . . . embodies to make strong, to corroborate, and only in a secondary sense to console. We often find it in our literature employed in that, its proper sense. (Richard Chenevix Trench, 1859–60)
❖*Comfortable*, susceptible of comfort. "For my sake, be *comfortable*." *As You Like It*. (Alexander Dyce, 1902)

**comical** Ill-tempered; blameable. (W. E. T. Morgan, 1881)
❖*Comical* has, in the [American] South, the peculiar meaning of 'strange, extraordinary.' (M. Schele De Vere, 1872)

**comma** Any short pause or delay; a slight hindrance or block. (Edward Lloyd, 1895)
❖"No levell'd malice infects one *comma* in the course I hold." William Shakespeare, *Timon of Athens*.

**commerce** Conversation. *Twelfth Night*. (C. H. Herford, 1902)
❖Familiar intercourse between the sexes. (Noah Webster, 1828)

**commode** A frame of wire, two or three stories high, fitted for the head, or fitted with tiffany or other thin silks. (John Dunton, 1694)
❖A kind of lady's head-dress in use in the time of William and Mary. (Edward Lloyd, 1895)

**common sense** The sense which is common to all the five, or the point where the five senses meet, supposed to be the seat of the soul, where it judges what is presented by the senses, and decides the mode of action. (E. Cobham Brewer, 1887)
❖In truth, this phrase, *common-sense*, meant once something very different from that plain wisdom, the common heritage of men, which now we call by this name . . . a sense which has the common bond of them all, and which passed its verdicts on the reports which they severally made to it. (Richard Chenevix Trench, 1859–60)

**compass** In archery, the curved path described by an arrow; the angle of elevation as determining this path. (James Murray et al., 1888–1928)

**compassionate** Lamenting, complaining. *Richard II*. (Alexander Dyce, 1902)

**competitor** A partner, confederate. "Our great *competitor*." *Antony and Cleopatra*. (Alexander Dyce, 1902)

**complexion** Of the face, the expression. (Michael Traynor, 1953)
❖The temperature of the humors in [a] man's body which causeth the colour; sometime it signifieth [cosmetic facial] painting used by women. (John Bullokar, 1616)

❖If fire predominates, the person is *bilious;* if air, he is *sanguine,* or full of blood; if earth, the body is *melancholic;* if water, it is *phlegmatic.* The first is hot and dry; the second, hot and moist; the third, cold and dry; and the last, moist and cold. (E. Cobham Brewer, 1887)
cf. *rude, yellow-belly*

**compost** A calendar of computation of astronomical and ecclesiastical data. "This present book [*Shepherd's Kalender,* 1656] is named the *compost,* for it comprehendeth fully all the compost and more, for the days, hours, and moments, and the new moons, and the eclipse of the sun and moon." (James Murray et al., 1888–1928)
❖A mixture, combination, or compound of any kind. (Edward Lloyd, 1895)

**comrades** Those who sleep in the same bed-chamber. It is a Spanish military term derived from the custom of dividing soldiers into chambers. The proper spelling is *camerades,* men of the same *camera,* chamber. (E. Cobham Brewer, 1887)
❖Sixteenth-century adaptation of Spanish *camarada,* originally "chamberful," thence "chamber-mate." (James Murray et al., 1888–1928)

**conceit** Thought, imagination. "A gentleman of good conceit." *As You Like It.* (Alexander Dyce, 1902)
❖*Conceited,* fanciful, ingenious; also, inclined to jest. (James Halliwell, 1855)
❖A laudatory term. (Thomas Fosbroke, 1843)

**concept** The object of an act of conception. (Joseph Angus, 1870)
❖Adaptation of Latin *conceptare,* to conceive in the womb [1600s]. (James Murray et al., 1888–1928)
cf. *womb*

**conclusion** An experiment; something from which a *conclusion* may be drawn. Noticed by Johnson, but not as disused, which it certainly is. We are not, therefore, to suspect Lancelot Gobbo of incorrect language when he proposes to *try conclusions* upon his old purblind father [in] *The Merchant of Venice.* (Robert Nares, 1859)

**concubine** No notice is taken in our dictionaries that the male paramour, as well as the female, was sometimes called by this name. (Richard Chenevix Trench, 1859–60)
cf. *maid, wench, womb*

**condescend** To agree; hence, *condescent*, an agreement. (James Halliwell, 1855)

❖"For which causes they all *condescended* upon their return to England." (John Stow, 1598)

❖A legal term, to state one's case; hence, *condescendence*, a statement of one's case; [from] Scotland. (Joseph Wright, 1896–1905)

**condominium** Joint rule or sovereignty; formed on Latin *dominicum*, lordship. (James Murray et al., 1888–1928)

**connive** To shut one's eyes to a thing that one dislikes but cannot help; to pretend ignorance; formed on *con*, together, and *nivere*, not found. (James Murray et al., 1888–1928)

❖When a man *connives* at some scandalous transaction, he need not be a participator in it—he simply *winks* at it. And the derivation of *connive* bears out this definition. The word comes to us, through the French, from the Latin *connivere*, to wink. (Basil Hargrave, 1925)

**constipate** To crowd together into a narrow room. (Samuel Johnson, 1755)

**continent** Something that holds or contains. "Tomb enough and *continent* to hide the slain." *King Lear*. [Also] *summary*. "The *continent* and summary of my fortune." *Hamlet*. Milton speaks of "the moist continent" of the moon. (C. T. Onions, 1911)

cf. *incontinent*

**conundrum** A low jest, a quibble. (John Walker, 1835)

cf. *quibble*

**convene** This is used in some parts of New England in a very strange sense, that is to be convenient, fit, or suitable. [For] example, "this road will *convene* the public," will *be convenient* for the public. (John Pickering, 1816)

**convent** An assemblage or gathering of persons; a company, specifically the twelve apostles; [1400s–1600s]. (James Murray et al., 1888–1928)

**convey** To steal. To manage secretly and artfully. "*Convey'd* himself as heir to the lady Lingare." *Henry V*. (Alexander Dyce, 1902)

❖*Conveyance*, dishonest practice. "I fear, there is *conveyance*." *1 Henry VI*. (C. H. Herford, 1902)

**coquette** A beau, a gallant, a general lover. (Edward Phillips, 1706)
❖[From] French *coqueter*, to cluck as a cock among hens. (Hensleigh Wedgwood, 1878)
❖At present, all our *coquets* are female. But . . . what once belonged to both sexes is now restricted to one. (Richard Chenevix Trench, 1859–60)
❖From French *coquart*, a prattler. (Samuel Johnson, 1755)
cf. *lover*

**cordial** A medicine that increases the force of the heart; any medicine that increases strength. (William Grimshaw, 1854)

**corn** In England, *corn* is a general term, and means all sorts of grain that are used for bread. . . . A correspondent says the term *corn* "among the English is more peculiarly applied to wheat." (John Pickering, 1816)
cf. *plum, rum*

**coroner** Literally a *crowner*, an officer whose original duty was to take charge of the property of the crown. (John Phin, 1902)
❖*Coronary*, the office of a *coroner*; adaptation of medieval Latin *coronaria*. (James Murray et al., 1888–1928)
cf. *laureate*

**corpse** Now only used for the body abandoned by the spirit of life, but once for the body of the living equally as of the dead. (Richard Chenevix Trench, 1859–60)
cf. *carcass*

**corsage** The body, as distinct from the limbs; the bust [1500s]. (James Murray et al., 1888–1928)

**cosmetic** One who practises the cosmetic art [1700s]. (James Murray et al., 1888–1928)
cf. *antics, pantomime, pedicure, rhetoric, zany*

**cosmic** Of this world; worldly [1600s]. (James Murray et al., 1888–1928)

**counterfeit** Now, to imitate with the purpose of passing off the imitation as the original, but no such dishonest intention was formerly implied in the word. (Richard Chenevix Trench, 1859–60)
❖A portrait, a likeness, a picture. *Merchant of Venice*. (Alexander Dyce, 1902)
cf. *facepainting, statue*

**courses** The natural purgations or cleansings most women have from fourteen to fourty-four. (Thomas Dyche and William Pardon, 1740)

**courteous** Having such manners as befit the *court* of a prince [from 1200s]. (James Murray et al., 1888–1928)
❖*Courting*, living at court. (Thomas Fosbroke, 1843)

**cousin** Kinswoman; a niece. *Troilus and Cressida*. (C. H. Herford, 1902)
❖Grandchild, nephew. *King John*. (Alexander Dyce, 1902)
❖Brother-in-law. *1 Henry IV*. (Alexander Dyce, 1902)
cf. *aunt, brother-in-law, foster-child, nephew, niece*

**cowlick** The term given to the lock of hair which costermongers and tramps usually twist forward from the ear; a large greasy curl upon the cheek, seemingly licked into shape. These locks are also called "number sixes," from their unusual shape. (J. C. Hotten, 1887)
❖A peculiar arrangement of the hair, which to fanciful men suggests the smooth and glossy appearance of a place licked by a cow. (M. Schele De Vere, 1872)

**cranky** Brisk, merry, jocund. (William H. Cope, 1883)
❖Sprightly, exulting, jocose. . . . The man in the village who is most conspicuous for dress, or who excels the rest of the villagers in the sports and pastimes held in estimation of them, is called, by way of pre-eminence, *the Cranky* [in] Durham. (John Brockett, 1825)
❖Full of quirks and pranks [in] Sussex and Hampshire. (R. E. G. Cole, 1886)

**cricket** A low wooden stool. The game of cricket was probably a development of the older game of *stool-ball*, a dairy-maid's stool being used for the wicket. Wedgwood suggests that the proper name for the bat was *cricket-staff*; [from] Anglo-Saxon *cricc*, a staff. (Robert Lawson, 1884)

**crimp** Detested agents who trepan seamen by treating, advancing money, &c. by which the dupes become indebted, and when well plied with liquor are induced to sign articles, and are shipped off, only discovering their mistake on finding themselves at sea robbed of all they possessed. (William Smyth, 1867)
❖One who ostensibly keeps a lodging-house for sailors but whose real occupation is to fleece the unwary of their wages; from Dutch *krimpe*, a confined place in which fish are kept alive till wanted. (James Stormonth, 1884)

**crispy** Curly, wavy, undulated [1300s–1800s]. (James Murray et al., 1888–1928)
❖"The quiet bay, whose little waves, *crisping* and sparkling to the moon-beams." (Walter Scott, *Guy Mannering*)

**croon** To bellow like a disquiet ox. It is also frequently applied to the cowardly and petted roaring of a disappointed child. [From] Dutch *kreunnen*, to groan. (John Brockett, 1825)
❖It appears to be one of the Low German words that came into Scottish in the Middle English period. (Michael Traynor, 1953)
cf. *ruddy*

**croquet** A shepherd's staff; dialect French. (Charles A. M. Fennell, 1892)

**cross-eyed** Squinting badly. (Robert Lawson, 1884)

**crotch** A bifurcation of road or river [1700s–1800s]. (James Murray et al., 1888–1928)

**crud** A term of endearment. A mother, addressing her child, said "Come here, white *crud.*" (Michael Traynor, 1953)
cf. *mumps, wench, whiteboy*

**cruel** *Cruel*, used . . . for 'great,' is one of the intensive expressions much affected by uneducated Americans, but not an Americanism. It was brought over from England in the early part of the seventeenth century. Thus, Pepys, in his diary, July 31, 1662, writes: "Met Captain Brown at the Rosebush, at which he was *cruel* angry." (M. Schele De Vere, 1872)

**crummy** Fat, in good condition. (Edward Peacock, 1877)
❖American slang for comely, pretty; a plump, full-figured girl in England [is] also described as *crummy.* (John Farmer, 1889)
cf. *bald, morbid*

**cummerbund** Such an article of dress is habitually worn by domestic servants, peons, and irregular troops, but any waist-belt is so termed; from Portuguese *kamar-band*, loin-cloth. (Henry Yule, 1886)
cf. *gee-string, sash*

**cunning** A feminine Americanism used when speaking of anything that is interesting or pretty. One's hand may have *cunning*, but a *cunning* foot would, in some cases awaken stirring memories. American ladies, however, would simply mean that the pedal extremity was small, shapely, pretty, or taking. (John Farmer, 1889)
❖The fact that so many words implying knowledge, art, skill, obtain in course

of time a secondary meaning of 'crooked knowledge, art which has degenerated into artifice, skill used only to circumvent,' . . . is a mournful witness to the way in which intellectual gifts are too commonly misapplied. (Richard Chenevix Trench, 1859–60)

❖Cunning once conveyed no idea of sinister or crooked wisdom. "The three persons of the Trinity," says a reverent writer of the fifteenth century, "are of equal *cunning*." (William Mathews, 1884)

**curious** This word is often heard in New England among the common farmers, in the sense of *excellent*, or *peculiarly excellent*, as in, "These are *curious* apples." (John Pickering, 1816)

❖Only an Americanism by survival. . . . It was once in frequent use by old English writers. (John Farmer, 1889)

❖*Curiosity*, in the time of Shakespeare, was a word that signified an over-nice scrupulousness in manners. "They mocked thee for too much *curiosity*." *Timon of Athens*. (Alexander Dyce, 1902)

**customer** One sitting officially at [a] customs [house], and not one repairing to a shop to purchase there, was a *customer* two and three centuries ago. (Richard Chenevix Trench, 1859–60)

**cute** Sharp, quick-witted. (Nathaniel Bailey, 1749)

❖With capacity for learning; having ability. (B. Lowsley, 1888)

❖Quick, intelligent, sly, cunning, clever. This word is probably an abbreviation of *acute*. (John Brockett, 1825)

**dad** To beat one thing against another. "He *dadded* his head against the wall." (Adam and Charles Black, 1851)
cf. *lather, rib-roast, spank*

**dainty** Large, as applied to inanimate objects; plump, and thriving, as regarding a child. (John Jamieson, 1879)
❖*Dainty*, strictly speaking, means a venison pastry, from the French *dain*, a deer; whence the Old French *dain*, delicate, nice. (F. Cobham Brewer, 1887)

**darn** To mend roads, in patches, with loose stones. (Michael Traynor, 1953)
cf. *botch*

**dashboard** A board or leathern apron placed on the fore part of a chaise, or other vehicle, to prevent water, mud, etc., from being thrown upon those in the vehicle by the horses. (William Whitney, 1889)

**davenport** A lady's drawing-room writing-table with drawers underneath, said to be after the Countess of Devonport. (James Stormonth, 1884)

**dead-beat** In clock and watch making, a term applied to a kind of escapement in which the seconds hand is made to stand still an instant after each beat without recoil. (Charles Annandale, 1897)

**dear** Fatal, mischievous, immediate, consequential; an enforcing epithet with not always a distinct meaning. (Thomas Fosbroke, 1843)
❖The word means 'most hateful' when derived from Anglo-Saxon *derian*, to hurt, and the Scotch *dere*, to annoy. (Basil Hargrave, 1925)
❖"Would I had met my *dearest* foe in Heaven." (William Shakespeare, *Hamlet*)
cf. *annoy*

**deceivable** So far as we use *deceivable* at all now, we use it in the passive sense, as liable to be, or capable of being, deceived. It was active when counted exchangeable with *deceitful*. (Richard Chenevix Trench, 1859–60)

**decimate** To select and put to death one in every ten of a body of soldiers guilty of mutiny or other crime, a practice in the ancient Roman army. (James Murray et al., 1888–1928)
❖To take [one-]tenth; to gather the tithe. (Thomas Blount, 1656)
❖It is extraordinary how loosely it is often used. Even in the newspapers, and certainly in common talk, it is not infrequently employed to express great slaughter of a body of men, with a complete indifference to the proportion killed. If the derivation of the word were borne in mind, such a mistake could not be made. It comes from the Latin *decem*, ten, and denotes a tenth part, or even figuratively, some approximation to that proportion. (Basil Hargrave, 1925)
cf. *captivate, ordeal*

**decrepit** Unable to make a noise. It refers rather to the mute voice and silent footstep of old age than to its broken strength. (E. Cobham Brewer, 1887)
❖From Latin *decrepitus*, noiseless (*de*, away from, and *crepitus*, a noise). (Edward Lloyd, 1895)

**decypher** To write after a strange manner, in so much as no man can read it. (Henry Cockeram, 1623)

**demerit** It was plainly a squandering of the wealth of the language that *merit* and *demerit* should mean one and the same thing. However, this might be justified by the fact that [Latin] *mereor* and *demereor*, from which they were severally derived, were scarcely discriminated in meaning. It has thus come to pass, according to the desynonymizing processes ever at work in a language, that *demerit* has ended in being employed only of ill desert, while *merit* is left free to good or ill, having predominantly the sense of the former. (Richard Chenevix Trench, 1859–60)

**depend** To hang down, to be suspended; from Latin *dependeo*, to hang down. "Long icicles *depend*." (Edward Lloyd, 1895)

**desire** To *desire* is only to look forward with longing desire. The word has lost the sense of regret or looking back upon the lost but still loved. (Richard Chenevix Trench, 1859–60)

**detest** To testify against; from Latin *testor*, to call to witness, *testis*, a witness. (Edward Lloyd, 1895)

**dexterity** The ability to use the right hand better or more expertly than the left; right-handedness; from Latin *dexteritas, dexter,* the right. (Edward Lloyd, 1895)
cf. *ambidextrous, left-handed, sinister*

**dialing** The art of making *dials* (plate marked with lines, where a hand, or shadows, show the hours); the knowledge of shadows. (John Walker, 1835)

**dialysis** A figure in Rhetoric by which syllables or words are divided. (John Phin, 1902)

**diaper** To draw flowers or arabesques upon cloths. (Joseph Worcester, 1881)
❖To decorate with a variety of colours; to embroider on a rich ground. (James Halliwell, 1855)
❖*Diaper'd,* diversified with flourishes or sundry figures; whence we call cloth that is so diversified, *diaper.* (Thomas Blount, 1656)

**diary** Daily experience. (Henry Cockeram, 1623)
❖Lasting for one day; ephemeral. Adopted from medieval Latin *diarius,* daily. (James Murray et al., 1888–1928)

**dicker** Ten hides of leather. (John Bullokar, 1616)

**dibs** A game played with the small knuckle bones taken from legs of mutton. These bones themselves are called *dibs.* (B. Lowsley, 1888)
❖*Dibs,* found in the eighteenth century, was probably a familiar shortening of *dibstones.* (James Murray et al., 1888–1928)

**diet** Board, keep; usually in the phrase, *wages and diet.* (Michael Traynor, 1953)
❖*Diet-drink,* drink prepared with medicinal ingredients. (John Ogilvie, 1865)
cf. *cheer, entertainment*

**digitize** To use with the fingers; to point with the fingers. (Edward Lloyd, 1895)

**dignity** In astrology, *dignities* are the advantages a planet has upon account of its being in a particular place of the Zodiack . . . by which means its influences and virtue are encreas'd. (Edward Phillips, 1706)

**dike** *Dike,* denoting a man in full dress . . . is a peculiar American cant term as yet unexplained. To be "out on a *dike*" is said of persons, mainly young men, who are dressed more carefully than usual, in order to pay visits or to attend a party. It is not unlikely that the term is merely a corruption of the obsolete *dight*, which meant 'decked out,' and is in this sense used by many Old English writers. (M. Schele De Vere, 1872)

**dilapidate** Adopted from Latin *dilapidare*, literally "to scatter, as if throwing stones," to throw away, destroy; from *lapidem*, stone; taken in English in a more literal sense than was usual in Latin. (James Murray et al., 1888–1928)

**dildo** The chorus of a song. "He has the prettiest love-songs for maids . . . with such delicate burthens of *dildos* and fadings." *Winter's Tale*. (John Phin, 1902)
cf. *ballad, burden, rhapsody*

**diligence** A public stage-coach [1700s–1800s]. Used for the passengers of a 'diligence.' (James Murray et al., 1888–1928)

**dine** To go to bed. (Harold Wentworth, 1944)
❖*Dine out*, to go without dinner. "I dined out today," would express the same among the very lower classes that "dining with Duke Humphrey" expresses among the middle and upper. (J. C. Hotten, 1887)

**diploma** An original document, as a matter of historical investigation or literary study. (James Murray et al., 1888–1928)
❖A letter or writing conferring some privilege, so called because they used formerly to be written on waxed tablets and folded together. (Samuel Johnson, 1755)

**disable** Our ancestors felt that to injure the character of another was the most effectual way of disabling him, and out of a sense of this they often used *to disable* in the sense of to disparage, to speak slightingly of. (Richard Chenevix Trench, 1859–60)

**disaster** The blast, stroke, or influence of an unfavourable or unlucky planet; an unpropitious portent or omen. (Edward Lloyd, 1895)
❖*Disaster* is being under an evil star (Greek *dus-aster*, evil star); an astrological word. (E. Cobham Brewer, 1887)
cf. *asterisk, dismal*

**disclose** To open. "Before their buttons (buds) be *disclos'd*." *Hamlet*. (Alexander Dyce, 1902)
❖To hatch. *Disclosing* is when the young birds just peep through the shells. (James Halliwell, 1855)

**discolored**  Deprived of colour; colourless. (Edward Lloyd, 1895)
cf. *remiss*

**diseases**  Our present limitation of disease is a very natural one, seeing that nothing so effectually wars against *ease* as a sick and suffering condition of body. Still, the limitation is modern, and by *disease* was once meant any malease, distress, or discomfort. "His double burden did him sore *disease.*" Spenser's *Fairy Queen.* (Richard Chenevix Trench, 1859–60)

**dismal**  Ill-boding, sinister. . . . The original application of the word is to the unlucky days *(dies mali)* of the medieval calendar. (C. T. Onions, 1911)
cf. *disaster*

**dither**  To quiver with cold. (Ralph Thoresby, 1718)
cf. *clumsy, starve*

**divot**  A piece of turf, ready cut and dried for burning. (Charles Mackay, 1888)
❖A thin, flat, oblong sod used in thatching or in covering stone walls. (Michael Traynor, 1953)
❖A slice of earth with the grass growing upon it; a sod such as are used in the North for roofing cottages, forming the edges of thatched roofs, the tops of dry-stone walls, etc. (James Murray et al., 1888–1928)
cf. *topsy-turvy*

**dizzy**  One addicted to dice; perhaps from *dicey. Measure for Measure.* (Alexander Dyce, 1902)

**docile**  Able to learn; easily taught; from Latin *doceo*, to teach. (Edward Lloyd, 1895)
cf. *document*

**doctor**  The seventh son of a family born in succession without a girl is always called the *doctor,* and is believed to be born with a special aptness for the healing art. (R. Pearse Chope, 1891)
❖*To doctor one,* to kill one; a phrase evidently borrowed from the prejudice of many of the vulgar against regular practitioners. (John Jamieson, 1879)
❖A sea-cook. The cook is, in fact, called the *doctor* in all [American] merchant ships. (Richard Thornton, 1912)

**document**  A lesson. (John Bullokar, 1616)
❖Now used only of the material, and not, as once, of the moral proof, evi-

dence, or means of instruction. (Richard Chenevix Trench, 1859–60)
❖From Latin *doceo*, to teach. (Edward Lloyd, 1895)
cf. *docile*

**doff** To lay aside one's clothes; to undress. (Edward Lloyd, 1895)
❖"The lads ran across the field *doff'd*," naked. (Alfred Easther, 1883)

**dog-biscuit** Coarse waste, or broken biscuits, sold for feeding dogs.
(Peter Simmonds, 1858)
cf. *kibble*

**dole** Grief, sorrow, lamentation; [from] Old French *dol, dole*, modern
French *deuil* [mourning]. By no means obsolete, as stated in Todd's [edition of]
Johnson['s dictionary]. Alms distributed at funerals are still called *doles*. (John
Brockett, 1825)
❖[From] Latin *dolor*, pain, grief. (Noah Webster, 1828)

**dollop** A packet or lump of tea, weighing six to eighteen pounds,
so packed for the convenience of smuggling. (William H. Cope, 1883)
❖A patch, tuft, or clump of weeds, etc. in a field. (James Murray et al.,
1888–1928)

**domino** A kind of hood or habit for the head worn by canons, and hence
also, a fashion of veil used by some women that mourn. (Randle Cotgrave, 1611)
❖A kind of loose cloak, apparently of Venetian origin, chiefly worn at masca-
rades. According to Littré [the modern gaming] sense came from the supposed
resemblance of the black back of each of the pieces of the mascarade garment.
Du Cange cites *domino* in Latin context in the sense of a covering of the head
and shoulders worn by priests in winter. (James Murray, 1888–1928)
❖A common ejaculation of soldiers and sailors when they receive the last lash of
a flogging. A *domino* means either a blow or the last of a series of things, whether
pleasant or otherwise, so the ejaculation savours somewhat of wit. The allusion
may be understood from the game of dominos. (J. C. Hotten, 1887)
cf. *chaperon*

**doom** To tax at discretion [in] New England. When a person fails to make a
return of his taxable property to the assessors of a town, those officers *doom* him,
that is, judge upon, and fix his tax according to their discretion. "The estates of
all merchants, shopkeepers, and factors shall be assessed by the rule of common
estimation, according to the will and *doom* of the assessors." *Massachusetts*

*Colony Law*, 1660. (John Pickering, 1816)

**dork**  A thick slice of bread. (Basil Hargrave, 1925)

**dorm**  To doze. A kind of half-sleep or cat-sleep. (Alfred Easther, 1883)
❖*Dormitory*, a burial-place; a cemetery. (Edward Lloyd, 1895)
❖*Dormitory*, tending to or causing sleep [1600s]. (James Murray et al., 1888–1928)

**double-header**  A railway train having two engines. (James Murray et al., 1888–1928)

**double-standard**  In economics, the phrase *double-standard* is used to signify . . . what is known as the *gold standard* on the one hand, and the *silver standard* on the other. Wherever the *double standard* is in use, a creditor is bound to accept payment of any sum in coins of either of the metals, gold or silver, which the debtor may choose to tender. (Edward Lloyd, 1895) cf. *soft money*

**downfall**  A fall of rain or snow. (Alfred Easther, 1883)
❖The descending waters of rivers and creeks. (William Smyth, 1867)

**downright**  Straight down; vertically downwards. (James Murray et al., 1888–1928)

**drab**  A thick woollen cloth of a dun colour, inclining to reddish brown; from Low Latin *drappum, drappus, cloth.* (Edward Lloyd, 1895)

**drape**  A cow which has one or more calves, but whose milk has dried up, and is likely to have no more. (Alfred Easther, 1883)

**draught**  The drawing of a bow; a bow-shot; also, the distance which a bow can shoot [1300s–1600s]. (James Murray, 1888–1928)

**draught-board**  A checkered board for playing *draughts* ["checkers" in America]. (Joseph Worcester, 1881)

**draughtsman**  One who draws up formal documents, as deeds, leases, &c. (Edward Lloyd, 1895)
❖A tippler. (Joseph Worcester, 1881)

**drawback**  Money paid back for ready payment; a kind of bounty allowed upon the exportation of foreign merchandise, upon which duties had been paid on the importation. (Richard Coxe, 1813)

❖Some kind of trick or performance. (Richard Thornton, 1912)

❖A gasp or loud inspiration, as in whooping-cough. (Joseph Wright, 1896–1905)

**drawl** To be slow in action; to dawdle; [related to] Dutch *dralen*, to loiter. (Edward Lloyd, 1895)
cf. *loiter*

**dread** To be reverenced in the highest degree; used in an address to a sovereign. *Dreadful*, originally, full of dread; not inspiring dread, but feeling it. It is sometimes followed by *of*, before the object of dread, [as] "*dreadful* of dangers that might him betide," in Spenser's *Fairy Queen*. (Edward Lloyd, 1895)

❖"Elizabeth, our *dread* sovereign and gracious queen." (Francis Meres, *Pallidas Tamia*, 1598)

❖*Dreadfully*, now that which causes dread, but once that which felt it. (Richard Chenevix Trench, 1859–60)

❖"Apprehend death no more *dreadfully*, but as a drunken sleep." *Measure for Measure*. (Alexander Dyce, 1902)

**drench** To drown. (Thomas Tyrwhitt, 1871)

❖To force down physic [medicines] mechanically; to purge violently. (Edward Lloyd, 1895)

❖A physick-drink for a horse. (John Kersey, 1772)

❖As *to fell* is 'to make to fall,' and *to lay*, 'to make to lie,' so *to drench* is 'to make to drink,' though with a sense now very short of 'to drown.' But *drench* and *drown*, though desynonymized in later English, were once perfectly [equivalent] to one another. (Richard Chenevix Trench, 1859–60)
cf. *physics*

**dresser** The bench in a kitchen on which meat is *drest*, or prepared for the table. (Samuel Johnson, 1755)

❖A long chest of drawers about three feet high, with an opening in the center for pots and pans, making a sort of kitchen table. [From] Teutonic *dressoor*, French *dressoir*, a side-board. (John Brockett, 1825)

**dribble** A servant, generally conjoined with the epithet *true*. "He's a *true dribble*," that is, one who is truly laborious and diligent. (William Carr, 1828) cf. *henchman*, *lout*, *servant*

**dribbling** A technical term in archery for an arrow too weakly shot to reach the mark. *Measure for Measure*. (C. H. Herford, 1902)

**drummer** A commercial traveller. The old-time peddlers and cheap jacks were in the habit of announcing their arrival in the town by the beating of drums; hence the term. So *drumming [up business]*, the solicitation of orders by commercial travellers. (John Farmer, 1889) cf. *cheap*, *rub-a-dub*, *tattoo*

**dull** Hard of hearing. (John Brockett, 1825)

**dumb-waiter** A piece of dining-room furniture, fitted with shelves, to hold glasses, dishes and plate. So called because it answers all the purposes of a waiter, and is not possessed of an insolent tongue. (E. Cobham Brewer, 1887) cf. *servant*, *tongue*

**dump** A mournful elegy. (Thomas Fosbroke, 1843)
❖Formerly the received term for a melancholy strain in music, vocal or instrumental. . . A *dump* appears also to have been a kind of dance: "He loves nothing but an Italian dump or a French brawl." (*Humour Out of Breath*, 1607). But whether *Devil's dumps* . . . be interpreted "devil's tunes" or "devil's dances," depends on whether it be thought to refer to the music preceding, or the dance following. (Robert Nares, 1859)
cf. *maggoty*

**dunce** A word introduced by disciples of Thomas Aquinas in ridicule of the disciples of John Duns Scotus. (Robert Hunter, 1894)

❖Duns Scotus (1265–1305) was . . . called *Duns* because he was from Dunce, in Berwickshire. He was a great supporter of the old theology against the new . . . and the classics. His followers were called *Dunsers,* and hence, it is asserted, *dunce* became a general name for any opponent of progress and learning. (Basil Hargrave, 1925)

**dungaree** In New York and Connecticut waters, a vessel used for transportation of *dung;* whence its name. (John Farmer, 1889)
cf. *manure*

**duplex** A name given to porter, or beer of more than ordinary strength, misunderstood as "double X," a survival in somewhat disguised form of the Latin word *duplex.* Thus, the fellows and postmasters of Merton College were forbidden by the statutes to drink *cervisium duplex,* or strong ale. (Robert Hunter, 1894)

**duplicity** The number *two.* (Noah Webster, 1828)

**Dutch** Till late in the seventeenth century, *Dutch* meant generally German, and a *Dutchman* a native of Germany, while what we now term a *Dutchman* was then a *Hollander.* In America, this with so many other usages is retained, and Germans are now often called *Dutchmen* there. (Richard Chenevix Trench, 1859–60)
❖Language—scientific, technical, or otherwise—which cannot be easily understood. . . . I have heard it said of children, when they gabble in the unknown tongue of childhood, that they talk *Double Dutch.* (Alfred Easther, 1883)
❖*Double-Dutch,* gibberish, jargon, or a foreign tongue not understood by the hearer. *Dutch* is a synonym for foreign, and *double* is simply excessive, in a twofold degree. (E. Cobham Brewer, 1887)
cf. *alien, far-fetched, outlandish, uncouth*

**eager** The physical and literal sense of *eager*, that is, sharp or acrid, has quite departed from the word. It occasionally retained this long after it was employed in the secondary meaning which is its only one at present. (Richard Chenevix Trench, 1859–60)
✦Sharp liquors, as beer, wine turned sour. Hence the compounds, *vinegar*, [and] *alegar*. (B. E., Gent., c. 1690)

**ear** A kidney, as the *ear of veal*. It is supposed to be so called from its resemblance to an ear, and being a name more delicate than a kidney, but it is probably a corruption of German *niere*, a kidney. The old name, presenting a less familiar idea, might be retained from delicacy, as the old French words mutton, veal, and pork are considered less offensive than sheep, calf ox, and pig, when these animals are brought to table. (John Brockett, 1825)
cf. *kidney*

**earmark** A hole cut in the ear of a sheep . . . to distinguish it from other animals. This is necessary when the cattle of several persons are put out to giste in a park. (Sidney Addy, 1888)
✦An 'ownery-mark.' (William Dickinson, 1881)
✦Cattle, hogs, and other animals are sometimes marked in the same way, by notching, clipping, or slitting the ear. (Cuthbert Johnson, 1844)
✦It seems to have been the custom for persons who could not write to make the same device [design, an *earmark*] with which they marked their sheep, do duty for their signature. (T. Lewis Davies, 1881)
cf. *marksman*

❖It seems to have been the custom for persons who could not write to make the same device [design, an *earmark*] with which they marked their sheep, do duty for their signature. (T. Lewis Davies, 1881)
cf. *marksman*

**eavesdrop** The water which falls in drops from the eaves of a house. (James Donald, 1877)
❖*Eavesdropping*, the dropping of water from the eaves. (Joseph Worcester, 1881)

**ebb** Nothing ebbs, unless it be figuratively, except water now. But *ebb*, oftener an adjective than anything else, was continually used in our earlier English with a general meaning of 'shallow.' There is still a Lancashire proverb, "Cross the stream where it is *ebbest*." (Richard Chenevix Trench, 1859–60)

**ecstasy** A state of excessive grief, distress, or anxiety; madness, distraction. "Better to be with the dead . . . than on the torture of the mind to lie in restless *ecstasy*." *Macbeth*. (Edward Lloyd, 1895)
❖We still say of madmen that they are 'beside themselves,' but *ecstasy*, or a standing out of oneself, is no longer used as an equivalent to madness. (Richard Chenevix Trench, 1859–60)
❖In the usage of Shakespeare and some others, it stands for every species of alienation of mind, whether temporary or permanent, proceeding from joy, sorrow, wonder, or any other exciting cause. From . . . wonder and terror, mixed with anger: "Follow them swiftly, and hinder them from what his *ecstasy* may now provoke them to do." *The Tempest*. (Robert Nares, 1859)
cf. *giddy, grin, melancholy, wrangle*

**effluvium** A stream of minute particles formerly supposed to be emitted by a magnet, electrified body, or other attracting or repelling agent, and to be the means by which it produces its effects. (James Murray, 1888–1928)
cf. *electron, hard-bodies*

**ejaculation** A short prayer in which the mind is directed to God on any emergency. (Charles Buck, 1835)
❖The hasty utterance of words expressing emotion [such as "Praise the Lord!"]. (James Murray, 1888–1928)

**elaborate** To produce with labour. (William Grimshaw, 1854)

**elegant** [As a substitute] for *excellent,* applied to articles of food and drink is common, as *elegant water, elegant beef, elegant butter.* (James Bartlett, 1849)
❖"The physicians call a medicine which contains efficient ingredients in a small volume, and of a pleasant or tolerable taste, an *elegant* medicine." (Vicesimus Knox, *Winter Evenings,* 1788)

**elder** The German *eltern* still signifies 'parents,' as *elders* did once with us, though it has quite let this meaning go. (Richard Chenevix Trench, 1859–60)

**electron** A name given to the sun, the supposed center and source of electricity. (Noah Webster, 1806)
❖A mixture of gold with a fifth part of silver. (Noah Webster, 1828)
cf. *effluvium, hard-bodies*

**elevate** There are two intentions with which anything may be lifted from the place which now it occupies; either with the intention of setting it in a more conspicuous position, or else of moving it out of the way, or figuratively, of withdrawing all importance and significance from it. We employ *to elevate* now in the former intention; our ancestors, for the most part, especially those whose style was influenced by their Latin studies, in the latter. (Richard Chenevix Trench, 1859–60)

**elf** To entangle in knots, such as *elf-locks.* It was supposed to be a spiteful amusement of Queen Mab and her subjects to twist the hair of human creatures, or manes and tails of horses, into hard knots which it was not fortunate to untangle. (Robert Nares, 1859)
cf. *imp*

**elopement** *Elopement* is when a married woman, of her own accord, departs from her husband and lives with an adulterer, whereby without voluntary submission or reconcilement to her husband, she shall lose her dower. . . . I am persuaded the word is taken from the Saxon *gelopan*, to depart from one place to dwell in another. (Thomas Blount, 1717)
cf. *adulterer*

**embassy** A message of any kind. (Edward Lloyd, 1895)

**embezzle** To mutilate, tamper with a document or writing of any kind; to impair or diminish by waste or extravagance; to squander, dissipate [1400s–1600s]. (James Murray, 1888–1928)
❖A man can now only *embezzle* another man's property, [but] he might once *embezzle* his own. Thus, while we might now say that the Unjust Steward *embezzled* his lord's goods (Luke 16:1) we could not say that the Prodigal Son *embezzled* the portion which he had received from his father, and which had become his own. But the one would have been as free to our early writers as the other. (Richard Chenevix Trench, 1859–60)

**emotion** Trouble of the mind. (Elisha Coles, 1713)
❖A disturbance. (John Kersey, 1772)

**engine** Intellect, genius, mental capacity. (Joseph Wright, 1896–1905)
❖Native talent, mother wit, genius; adaptation of Old French *engin*, Latin *ingenium*; whence, *ingenius* [1300s–1700s]. (James Murray, 1888–1928)
❖"And she shall file our *engines* with advice." *Titus Andronicus*. The allusion is to the operation of the file which, by conferring smoothness, facilitates the motion of the wheels which compose an *engine*. Here, *file our engines* is equivalent to "sharpen our wits." (Alexander Dyce, 1902)

**English** To translate into the English English. (Noah Webster, 1828)
cf. *romance, transfusion*

**engrave** To entomb. (James Murray, 1888–1928
❖"In thy death *engrave* me." (Phineas Fletcher, *Poetical Miscellanies*, 1633)

**enormous** Abnormal, unusual, extraordinary, unfettered by rules; hence, mostly in a bad sense, strikingly irregular, monstrous, shocking. (James Murray et al., 1888–1928)
❖Disordered, confused, perverse; wicked in an exceeding degree; [from] Old French *enorme*, Latin *enormis* (*e*, out, away, and *norma*, a rule). (Edward Lloyd, 1895)

**ensure** None of our dictionaries, as far as I can observe, have taken notice of an old use of this word, namely to betroth, and thus to make *sure* the future husband and wife to each other. (Richard Chenevix Trench, 1859–60)

**entertainment** Food and lodging. I have seen on a sign-board, "*Entertainment* here for man and beast." (Michael Traynor, 1953)
cf. *cheer*

**entitle** To obligate. "After he had done so much for us, we felt *entitled* to do this for him." (Harold Wentworth, 1944)
❖*Entitlement*, a name. "What may be your *entitlements?*" [was] frequently used by illiterate whites for "What is your name?" (Harold Wentworth, 1944)

**epicure** Now applied only to those who devote themselves, yet with a certain elegance and refinement, to the pleasures of the table. Lord Bacon and others, the followers of Epicurus . . . are often called *epicures*, after the founder of their sect. From them, it was transferred to all who were, like them, deniers of a divine providence, and this is the common use of it by our elder divines. But, inasmuch as those who have persuaded themselves that there is nothing above them, [they] will seek their good, since men must seek it somewhere, in sensual delights. The name has been transferred by the true moral instinct which is continually at work in speech, from the philosophical speculative atheist to the human swine, for whom the world is but a feeding-trough. (Richard Chenevix Trench, 1859–60)

**equal** The ethical sense of *equal* as fair, candid, just, has almost, if not altogether, departed from it. (Richard Chenevix Trench, 1859–60)
❖"The gods have been most *equal*." *Two Noble Kinsmen* (Alexander Dyce, 1902)

**equivocate** The calling [of] two or more different things by one and the same name (*æque vocare*) is the source of all error in human discourse. He who wishes to throw dust in the eyes of an opponent, to hinder his arriving at the real facts of a case, will often have recourse to this artifice; and thus 'to equivocate' and 'equivocation' have attained their present secondary meaning, very different from the original, which was simply the naming of two or more different things by one and the same word. (Richard Chenevix Trench, 1859–60)

❖From Latin *æquus*, equal, and *voco*, to call. (Edward Lloyd, 1895)

**escapade** Of a horse, a throwing off of control; a fit of plunging and rearing. (James Murray et al., 1888–1928)

**essay** There is no particular modesty now in calling a treatise or dissertation an *essay*. But from many passages it is plain that there was once, which indeed is only agreeable to the proper meaning of the word, an *essay* being a trial, proof, specimen, taste of a thing, rather than the very and completed thing itself. (Richard Chenevix Trench, 1859–60)

**estuary** A place where water boils up; [from] Latin *æstuarium*, a creek, *æstuo*, to boil with heat. (Edward Lloyd, 1895)

**ethnic** Heathen, pagan. (William Grimshaw, 1854)
cf. *heathen*

**etiquette** The word means a 'ticket or card,' and refers to the ancient custom of delivering a card of directions and regulations to be observed by all those who attended court. (E. Cobham Brewer, 1887)
❖The word originally signifie[d] a pointed stick, just such, no doubt, as a gardener may fix in a flower-pot after writing upon it some singularly distorted botanical name. We have but to replace the Old French *s* before the first *t* in the word [*etiquette*] to see how closely cognate *estiquette* is with *stick*. From this first meaning, it came in the form of *ticket* to signify the same thing as *label*. (W. L. Blackley, 1869)
cf. *label, ticket*

**evening** In the [American] South and West, *evening* commences at noon, there being no *afternoon*, as that term is understood in England. At sunset, *night* commences. (John Farmer, 1889)

**even keel** A ship is properly said to be on an *even keel* when she draws the same water abaft [behind] and forward. The term is sometimes used, though inaccurately, to denote that she is not inclined to either side, but is upright. (John Ogilvie, 1865)

**exalted** Of the pulse, high, rapid. *Exaltation*, in the older chemistry and physiology, the action or process of refining or subliming; the bringing a substance to a higher degree of potency or purity; an instance of the same. (James Murray et al., 1888–1928)
❖It is this *exaltation* of the sulphurous part in strawberries, that gives them their agreeable, vinous taste. (Ephraim Chambers, 1727–51)

**exasperate** To add harshness to language, sounds, etc. (James Murray et al., 1888–1928)
❖To over-aspirate the letter *H*, or to aspirate it whenever it commences a word, as is commonly done by under-educated people who wish to show off their breeding. (J. C. Hotten, 1887)

**excellency** This title is, in America, given by courtesy to governors of states. (John Farmer, 1889)

**exchequer** A chess-board; hence, the game of chess itself; from Old French *eschequier*, *eschec*, "check" at chess, Low Latin *scaccarium*, a chessboard. (Edward Lloyd, 1895)

**excrement** Hair, beard, and other things growing out of the body. The etymological meaning of *excrement* is "something which grows out," and it is in this sense that it is used in Shakespeare. (John Phin, 1902)
❖"It will please his Grace, by the world, sometime to lean upon my poor shoulder and with his royal finger, thus dally with my *excrement*, with my mustachio." (William Shakespeare, *Love's Labour's Lost*)
cf. *flatulent, lax*

**exorbitant** Deviating from the course appointed or rule established; overstepping rule or propriety; from Latin *exorbitans*, *exorbito*, to go out of the track (*ex*, out, and *orbita*, a track). (Edward Lloyd, 1895)

**expectorate**  To express from the breast. (William Grimshaw, 1854)
❖Of Latin *expectoro*, *ex*, out, and *pectoris*, the breast. (Edward Lloyd, 1895)

**expletive**  A word not necessary to the sense, but merely to fill up the measure of verse, or give roundness; [from] Latin *expletivus*, *expleo*, to fill. (Joseph Worcester, 1881)
❖An *expletive person* or *thing*, one that merely serves to fill up space. (James Murray et al., 1888–1928)

**explode**  To drive out with clapping the hands. (John Bullokar, 1616)
❖All our present uses of *explode*, whether literal or figurative, have reference . . . to bursting with noise, and it is for the most part forgotten, I should imagine, that these are all secondary and derived. To *explode*, originally an active verb, mean[t] to drive off the stage with loud clapping of the hands, and that when one of our early writers speaks of an *exploded heresy*, or an *exploded opinion*, his image is not drawn from something which, having burst, has perished so. But he would imply that it has been contemptuously driven off from the world's stage—the fact that *explosion* in this earlier sense was with a great noise, being the connecting link between that sense and our present [one]. (Richard Chenevix Trench, 1859–60)

**extenuating**  The action of the verb *extenuate*, to make the body thin or lean, to render emaciated or shrunken. (James Murray et al., 1888–1928)

**exterminate**  This now signifies to destroy, to abolish, but our fathers, more true to the etymology, understood by it to drive men out of and beyond their own borders. (Richard Chenevix Trench, 1859–60)

**extravagant**  Straying beyond the bounds; vagrant, roving about. "The *extravagant* and erring spirit." (Alexander Dyce, 1902)

**eye-glass**  The lens of the eye. *Winter's Tale*. (John Phin, 1902)

**fabulous** Dealing in, or belonging to *fables*, fiction or falsehood. (Daniel, Fenning, 1775)

**facepainting** The art of drawing portraits. (Samuel Johnson, 1755) cf. *counterfeit, local color, statue*

**facetiousness** *Facetiousness* has already acquired the sense of buffoonery, of making ignoble mirth for others . . . while there was a time when it could be ascribed in praise to high-bred ladies of the court and to grave prelates and divines. (Richard Chenevix Trench, 1859–60)

**faggot** A badge worn in times of Popery on the sleeve of the upper garment of those who had recanted and abjured what the then powers called 'heresy.' (Thomas Fosbroke, 1843)

❖A naughty child. (Angelina Parker, 1881)

❖*Faggot of misery*, a contemptuous epithet for a female. (John Brockett, 1825)

**fairy** In whatever latitude we may employ *fairy* now, it is always restricted to the middle beings of the Gothic mythology, being in no case applied, as it used to be, to . . . classical [Greek] antiquity. (Richard Chenevix Trench, 1859–60)

**fallow** Light brown, with a yellow or reddish tinge [1000–1800]. "You *fallow* greyhound." *Merry Wives of Windsor.* (Alexander Dyce, 1902)

**familiar** Pertaining to a *family*. (Noah Webster, 1828)
❖It is not a good sign that the *family* has now ceased to include servants. But for a long while, the word retained the largeness of its classical use, indeed it has only very recently lost it altogether. (Richard Chenevix Trench, 1859–60)

**fanatic** A word applied to the priest or other official whose business it was to give responses from the sanctuary to such as consulted the deity or oracle; from Latin *fanaticus*, inspired, beside oneself. (Hensleigh Wedgwood, 1878)
❖Those transported with "temple madness." Among the Romans, there were certain persons who attended the temples [*fanum*] and fell into strange fits, in which they pretended to see spectres, and uttered what were termed "predictions." (E. Cobham Brewer, 1887)

**fang** The talons of a fowl. *To fang*, to grip or hold fast. (Adam and Charles Black, 1851)

**farce** A composition of different foods; seasoning, stuffing, of meat; "force-meat" [late 1300s–1900s]. (Edward Lloyd, 1895)
❖*Farces*, meat chopped small, and well-spiced. (George Crabb, 1830)

**far-fetched** Brought from places at a great distance; sought with care and pains. (Charles Annandale, 1897)
cf. *barbaric, outlandish, uncouth*

**farthing** The word means literally 'a fourth part,' being derived from the Anglo-Saxon *feorth*, fourth. . . . A *farthing* was once the fourth part of a *noble*, a gold coin . . . and also indicated a division of land. In old days, a penny was nicked right across with two transverse lines, so that it could be divided into two or four parts. (Basil Hargrave, 1925)
cf. *nick*

**fascination** A bewitching by the eye. (Elisha Coles, 1713)
❖This was anciently supposed a peculiar quality of the eye, and many remedies or amulets were supposed to charm away its power. (Francis Douce, 1807)
cf. *gloat, overlook*

**fast and loose** This was a cheating game much practised in Shakespeare's time, whereby gipsies and other vagrants beguiled the common people of their money, and hence very often seen at fairs. Its other name was "Pricking at the Belt." . . . A leather belt was made up into a number of intricate folds and placed edgewise upon a table. One of the folds was made to resemble the middle of the girdle, so that whoever could thrust a skewer into it would think he held it fast to the table, whereas when he had done so the person with whom he plays may take hold of both ends and draw it away. *Love's Labour's Lost.* (John Phin, 1902)

**fastidious** Causing disgust; loathsome; difficult to please; from Latin *fastidiosus*, disdainful, disgusting, *fastidium*, loathing. (Edward Lloyd, 1895)

**father-in-law** *Father-in-law* and *mother-in-law* [are] invariably used for *step-father* and *step-mother*. (Angelina Parker, 1881) cf. *aunt, brother-in-law, cousin, foster-child, nephew, niece*

**faucet** The enlarged end of a pipe to receive the spigot end of the next section. (Edward Knight, 1874)

**faux pas** An act which compromises one's reputation, specially a woman's lapse from virtue; from French *faux*, false, and *pas*, step. (James Murray et al., 1888–1928)

**favour** To resemble, to have a similar countenance or appearance. "He *favours* his father." (John Brockett, 1825)
❖Appearance. "I know your *favour* well." *Twelfth Night.* (C. H. Herford, 1902) cf. *blush*

**feather** The rising of cream on the surface of a cup of tea or coffee. (M. Schele De Vere, 1872)

**fellowship** This word is regarded by many lexicologists as part of the stock-in-trade of religious cant. . . . Religious newspapers have, however, so popularized the phrase that it is no longer confined to matters theological. *To fellowship* signifies to hold communion with those sharing identical views as to religious doctrine and discipline. Used passively, a man would be said *to fellowship with* others, actively *to fellowship* them. (John Farmer, 1889)

**felon** A brave man, a warrior [1400s]. (James Murray et al., 1888–1928)

**fend** To be industrious. . . . It is also used in allusion to the state of health, as "How *fends* it?" How are you in health? *Fendy*, good at making a shift, warding off want. *Fend* is an old word for support. (John Brockett, 1825)
❖*Fender*, a careful provider. A cow or horse which takes pains to find all the choice or eatable portions of a meadow is a good *fender*. (Alfred Easther, 1883)

**fermentation** The sixth process in alchemy, the mutation of any substance into the nature of the ferment, after its primary qualities have been destroyed. (James Halliwell, 1855)

**field-day** A day when troops are drawn out for instruction in field exercises. (Daniel Lyons, 1897)
❖A day when explorations, scientific investigations, &c., as of a society, are carried on in the field. (William Whitney, 1889)

**fierce** Brisk, gay; used of a cheerful child, even of an infant or of a recovering invalid, or of an animal, however inoffensive. A frog, from its bright colour, is as *fierce* as a viper. (Edward Gepp, 1923)

**filibuster** The word is equivalent to the English *freebooter*, or lawless adventurer. (John Farmer, 1889)
❖Originally one of a number of buccaneers who infested the West Indies seas, preying on the Spanish commerce with South America; now applied to any lawless military adventurer, especially one in quest of plunder; from Dutch *vrijbuiten*, to rob, plunder [late 1700s–1800s]. (Edward Lloyd, 1895)

**find oneself** To provide for oneself. When a laborer engages to provide himself with victuals, he is said to *find himself*, or to receive day wages. (James Bartlett, 1849)

**fireworks** The quaint substitute which New Englanders not unfrequently use for *matches*. (M. Schele De Vere, 1872)

**first-rate** The highest of the rates by which vessels of war are distinguished by size and equipment [late 1600s–1800s]. (James Murray et al., 1888–1928)

✦In the United States, *first-rate* is used by the mass of people, and with an unbounded license, even where no rating is possible. (M. Schele De Vere, 1872)

**flabby**  Damp, clammy [late 1700s–1800s]. (James Murray et al., 1888–1928)

**flagrant**  Burning. (John Minshew, 1627)
✦Glowing, flaming. (John Walker, 1835)
✦From Latin *flagrans*, *flagro*, to burn. (Edward Lloyd, 1895)

**flamboyant**  Flaming, blazing; [adopted from] French *flamboyant*, flaming. (Edward Lloyd, 1895)
✦Of wavy form, suggesting the outline of a flame [1800s]. (James Murray et al., 1888–1928)
✦A term applied to the decorated and very ornamental style of architecture of French invention and use [that has] waving arrangements of the tracery of the windows, panels, &c. (Robert Hunter, 1894)
cf. *vagina*

**flashy**  Over-moist, watery; hence, insipid. (Joseph Wright, 1896–1905)
✦In Virginia, used of anything that is unproductive, acid, or sour. Thus, crab-apples would be called *flashy*. (John Farmer, 1889)

**flat-footed**  Firm-footed, resolute. (James Bartlett, 1849)
✦A synonym for honesty, earnestness, resolution. A man who is thorough, whose heart and soul are devoted to the interests of his party, is said to be *flat-footed*, and politically, no higher praise can be bestowed upon a man. The term is Western in origin, and the simile, of course, is that of a man standing firmly, with his back to a wall, resolved to accomplish his purpose. (John Farmer, 1889)

**flatulent**  Of the nature of wind. (Edward Lloyd, 1895)
✦"The spring and autumn . . . are the most *flatulent* seasons of the yeere." (R. Bohun, *Wind*, 1671)
cf. *excrement*, *wind-breaker*

**flavour**  That quality in anything which pleases the smell; odour, fragrance. A bright hue or colour; from Low Latin *flavor*, yellow coin, Latin flavus, *yellow*. (Edward Lloyd, 1895)
cf. *taste*

**flaws** These are sudden gusts of wind. It was the opinion, says Warburton, "of some philosophers that the vapors being congealed in the air by the cold, which is most intense in the morning, and being afterwards rarefied and let loose by the warmth of the sun, occasion those sudden and impetuous gusts of wind which were called *flaws*." Thus he comments on the following passage in *2 Henry IV*: "As humorous as winter, and as sudden as *flaws* congealed in the spring of day." (T. F. Thiselton Dyer, 1884)
❖I have myself heard the word used to signify both thin cakes of ice and the bursting of those cakes. (Alexander Dyce, 1902)
❖From the Gaelic *fluich*, a rainstorm. (Charles Mackay, 1888)

**flea-bitten** A Texas term to describe the color of a horse, or other animal dotted with minute specks of black and white, like salt and pepper. (John Farmer, 1889)

**flicker** This and *flutter*, are thoroughly desynonymized now; a flame *flickers*, a bird *flutters*, but it was not so once. (Richard Chenevix Trench, 1859–60)

**flippant** Nimble, moving lightly or alertly; easily moved or managed; light to the hand; pliant, flexible, limber [1600s]. (James Murray et al., 1888–1928)

**flirt** A jeer; to *flirt* at one, to jeer him. (John Kersey, 1772)
❖A quick elastic motion or jerk; a sudden throw or cast. To throw with a quick, elastic motion or jerk; to fling. (Edward Lloyd, 1895)

**floss** Untwisted filaments of the finest silk, used in embroidery or satin. (Robert Hunter, 1894)

**fluent** Which floweth or aboundeth. (John Bullokar, 1616)
cf. *courses*

**flunkey** A servant in livery, metaphorically applied to a person who abjectly flatters the great. Thackeray and Carlyle in our own day have made it classical English, although the most recent lexicographers have not admitted it or its derivative *flunkeyism* to the honours of the dictionary. The word is supposed to be derived from the Gaelic *flann*, red, and *cas*, a leg or foot . . . applied to the red or crimson plush breeches of footmen. (Charles Mackay, 1888)
cf. *knave, lackey, lout, slut*

**fly-boy** The boy in a printing office who lifts the printed sheets off the press. He is called the *fly-boy* because he catches the sheets as they *fly* from the tympan. (E. Cobham Brewer, 1887)
❖A boy who sells fly-papers. (James Murray et al., 1888–1928)

**fly-by-night** "You old *fly-by-night*," an ancient term of reproach to an old woman, signifying that she was a witch. (Francis Grose, 1796)
❖A bird which flies overhead in the night and is considered to be a forewarner of death. (Joseph Wright, 1896–1905)
❖A sort of square-sail, like a studding-sail, used in sloops when running before the wind. (William Smyth, 1867)

**fogey** A nickname for an invalid soldier, derived from the French word, *fougueux*, fierce or fiery. (Francis Grose, 1796)
❖It seems most probable that it comes from *foggy*, misty, hazy intellect, unable to see things that are obvious to clearer minds. Or it may be from Gaelic *fogaire*, an exile, a banished man. (Charles Mackay, 1888)

**fond** Silly, stupid, idiotical. Luscious, fulsome, disagreeable, sweet in taste or smell. (William Holloway, 1838)
❖*Fond* retains to this day, at least in poetry, not seldom the sense of foolish, but a *fondling* is no longer a fool. (Richard Chenevix Trench, 1859–60)
❖*Fondness*, foolishness. (C. Clough Robinson, 1876)
❖*Fondle*, to treat with fond indulgence. (James Murray et al., 1888–1928)
❖*Fondle*, to be over-fond; to make much of. (John Kersey, 1772)
cf. *giddy*

**footing** An entertainment given on entering at a school, or on any new place or office. (John Brockett, 1825)
❖*To pay one's footing*, to pay a fine or forfeit on doing anything for the first time, or on being admitted to a trade, place of work, society, &c. (Edward Lloyd, 1895)
cf. *garnish*

**footstool** A pillar's lowest part. (Henry Cockeram, 1623)
cf. *podium, vagina*

**forefront** The forehead. (James Halliwell, 1855)

**forehanded** In English dictionaries, the meaning of this word is given as 'early, timely,' with a supplementary signification of 'easy circumstances.' This last meaning is rarely heard in England, but is perfectly colloquial in America. (John Farmer, 1889)

**forerunner** One who runs before, especially one sent to prepare the way, and herald a great man's approach; a harbinger; a guide. First used figuratively as a rendering of Latin *præcursor*, especially of John the Baptist as the "*forerunner* of Christ" about 1300. (James Murray et al., 1888–1928)
cf. *harbinger*

**forgery** The action or craft of forging metal [1600s]. A piece of forged [metal] work [1800s]. (James Murray et al., 1888–1928)

**for God's sake** A curious mode of stating that a thing is thoroughly or well done, and probably of Puritan . . . derivation. Thus, such quaint phrases are sometimes heard as, "that orchard was planted *for God's sake*," or similarly, "a building is erected *for God's sake*," the meaning in each case being simply that the work was effectively done. (John Farmer, 1889)

**forlorn** Thin, lean. "He was so *forlorn* that his dimensions . . . were invisible." *2 Henry IV.* (Thomas Fosbroke, 1843)

**formal** It is curious to trace the steps by which *formality*, which meant in the language of schools the essentiality, the innermost heart of a thing, that which gave it its *form* and shape, should now mean something not merely so different, but so opposite. (Richard Chenevix Trench, 1859–60)

**fornicate** Vaulted like an oven or furnace. From Classical Latin *fornix*, an arch, a brothel. [Derived from ancient Roman brothels, commonly found in vaulted, subterranean portions of buildings.] (Edward Lloyd, 1895)
cf. *stew*

**forty** The familiar number on many occasions where no very exact reckoning was necessary. Anciently adopted to express a great many, [as] "these *forty* years." *Richard II.* (Alexander Dyce, 1902)
❖"And the rain was upon the earth for *forty* days and *forty* nights." (Genesis 7:12)
cf. *baker's dozen, quarantine*

**forty-niner** One who favored the 49th parallel of latitude as a compromise Oregon boundary line [1846]. (Mitford Mathews, 1956)

**foster-child** A child nursed by a woman not the mother, or bred by a man not the father. (Edward Lloyd, 1895)
❖*Foster-brother*, a male child nursed at the same breast, or fed by the same nurse, but not the offspring of the same parents. (Edward Lloyd, 1895)
❖*Foster-mother*, a nurse. (William Grimshaw, 1854)
cf. *aunt, brother-in-law, father-in-law, genealogy nephew, niece*

**foul** The past participle of [Saxon] *fylan*, to file, which we now write *to defile*. (John Horne Tooke, 1840)

**franchise** A sanctuary or asylum for persons liable to be arrested. In ordinary language, freedom, liberty. An immunity or exemption from ordinary jurisdiction. (Edward Lloyd, 1895)
❖Frankness; generosity; Old French. (Thomas Tyrwhitt, 1871)

**frank** A signature placed on a letter, entitling it to pass through the post free of charge. The privilege of *franking* letters was enjoyed by all members of Parliament up to 1840, when it was abolished by the same act which established penny postage. . . . From Low Latin *francus*, free, Old High German *franks*, a freeman. (Edward Lloyd, 1895)

**fraud** A person is called a *fraud* . . . when he disappoints expectations. Thus, an actor of whom great things have been heard, but who should be judged not so clever as has been anticipated, would be described as a *fraud*, but certainly not with the idea of attributing actual dishonesty to him. So a picture, or a book or play which proved disappointing is called a *fraud* without necessarily attributing any trickery to the painter or author. In fact, the word is often applied to a landscape or other natural object or phenomenon. For instance, the constellation of the Southern Cross has before now been called a *fraud* by those Americans who see it for the first time under unfavourable conditions. (John Farmer, 1889)

**Frenchman** Anciently used for every stranger. (Thomas Blount, 1717)
cf. *far-fetched, outlandish, uncouth*

**fresh liquor** Unsalted lard. (Angelina Parker, 1881)
cf. *lard*

**freshwater** Unpractised, raw, unskilled. (Edward Lloyd, 1895)
❖*Fresh-water soldier*, a raw, inexperienced warrior. (John Kersey, 1772)

**frightful** Now always active, that which inspires fright, but formerly as often passive, that which is, or is liable to be, frightened. "The wild and *frightful* herds, not hearing other noise, but this of chattering birds, feed fairly on the lawns." Drayton's *Polyolbion*, 1612. (Richard Chenevix Trench, 1859–60)

**frigid** A weak disabled husband; cold, impotent. (B. E., Gent., c. 1690)

**frog** A young horse, more than one, but less than two years old. (Edward Lloyd, 1895)
cf. *hog, kittie*

**fun** A cheat or slippery trick. (B. E., Gent., c. 1690)
❖Past tense and past participle of *to find*. (Alfred Easther, 1883)
❖*Funny*, shy, disagreeable, capricious, ill-tempered. (Joseph Wright, 1896–1905)

**funeral** *Funeral* means a torchlight procession, from the Latin *funís*, a torch, because funerals among the Romans took place at night by torchlight, that magistrates and priests might not be violated by seeing a corpse, and so be prevented from performing their sacred duties. (E. Cobham Brewer, 1887)

**funk** A strong rank smell, as that of tobacco. (Hensleigh Wedgwood, 1878)
❖A coward. (James Bartlett, 1849)
❖*Funky*, easily frightened; timid. (Edward Lloyd, 1895)
❖*Funky*, short-tempered; apt to take offence. (John Jamieson, 1879)

**furniture** This word formerly signified any kind of moveable property. A country well-stocked with animals, &c. is said to have "good *furniture*." (James Halliwell, 1855)
❖Dress, equipment. *Taming of the Shrew*. (C. H. Herford, 1902)
❖The harness, housings, trappings, etc. of a horse or other draught animal; similarly, the hood, bells, etc. of a hawk. (James Murray et al., 1888–1928)
cf. *apparel*

**gabardine** A shepherd's coarse frock. (Nathaniel Bailey, 1749)
❖Any mean dress. (Samuel Johnson, 1755)
❖Cotgrave calls it "a cloak for rainy weather." (Thomas Fosbroke, 1843)
❖In *The Tempest*, Shakespeare has Trinculo come upon Caliban in the storm, for protection creep under his *gabardine*, whence the word is sometimes used to mean 'protection.' (Joseph Shipley, 1955)
❖Sometimes called a "cow-gown," formerly worn by labouring men in many countries, now fast disappearing. (W. D. Parrish and W. F. Shaw, 1887)
❖From the German *gave*, because 'tis usually *given* to servants every year. (Thomas Blount, 1717)
❖In the Middle Ages, a long loose coat or cassock, rendered obligatory on the Jews to wear. (James Stormonth, 1884)

**gags** *Gags*, in theatrical parlance, are interpolations. When Hamlet directs the clowns to say no more "than is set down," he cautions them against indulgence in *gags*. [From] Dutch *gaggelen*, to cackle. (E. Cobham Brewer, 1887)

**galaxy** Bright circle in the sky caused by the reflection of the stars. (Thomas Blount, 1656)
cf. *moon, solarium*

**galoshes** Wooden shoos or patens made all of a peece, without any latchet or type of leather, and worn in France by the poor clowns in winter. (Thomas Blount, 1656)
❖From French *galoche*, a wooden shoe, from Low Latin *calopedia*, a clog. (Edward Lloyd, 1895)

**gamut** A word fast becoming obsolete in England, and meaning the [musical] scale. It is derived from *gamma*, the Greek name of the letter G, which was adopted by Guido d'Arezzo, as the lowest note of his system, and thence became employed for the entire compass of a voice or instrument. (George Grove, 1902)

**garb** One of many words whereof all the meaning has run to the surface. A man's dress was once only a portion, and a very small portion, of his *garb*, which included his whole outward presentment to other men. Now it is all. (Richard Chenevix Trench, 1859–60)

**garbage** The fat, tripe, entrails, &c. of cattle; of *garble*, to cleanse [1400s–1700s]. (Nathaniel Bailey, 1749)
cf. *fresh liquor*, *garble*, *lard*

**garble** Books only are *garbled* now, and *garbled* extracts are extracts which have been dishonestly made, which have been so shifted, mutilated, and otherwise dealt with that, while they are presented as fair specimens, they convey a false impression. It is not difficult to trace the downward progress of the word. It is derived from the Low Latin *garba*, a wheatsheaf, and *garbellare*, to sift or cleanse corn from any dust or rubbish which may have become mingled with it. It was then applied to any separation of the good from the bad . . . and used thus, especially of spices . . . of selecting the worse and dismissing the better. (Richard Chenevix Trench, 1859–60)

**garish** Splendid, shining. "And pay no attention to the *garish* sun." *Romeo and Juliet*. (Alexander Dyce, 1902)

**garland** At present, we know no other garlands but of flowers. But *garland* was at one time a technical name for the royal crown or diadem, and not a poetical one, as might at first sight appear. (Richard Chenevix Trench, 1859–60)
cf. *laureate*

**garnish** A fee given by a prisoner to his keepers and fellows at his first admittance. (John Kersey, 1772)
❖"It was a custom of the place for every prisoner, upon his first arrival, to give something to the former prisoners to make them drink. This, he said, was what they called *garnish*." Henry Fielding's *Amelia*, 1751. (Edward Lloyd, 1895)
cf. *footing*

**gash** Talkative. Jamieson defines the word as a verb, "to talk much in a confident way, to talk freely and fluently," and as an adjective, "shrewd, sagacious." It seems derivable from the Gaelic *gais* (pronounced *gash*) a torrent, an overflow, the English *gush*, an overflow or torrent of words, and hence by extension of meaning applied to one who has much to say on every subject. (Charles Mackay, 1888)
❖Solid, sagacious; one with a long chin we call *gash-gabbet*, or *gash-beard*. (Adam and Charles Black, 1851)

**gasoline** A volatile inflammatory liquid . . . employed for the purposes of heating and illumination. (James Murray et al., 1888–1928)
❖From Latin *oleum*, oil. (Daniel Lyons, 1897)

**gather** A calf's gather, the entrails, as the heart, liver, &c. (Edward Lloyd, 1895)
cf. *pluck*

**gaudy** Of fare, luxurious [1500s]. (James Murray et al., 1888–1928)
❖*Gaudy night*, a feast night. (Thomas Fosbroke, 1843)

**gawk** To romp, applied to girls who are too fond of the society of men, and who either play roughly themselves or suffer men to play roughly in their company. The word is probably a variety of *geck*, to sport or mock. (Charles Mackay, 1888)
cf. *tomboy*

**gay** Pretty well; a common answer to the salutation, "How are you?" Gay, tolerable. Also considerable. "A *gay* while." (John Brockett, 1825)

**gazebo** A turret or lantern on the roof of a house for the purpose of commanding an extensive prospect. . . . A projecting window or balcony [1700s–1800s]. (James Murray et al., 1888–1928)
cf. *lantern*

**gazette** Originally an Italian word meaning a small coin current at Venice. Newspapers, being first published there, and being sold for a *gazette* coin, came to be called *gazettes*. Johnson says that in the eighteenth century the pronunciation of the word was frequently GAHZ-ette. (Robert Hunter, 1894)
❖*Gazetteer*, a writer of news; a journalist. (William Whitney, 1889)

**gee-string** An Indian's waist-band. (Richard Thornton, 1912)
❖A breech-cloth [from the 1800s]. (Mitford Mathews, 1956)
cf. *cummerbund, sash*

**gelding** Restrained at present to horses which have ceased to be entire, but until *eunuch*, which is of somewhat late adoption, had been introduced into the language, serving the needs which that serves now. (Richard Chenevix Trench, 1859–60)

**genealogy** Progeny, offspring [1500s–1700s]. (James Murray et al., 1888–1928)
cf. *foster-child, generous*

**generous** We still use *generous* occasionally in the sense of highly or nobly born, but *generosity* has quite lost this in its earlier sense, and acquired a purely ethical meaning. (Richard Chenevix Trench, 1859–60)
❖From Latin *generosus, genus*, race, family [originally introduced in Shakespeare's *Love's Labour's Lost*]. (Edward Lloyd, 1895)
❖Strong, full of spirit, as a *generous* wine. (Noah Webster, 1828)
cf. *genealogy, ilk*

**gentle** To ease, soften, or sooth. A survival of Elizabethan English. Also applied to the taming of horses by kind treatment. (John Farmer, 1889)
❖*To gentle* received a new application when Mr. Rarcy practised and taught the art of *gentling* horses. (M. Schele De Vere, 1872)
❖Enchanted or haunted by the fairies; a *gentle plant*, one which the fairies regard as peculiarly their own, and with which it is dangerous for humans to interfere. Hence, the phrase, the "gentle people," the fairies. (Michael Traynor, 1953)

**german** Related. One approaching to a brother in proximity of blood; thus the children of brothers and sisters are called *cousins german*. [From] French *germain*, Latin, *germanus*. (Samuel Johnson, 1755)
cf. *carnal, cousin*

**gestation** Now a technical word applied only to the period during which the females of animals carry their young, but acknowledging no such limitation once . . . [when it meant a body] being carried in a coach, litter, upon

horseback, or in a vessel in the water. (Richard Chenevix Trench, 1859–60)
❖*Gesture*, the carriage of the body; from Latin *gesturus, gero*, to carry. (Edward Lloyd, 1895)

**gibberish** Cant, the private language of rogues and gypsies. Derived by Skinner from French *gaber*, to cheat; but as it was anciently written *gebrish*, it . . . originally implied the jargon of *Geber* and his tribe. (Richard Coxe, 1813)
cf. *jargon*

**giddy** Mad, insane, foolish; [from] Old English *gidig*, insane; apparently from Old Teutonic *gudo*, God; the primary sense thus appears to be 'possessed by God,' [akin to] Old English *ylfig*, insane, literally 'elf-possessed,' similarly formed on *ælf*, elf [1000–1300]. (James Murray et al., 1888–1928)
❖*To go giddy*, to go in a passion. (James Halliwell, 1855)
❖Wild, heedless; from Anglo-Saxon *gyddian*, to sing, to be merry; from *gyd*, a song. (Edward Lloyd, 1895)
cf. *ecstasy, fond, melancholy, silly, teen*

**giggle** To be restless and uneasy, generally applied to children. (Joseph Wright, 1896–1905)
❖From Bavarian *gigken*, to utter inarticulate sounds, either in stuttering [or] retching. (Hensleigh Wedgwood, 1878)

**gimpy** As used colloquially for sprightly or active, this word, which is provincial in England, . . . may be classed among Americanisms. (John Farmer, 1889)

**girls** Young persons, either male or female; Saxon. (Thomas Tyrwhitt, 1871)
❖A diminutive of a root *gir*, a little child, and this of either sex. In Old English, a 'knave girle' occurs in the sense of boy. (Richard Chenevix Trench, 1859–60)
cf. *maid, street-walker, wench*

**glade** The name given originally to a part of the water which is not frozen over, though surrounded by ice—from the analogy to the *glade*, an opening in the woods—has been subsequently applied in New England to smooth ice. (M. Schele De Vere, 1872)
cf. *shade*

**glamour** Enchantment, witchcraft, fascination, once supposed to be from the Gaelic *glac*, to seize, to lay hold of, to fascinate, and *mor*, great; whence "great fascination," or magic, not to be resisted. Lord Neaves thought the word was a corruption of *grammar*, in which magic was once supposed to reside. (Charles Mackay, 1888)

❖A kind of haze covering objects, and causing them to appear differently from what they really are; [from] Icelandic *glamr*, a legendary ghost spirit. (Edward Lloyd, 1895)

❖When devils, wizards, or jugglers deceive the sight, they are said to "cast glamour" over the eyes of the spectator. (Adam and Charles Black, 1851)

❖From Danish *glimmer*, glitter, false lustre. (James Stormonth, 1884)

❖*Glamorous*, supernatural. (Joseph Wright, 1896–1905)

cf. *fascination, overlook, overshadow*

**glee** Music. Before our Anglo-Saxon and Scandinavian ancestors had learned to borrow from Norman-French or from Latin words to express old and familiar meanings, they had, necessarily, a word for the art of music. That word was *glee*, which by the progress of change and corruption, has come to signify that state of mind which music is so calculated to produce, joyfulness and pleasure. (Charles Mackay, 1874)

cf. *music*

**glib** Of machinery, smooth, slippery. Figuratively, cunning, slippery in dealings. Used to describe polished talk of sly, cunning persons. (Michael Traynor, 1953)

❖To castrate; supposed to be from *making smooth*, which is the effect of that operation on men. *To glib* is still said to be current in some counties in this sense. (Robert Nares, 1859)

❖A man who wears a *glib*, a thick mass of hair on the forehead and over the eyes, formerly worn by the Irish. Act 28 of Henry VIII [stated], "No person . . . shall . . . use the wearing of haire upon their heads, like unto long lockes, called *glibbes*." (James Murray et al., 1888–1928)

**gloat** To gaze with any warm or burning passion or sensation. (John Ogilvie, 1865)

❖From Icelandic *glotta*, to grin, Danish *gloe*, to glow, to stare. (Edward Lloyd, 1895)

cf. *fascination*

**glorious** Boastful, ostentatious; proud, haughty [1300s–1700s]. (James Murray et al., 1888–1928)
cf. *spread-eagle, stout*

**glut** *Glut*, a large wooden wedge, has been preserved in New England. It is, after all, but a small application of the general sense of *glut*, which means the complete filling of a passage, in this case accomplished by the wedge. (M. Schele De Vere, 1872)

**go-between** A servant who does part of the work of a housewife and part of a cook. (Joseph Wright, 1896–1905)
cf. *dribble, housewife*

**go-cart** A machine in which children are enclosed to teach them to walk, and which they push forward without danger of falling. (Samuel Johnson, 1755)

**god-send** Term used in the Orkney and Shetland Islands to denote the wreck which is driven ashore by the waves. (John Jamieson, 1879)
❖Flotsam and jetsam coming ashore. (Alexander Warrack, 1911)
❖The wreck of a ship; Kentish coast. (Samuel Pegge, 1814)

**good-mannered** A meadow that abounds in sweet grasses is said to be *good-mannered*. (John Walker, 1835)

**goosed** *To be goosed* signifies to be hissed while on the stage. (J. C. Hotten, 1887)

**gossip** One who answers for the child in baptism; from Saxon *god* and *syb*, relation, affinity. (Samuel Johnson, 1755)
❖It would be interesting to collect instances in which the humbler classes of society have retained the correct use of a word, which has been let go by those who would rather claim to be guardians of the purity than of their native tongue. *Gossip* is one, being still used by our peasantry in its first and etymologi-

cal sense, namely as a sponsor in baptism—one *sib*, or akin in God. . . . *Gossips*, in this primary sense, would often be intimate and familiar with one another . . . and thus the word was applied to all familiars and intimates. (Richard Chenevix Trench, 1859–60)

**graft** *To graft* is one of the many words by which the Sons of Crispin [cobblers] love to express the different modes of repairing boots. This term is generally applied when new soles are added, and new leather is sewn on all around. (M. Schele De Vere, 1872)
cf. *revamp*

**grail** A single-cut file, having one curved face and a straight one, used by comb-makers. (Edward Knight, 1874)

**grammar-school** A school in which learned languages, as Greek and Latin, are grammatically taught. (Joseph Worcester, 1881)
❖Schools, of which many English towns have one, founded in the sixteenth century or earlier for the teaching of Latin. (James Murray et al., 1888–1928)

**gregarious** Of classes or species of animals living in flocks or communities, given to associate with others of the same species; formed of Latin *gregarius*, from *greg*, *grex*, flock, herd [1600s–1800s]. (James Murray et al., 1888–1928)

**grin** Of persons or animals, to draw back the lips and display the teeth, as an indicator of pain or anger. "As the wolfe doth *grin* before he barketh." *Venus and Adonis* [1000–1800s]. (James Murray et al., 1888–1928)

**gripe** A rogue in bowling-alleys who lays bets with the crowd. (A. V. Judges, 1930)

**grocery** Though sometimes applied to a grocery store, the term is too often, in the [American] Southwest especially, only another name for a drinking saloon, and "groceries" then take the form of ardent spirits. (John Farmer, 1889)
❖Grocers, by the Statute 37, Edward 3, were those that *engrossed* merchandize. Now it is a particular trade, well known. (Thomas Blount, 1717)
❖Once called a *pepperer*, and still in French *épicier*. (Samuel Pegge, 1844)

**groin** A swine's snout. The mouth or muzzle of any animal. (Joseph Wright, 1896–1905)
❖A froward, grunting look. (Elisha Coles, 1713)

**groovy** Settled in habit; limited in mind. (John Farmer and W. E. Henley, 1890–1904)
❖"Schoolmasters, as a class, are extremely *groovy.*" (*Blackwell Magazine*)

**grope** Now to feel for, and uncertainly, as a blind man or one in the dark; but once simply to feel, or grasp. (Richard Chenevix Trench, 1859–60)
❖*Groping,* a mode of catching trout by tickling them with the hands under rocks or banks. (William Carr, 1828)

**grout** Coarse meal. (William Grimshaw, 1854)

**grubby** Old-fashioned. (J. C. Hotten, 1887)

**grudge** To think much of; to envy. (Nathaniel Bailey, 1749)
❖It formerly implied open utterances of discontent and displeasure with others, and did the work which *to murmur* does now. Traces of this still survive in our Bible. (Richard Chenevix Trench, 1859–60)
cf. *grungy*

**gruesome** Of weather, dull, cloudy, heavy. (Joseph Wright, 1896–1905)
cf. *shabby*

**gruff** To sleep restlessly; to snore. (Alexander Warrack, 1911)
❖A short, thick, well-dressed man. (John Mactaggart, 1824)
❖Applied to bulky goods; probably [from] the Dutch *grof,* coarse. (Henry Yule, 1886)

**grungy** A deep revengeful feeling; a grudge. A 'nisgal' or underling, the smallest of a brood of poultry. Used originally of the smallest pig in a litter. (Joseph Wright, 1896–1905)
cf. *grudge*

**guilt** The old idea, so ingrained in human nature that it still persists, that wrong-doing can be expiated by the payment of money, or its equivalent, is strangely exemplified in the word *guilt.* It comes from the Anglo-Saxon *gylt,* which means a fine. (Basil Hargrave, 1925)
cf. *smart-money*

**guinea-pig** A special juryman who is paid a guinea a case; also a military officer assigned to some special duty, for which he receives a guinea a day, are sometimes so called. A *guineapig* is neither a pig nor a native of Guinea. . . . A *guineapig*, in the Anglican Church, is a clergyman without cure, who takes occasional duty for a guinea a sermon. (E. Cobham Brewer, 1887)

❖A man who lives by getting himself placed upon the boards of companies whose business he can have neither the time nor the qualifications to assist in directing is a *guinea pig*. (A. J. Wilson, 1895)

❖This was a nickname given to midshipmen or apprentices on board Indiamen in the eighteenth century, when the command of such a vessel was a sure fortune, and large fees [in *guineas*] were paid to the captain with whom the youngsters embarked. (Henry Yule, 1886)

**guzzle** To eat loudly, hastily, and clumsily. (J. C. Hotten, 1887)

**gymnasium** A school or place of instruction for the higher branches of literature and science. Latin, from Greek *gumnazo*, to train naked [1600s–1800s]. (Edward Lloyd, 1895)
cf. *grammar-school*

**haberdasher** A pedlar; [from] Old French *hapertas*, pedlars' wares, from the bag in which they were carried. (Robert Hunter, 1894)
cf. *cadger, clothier*

**hackle** A cone-shaped covering of straw placed over bee-hives to protect them from wet and cold. (Georgina Jackson, 1879)

**hag** One of many words applied formerly to both sexes, but now restrained only to one. "And that old *hag* with a staff, his staggering limbs doth stay." Golding's translation of Ovid's *Metamorphosis*. (Richard Chenevix Trench, 1859–60)
cf. *concubine, maid, wench*

**haggle** To harass oneself with work, often applied to energetic preachers. (Angelina Parker, 1881)
❖*Haggler*, an upper farm servant who looks after his master's horse and the stock on Sundays. (W. H. Long, 1886)

**half-and-half** A mixture of beer or porter, and ale. (Joseph Worcester, 1881)

**half-seas-over** Originally a nautical phrase signifying half-way in one's course; hence, generally half-way. (Robert Hunter, 1894)
❖Figuratively, half through with a matter [1500s–1800s]. (James Murray et al., 1888–1928)

**hallmark** The mark on gold or silver articles after they have been assayed. Every article in gold is compared with a given standard of pure gold. This standard is supposed to be divided into twenty-four parts called *carats*. . . . Standard silver consists of thirty-seven parts of pure silver and three of pure copper. (E. Cobham Brewer, 1887)

**hammock** In Florida, a term given to a particular kind of land. The low *hammocks* are the richest in the country, and are capable of producing, for many successive years, rich crops of sugar, corn, hemp, or other equally exhausting productions. In their primitive state, they are clothed with so heavy a growth of timber and underwood that the task of clearing them is appalling. (James Bartlett, 1849)

**handful** As much as the arms will embrace. A palm; four inches. (Noah Webster, 1828)
cf. *hug*

**hand-grenade** A glass bottle containing a chemical to be broken in order to extinguish a fire [late 1800s]. (James Murray et al., 1888–1928)
❖From French *grenade*, a pomegranate. (Hensleigh Wedgwood, 1878)

**hand-in-hand** Balanced. *Cymbeline*. (C. H. Herford, 1902)

**hand-me-downs** Ready-made clothing. (John Farmer, 1889)

**handsome** Now referred exclusively to comeliness, either literal or figurative. It is, of course, closely connected with *handy*, [and] indeed differs from it only in termination, and in all early uses means 'having prompt and dexterous use of the hands.' (Richard Chenevix Trench, 1859–60)

**hanky-panky** Jugglery, legerdemain; an arbitrary formation probably related to *hocus pocus*, *hokey pokey*. (James Murray et al., 1888–1928)
cf. *juggle*, *prestigious*

**harbinger** This word belongs at present to our poet[ry] and to that only, its original significance being nearly or quite forgotten, as is evident from the

inaccurate ways it has come to be used, as though *harbinger* were merely one who announced the coming, and not always one who prepared a place and lodging, a 'harbour' for another. He did indeed announce the near approach, but only as an accidental consequence of his office. (Richard Chenevix Trench, 1859–60)
cf. *forerunner*

**hard and fast** Said of a ship on shore. (William Smyth, 1867)

**hard-bodies** In *Natural Philosophy*, such bodies as do not yield to any pressure or percussion whatever, or whose particles resist the action of any external force tending to alter their relative positions. They are thus distinguished from *soft bodies* and from *elastic bodies*. (John Ogilvie, 1865)
cf. *effluvium, electron*

**hard-nosed** Having little or no sense of smelling [a hunting term]. (James Halliwell, 1855)

**hard up** Said of the tiller when it is put as far as possible to windward, so as to turn the ship's head away from the wind; usually as a command. (James Murray et al., 1888–1928)

**hardy** When speaking of persons, *hardy* means always now 'enduring, indifferent to fatigue, hunger, thirst heat, cold,' and the like. But it once had a far more prevailing sense of 'bold,' which now only remains to it in connection with things, as we should speak of a *hardy*, meaning a bold assertion, though never now of a *hardy* if we intended a bold or daring person. (Richard Chenevix Trench, 1859–60)

**harmonica** A musical instrument invented by Benjamin Franklin, consisting essentially of tuned or musical glasses so arranged as to be conveniently played upon, originally by rubbing the edges with the moistened finger. (Mitford Mathews, 1956)
❖The essential difference between this instrument and the former ones was that the pitch of the tone was produced by the size of the glasses, and not their containing more or less water; and that chords could be produced of as

many notes as the fingers could reach at once. Franklin calls it the *armonica*, but it seems to have been generally known as *harmonica*. (George Grove, 1902)
cf. *tuba*

**harness** *To die in harness*, a common English phrase, meaning to die in action, to die with one's armor on, *harness* being a now obsolescent word for armor. (William Walsh, 1900)

**hassle** To pant, breathe noisily. (Harold Wentworth, 1944)

**hatter** In Old English and provincial English, to entangle; to weary out; to wear out; to harass. . . . *To work as hard as a hatter*, perhaps corrupted from 'hard as to hatter,' meaning to work so hard as to weary out or wear out—the familiar saying thus having no connection with that of the trade of a hatter. The same explanation may be given to 'mad as a hatter.' (James Stormonth, 1884)

**havoc** *Havoc* is Anglo-Saxon for 'hawk,' and originally *to cry havoc* was a cry of encouragement in falconry to a hawk when loosed upon its prey. In the later Middle Ages, it was a military cry to general massacre. The cry was forbidden on pain of death in the ninth year of Richard II. It was through this custom and cry that a word, originally meaning a falcon, came to mean general and relentless destruction. (William Walsh, 1900)

**hearse** The *hearse* was the frame or stand on which the body lay. (George Craik, 1886)
❖This term is derived from a sort of pyramidal candlestick, or frame for supporting lights. . . . It was not, at first, exclusively part of funeral display, but was used in the solemn services of the holy week. Chaucer appears to use the term *herse* to denote the decorated bier, or funeral pageant, and not exclusively the illumination. (Walter Skeat, 1879–82)

**heart-strings** The tendons or nerves supposed to brace and sustain the heart [1400s–1800s]. (Samuel Johnson, 1755, and John Redman Coxe, 1817)

**heathen** Literally, 'a dweller on the heath,' in the open country. The term was applied by the dwellers in towns to those who were cut off from urban civilisation, and it acquired its modern theological sense when the towns were Christian and the country chiefly of the older faith. (Basil Hargrave, 1925)
cf. *flunkey, knave, lackey, villain*

**heckle** To dress flax. *Heckler*, a flax-dresser. [From] Teutonic *hekelaer*. (John Brockett, 1825)

**hell on wheels** This expression originated during the building of the Union Pacific Railway in 1867. As the rails were laid westward, the honky-tonks, gambling halls, and harlots were loaded on flatcars and moved to the new terminals. (Ramon Adams, 1946)

**hemp** Mischief. Apparently based on the idea of a gallows-rope. Hence, in some parts a *hemp* is a troublesome person. (Edward Gepp, 1923)
cf. *lace*

**henchman** A servant; one who stands at one's *haunches*. It is said that Old English *hengst*, a horse, is a probable derivation, thus meaning 'groom,' or one that attends his master's horse. (James Stormonth, 1884)
cf. *dribble, lackey, lout, pioneer*

**herself** Himself; used by High-landers. (Joseph Wright, 1896–1905)

**heyday** An expression of frolic and exultation. (Joseph Worcester, 1881)
✧[From] Saxon *heh-dœg*, high-day. (E. Cobham Brewer, 1887)

**hide** This word is at present only contemptuously applied to the skin of man, being reserved almost exclusively for that of beasts, but it had once the same extent of meaning. (Richard Chenevix Trench, 1859–60)
cf. *spine*

**highball** A signal given a railway engineer to proceed. No doubt the expression in this sense arose from the use on railroads of a semaphore signal of which a ball formed a part. When the ball was high, it was a signal to the engineer to go ahead. (Mitford Mathews, 1956)

**high-jinks** Formerly in Scotland, boisterous and hilarious merriment, in which the dice were thrown to determine the person on whom some ludicrous penalty should be imposed. (William Walsh, 1900)

❖Most frequently, the dice were thrown by the company, and those upon whom the lot fell were obliged to assume and maintain for a time a certain fictitious character, or to repeat a certain number of fescennine [obscene] verses in a particular order. If they departed from the character assigned, they incurred forfeits, which were compounded for by swallowing an additional bumper. (James Stormonth, 1884)

❖A covetous man may save money and get himself as drunk as he can desire in less than an hour's time. (William Hone, 1832)

❖Probably derived from Anglo-Saxon *hige*, haste, and *jink*, to dodge, cheat, or make believe. (William Scott, 1791)

**high-minded** At a comparatively high mental level. (Robert Lawson, 1884)
❖Uppish, arrogant. (Michael Traynor, 1953)

**hobnob** Explained by some, [to] have or have not, hit or miss; by others, less probably . . . happen or not happen. [Introduced in] *Twelfth Night*. (Alexander Dyce, 1902)
❖A drinking to each other or together. (James Murray et al., 1888–1928)
cf. *symposium*

**hodgepodge** A commixture of lands. (Edward Lloyd, 1895)
❖The term is generally applied in reference to settlements by which a power is given to parents of appointing a fund among his or her children, wherein it is provided that no child . . . shall be entitled to any share in the appointed portion without bringing his or her own share into *hotchpotch*. (Robert Hunter, 1894)

**hog** A sheep before its first shearing. (Edward Sutton, 1881)
cf. *frog, kittie, squab*

**hoity-toity** Giddy, frolicsome, flighty; [from] French *haute tête*, high head. (William Carr, 1828) ❖An expression frequently used to soothe cows when they are being milked [with] vowels drawn out to a great length. Used also as a verb. (R. Pearse Chope, 1891)
cf. *giddy, tomboy*

**holocaust** A sacrifice wherein the whole beast is offered, and no part reserved. (John Bullokar, 1616) ❖A sacrifice wholly consumed by fire [1200s–1800s]. (James Murray et al., 1888–1928)

**homicide** A manslayer. (John Bullokar, 1616)
cf. *cosmetic, manslaughter, pedicure, politics, rhetoric*

**honeymoon** The term is said to have arisen from an old Teutonic practice of drinking a honey-like liquid, metheglin, for thirty days after marriage. . . . The honeymoon, during which the bridegroom keeps his bride away from her relatives and friends, may be a survival from marriage by capture. (Robert Hunter, 1894)

**hoodwink** To blindfold with a hood or cloth. (Edward Lloyd, 1895)

**hooker** These ho[o]kers, or angglers, be peryllous and most wicked knaves. . . . They customarily carry with them a staffe of five or six foote long, in which, within one ynch of the top thereof is a lytle hole bored through, in which hole they putte an yron hook, and with the same they wyll pluck unto them quickly any thing that they may reche ther with. (Thomas Harman, 1567)
cf. *bribery, thief*

**hospital** [From] Latin *hospitum*, a lodging for strangers; *hospitalis*, connected with guests, from *hospes*, landlord, entertainer, host, and conversely the person entertained, guest. (Hensleigh Wedgwood, 1878)
❖Houses erected for the relief of pilgrims, poor, and impotent people. (Elisha Coles, 1713)

**hostage** [An] inn. (A. V. Judges, 1930)

**housewife** A term of reproach; a hussy, a wanton, a minx, a strumpet. "Wild cats in your kitchen . . . and *housewives* in your bed." *Othello*. (Alexander Dyce, 1902)
cf. *queen*

**hovel** An outhouse. This is the word's first meaning [1400s], with no sense of squalor. It may be apart of the house used as an outhouse. (Edward Gepp, 1923)
❖The hood of a smith's forge [1600s]. (James Murray et al., 1888–1928)

**hubbub** A noisy game, somewhat like dice, played by Indians in colonial New England. (Mitford Mathews, 1956)
❖ "Hubbub . . . was accompanied by a continual shouting of *Hub-bub!*" (*Notes and Queries*, 1887)

**hug** The utterance induced by the shudder of cold is represented in different dialects by the interjection *ugh!* From this interjection is formed Dutch *huggeren*, to shiver. From the same source, the English *hug* signifies the bodily attitude produced by the sensation of cold when we shrug together into a heap with the back rounded and the arms pressed upon the breast. The reference to cold [was] afterwards lost, and the word is applied to the mere pressure of anything between the arms, against the breast. (Hensleigh Wedgwood, 1878)

**humble** *To humble barley*, to break off the beards or awns. [From] Suio-Gothic (Swedish) *hamla*, to mutilate. Allied to this is a *hummelled-cow*, a cow without horns. (John Brockett, 1825)

**humble pie** A pie made of the *umbles*, or entrails of the deer . . . undoubtedly influenced by the adjective, *humble*. The origin of the phrase, "to eat *humble-pie*," is said to be that at hunting-feasts, while the lord and his guests ate of the venison pasties, humble-pie only was placed before the huntsmen and their dependents. (Robert Hunter, 1894)
cf. *gather, lights, pluck*

**humorous** Perverse, capricious. "A vain, giddy, shallow, *humorous* youth." *Henry V.* (Alexander Dyce, 1902)
❖The four 'humours' in a man, according to the old physicians, were blood, choler, phlegm, and melancholy. So long as these were duly mixed, all would be well. But so soon as any of them duly preponderated, the man became 'humourous,' one humour bearing too great a sway in him. As such, his conduct would not be according to the received rule of other men, but have something peculiar, whimsical, self-willed in it. In this, the self-asserting character of the 'humourous' man lay the point of contact . . . between the modern use of 'humour' and the ancient. (Richard Chenevix Trench, 1859–60)
❖*Humourist*, one that is full of *humours*, or conceits. (Edward Lloyd, 1895)

**hump** A great amount. *To think a hump of* is to think much of. A dialect preservation of its Teutonic basis, a lump, hunch. (Edward Gepp, 1923)
❖*To hump oneself*, to bestir oneself; to be expeditious. *Hump yourself* is a frequently heard injunction to "Be sharp! Look alive!" (John Farmer, 1896)

**hunch** A lump; a large slice, especially of victuals. A misshapen piece, in contradistinction to a slice. A solid piece of meat or cheese would be called "a great hunch"; a "hunch of bread" is a large irregular piece, generally cut angularly from the corner of a loaf. (Anne E. Baker, 1854)
❖A thrust or shove; to *hunch* one, to thrust him with the elbows. (Edward Lloyd, 1895)
❖To gore with the horns. (James Halliwell, 1855)
cf. *lunch, snack*

**hundred** A part of a shire, so called . . . because it was composed of a hundred families. (Thomas Blount, 1717)
cf. *lathe*

**hungarian** An old cant term, generally meaning an hungry person, but sometimes a thief or rascal of any kind. (James Halliwell, 1855)
❖*Hungarian* is a cant term of doubtful origin, perhaps from the freebooters of Hungary, or perhaps it is equivalent to "gipsy," for the parts of Europe in which it is supposed that the gipsies originally appeared were Hungary and Bohemia. "O base *hungarian* wight, wilt you the spigot wield?" *Merry Wives of Windsor.* (Alexander Dyce, 1902)

**hustle** To shrug the shoulders. (Joseph Wright, 1896–1905)
❖To emit such a sound as an infant does when highly pleased, or a cat, when it is said to purr. (John Jamieson, 1879)

**hyena** A beast like a wolf, accounted the subtlest of all beasts, [capable of] changing sex often and counterfeiting man's voice. (Elisha Coles, 1713)
cf. *antelope, reptile*

**hyper** A New England word for *to be busy*. "I must *hyper* about and get tea." (M. Schele De Vere, 1872)

**hypochondria** The upper side of the belly about the short ribs; *hypochondriac*, belonging to the *hypochondria*, or troubled with a windy melancholy in those parts. (Edward Lloyd, 1895)
cf. *flatulent, melancholy*

**ignoramus** *Ignoramus* is a word properly used by the grand inquest, empannelled in the inquisition of causes criminal and publick . . . whereby any crime is offered to their consideration. When they mislike their evidence as defective or too weak to make good the presentment, all inquiry upon the party for that fault is thereby stopped. (Richard Coxe, 1813)
❖Hence *ignoramus'd*, freed from prosecution by the *ignoramus* of the Grand Jury [1400s]. (Joseph Worcester, 1881)

**ilk** *Of that ilk* is in Scotland exclusively applied to a gentleman whose family name is the same as that of his estate. Menzie of Menzies is an example. The number of families to whom the title is applicable is extremely limited, and it is regarded as more honorable than those of the new-made nobles. (William Walsh, 1900)
cf. *generous, madam, slogan*

**illegitimate** An *illegitimate person*, one unable to read or write. (Joseph Wright, 1896–1905)

**imbibe** To admit into the mind. (Samuel Johnson, 1755)
❖To receive by education. (Edward Lloyd, 1895)

**immense** A thing is *immense* when very good, which can hardly be said of the form of speech itself. A vulgar perversion of the language, which has gained some acceptance in England also. (John Farmer, 1889)

**imp** Shakespeare, in *Love's Labour's Lost*, makes Armando say, "Sadnesse is one and the selfe same thing, dear *impe*." Upon this passage, Dr. Johnson says, "*Imp* was antiently a term of dignity. Lord Cromwell, in his last letter to Henry VIII, prays for the *imp*, his son. . . . *Imp* is the past participle of the Anglo-Saxon verb *impan*, to plant, to graft. (John Horne Tooke, 1840)
❖An addition, an insertion. In hawking, to insert a new feather in place of

a broken one. (James Halliwell, 1855)

❖The word is derived from the Greek *emphuo*, to graft . . . and is now usually taken to denote a little devil or wicked spirit. But formerly it retained a scion of nobility, [as] an offspring, a child. . . . In an old devotional book, we have, "Let us pray for the king's most excellent majesty, and for his beloved son, Edward our Prince, that most angelic *imp*." (Basil Hargrave, 1925)

cf. *elf*

**improve**  To make progress in that which is evil; to grow worse. . . . This word is sometimes used in this country instead of to *use*, to *occupy*, or to *employ*, in a manner deemed improper and even ludicrous, as "to *improve* a person as a witness." (Joseph Worcester, 1881)

❖The part of a discourse intended to enforce and apply the doctrines is called the *improvement*. (James Bartlett, 1849)

❖*Improvement*, of a sermon, the conclusion. (John Pickering, 1816)

**incarnation**  A making flesh to grow; [related to] *incarnate*, in surgery, to fill up with new flesh. (John Kersey, 1772)

cf. *carnation*

**incense**  Now, to kindle anger only, but once to kindle or inflame any passion, good or bad, in the breast. Anger, as the strongest passion, finally appropriated the word. (Richard Chenevix Trench, 1859–60)

cf. *giddy*, *grin*, *wrangle*

**incontinent**  Immediately, forthwith, at once. (Joseph Wright, 1896–1905)

❖One who indulges in sexual passion unlawfully. (Joseph Worcester, 1881)

cf. *continent*, *libido*, *wrangle*

**incubation**  The practice of sleeping in a temple or sacred place for oracular purposes. (James Murray et al., 1888–1928)

**incumbent**  A person that is in present possession of a church-living. (John Kersey, 1772)

**index**  Whatsoever directs, [such as] the fore-finger, hand of a clock, &c. (Elisha Coles, 1713)

❖A finger or arm of a balance or measuring apparatus, which moves along a graduated scale; a finger-post which points out the road to any place. (Edward Lloyd, 1895)

❖The *index* was formerly prefixed to a book. . . . It was used generally for 'prelude,' or anything preparatory [1600s]. (Joseph Worcester, 1881)

**infantry** Children. Ben Jonson. (James Halliwell, 1855)

**infield** Arable land which receives manure, and is perpetually in crop; Scotland, Cumberland, Cheshire. (Joseph Wright, 1896–1905) cf. *manure, outfield*

**ingrained** Dyed with grain. . . . *Ingrain-carpet,* a carpet manufactured from wool or woollen dyed in the grain before manufacture. (Edward Lloyd, 1895)

**inlaid** In easy circumstances; rich, or well to pass. (Francis Grose, 1796) ❖A man is said to be *inlaid* when he has been able to save and invest his ill-gotten gains. (John Farmer, 1889)

**inlaw** To clear from outlawry; to restore. (Noah Webster, 1806)

**inning** A harvest or gathering in of corn. Lands enclosed when recovered from the sea are called *innings.* (James Halliwell, 1855)

**insolent** The *insolent* is, properly, no more than the unusual. This, as the violation of the fixed law and order of a society, is commonly offensive, even as it indicates a mind willing to offend, and thus *insolent* has acquired its present meaning. But for the poet, the fact that he is forsaking the beaten track, . . . in this way to be *insolent,* or original, as we should now say, may be his highest praise. (Richard Chenevix Trench, 1859–60)

**instill** To drop or pour in. (Max Müller, 1863)

**intend**  To stretch out, extend, expand, increase, intensify; a group of senses of late introduction, immediately from Latin [1600s]. (James Murray et al., 1888–1928)
❖Used curiously to express a desire or expectation in matters beyond one's own control. (Alfred Easther, 1883)

**intoxicate**  To poison. (James Halliwell, 1855)
cf. *pot-shot*

**investment**  The act of putting clothes or vestments on; concretely, clothing, robes, vestments. [Introduced in] Shakespeare's *2 Henry IV*, 1597. (James Murray et al., 1888–1928)

**jacket** "He proceeded home by a *jacket* way," is a peculiar usage and essentially American, the meaning being that the road is roundabout. It is difficult to imagine what connection there is in this case between the word and the idea conveyed by it, except it be that a *jacket* surrounds or goes about the body. (John Farmer, 1889)

**jargon** Properly, the chattering of birds, analogous to forms like Anglo-Saxon *cearkian*, Old English *chark*, *chirk*, to creak, chirp, . . . [From] French *jargonner*, to gaggle as a goose; *jargouiller*, to warble, chirp or chatter. . . . Hence, figuratively for an utterance of sounds not understood. (Hensleigh Wedgwood, 1878)
cf. *gibberish*

**jay** A loose woman. "To know turtles from *jays*." *Merry Wives of Windsor*. (Alexander Dyce, 1902)

**jealous** Devoted, eager, zealous [1300s–1600s]. (James Murray et al., 1888–1928)
❖We look on *jealousy* as an odious failing, and the jealous person as possessing a miserable disposition, and if we be ignorant that the word in its general sense means zealous, we find a trial to our faith in reading that the Lord our God is a *jealous* God. (W. L. Blackley, 1869)
cf. *revenge*

**jetty** That part of a building which shoot[s] forward beyond the rest. An outnooke. *Macbeth*. (Alexander Dyce, 1902)

**jig** There can be no doubt that in the present passage, Shakespeare alludes to a theatrical *jig*, which was the technical term for a coarse sort of comic entertainment usually performed after the play. "He's for a *jig*." *Hamlet*. (Alexander Dyce, 1902)

**jilt** A woman accomplice of a thief, who entices the victim and occupies his attention whilst he is being robbed. (John Farmer, 1889) cf. *bribery*, *thief*

**job** A sudden stab with a pointed instrument. This seems to be nearly the original sense. (Noah Webster, 1828)
❖To peck at, as a bird; to thrust at so as to stab or pierce; [1560s-1800s]. (James Murray et al., 1888–1928)

**jockey** A man that deals in horses. A cheat; a trickish fellow. From *jack*, the diminutive of John, comes *Jackey*, or as the Scotch [say it] *jockey*, used for any boy, and particularly for a boy that rides race-horses. (Samuel Johnson, 1755)
❖The verb *to jockey*, signifying to cheat, to trick, is in Johnson's and other dictionaries. A friend informs me that it is a coarse but well known colloquial word in England. (John Pickering, 1816)

**jolly** For a long time after its adoption into the English language, *jolly* kept the meaning of 'beautiful,' which it brought with it from French, and which *jolie* in French still retains. (Richard Chenevix Trench, 1859–60)
❖Amorous, wanton, lustful; of animals, in heat [1300s–1600s]. (James Murray et al., 1888–1928)

**juggle** To play tricks by sleight-of-hand. (Hezekiah Burhans, 1833)
❖*Juggling*, the practice of magic, or of legerdemain; conjuring; the practice of trickery or deception [1300s–1800s]. (James Murray et al., 1888–1928)
❖It is certain that *joke* and *jocular* . . . are from the same root as *juggle*, perhaps Chaldee *hukk*, or *chuk*, to laugh, to play, to sport. (Noah Webster, 1828)
cf. *hanky-panky*, *prestigious*

**jungle** The native word means, in strictness, only waste, uncultivated ground. . . . The Anglo-Indian application is to forest, or other wild growth, rather than to the fact that it is not cultivated. From Anglo-Indian it has been adopted into French as well as English. (Henry Yule, 1886)

**junkets** Cakes or sweetmeats; any sort of delicious fare; *to go junketing*, to entertain one another with banquets or treats. *Taming of the Shrew.* (John Kersey, 1772)
cf. *banquet*

**junky** Stout, sturdy [in] Scotland. (Joseph Wright, 1896–1905)

**justify** To inflict capital punishment, to execute. (Joseph Wright, 1896–1905)
cf. *baffle, ostracize*

**kennel** The hole of a fox. *Unkennel*, to drive from his hole; to rouse from his retreat. (William Grimshaw, 1854)
cf. *rumpus*

**kibble** Sweepings, as from garden paths and court yards. (B. Lowsley, 1888)
cf. *dog-biscuit*

**kidney** Disposition, principles, humour. (John Brockett, 1825)
❖The use of this word seems to have risen from Shakespeare's phrase, "A man of my *kidney*," where Falstaff means, "a man whose kidneys are as fat as I am." (Joseph Worcester, 1881)
❖"Of the same *kidney*," of a like sort. [Hotten's] *Slang Dictionary* has "two of a *kidney*, or two of a sort, as like as two pears, or two kidneys in a bunch." A little knowledge of the original language of the British people would show the true root of the word to be the Gaelic *ceudna* (pronounced *keudna*), of the same sort. (Charles Mackay, 1888)
cf. *ear, liver, spleen, stomach*

**kilt** To lift one's petticoats or other clothes to keep them clean and dry while on a walking journey. From this came the familiar "kilt." (Charles Mackay, 1874)

**kindly** Nothing ethical was connoted in *kindly* once. It was simply the adjective of *kind*. (Richard Chenevix Trench, 1859–60)
❖Natural. "The other daughter will use thee *kindly*." (*King Lear*) The Fool uses the word *kindly* here in two senses; it means 'affectionately,' and 'like the rest of her kind.' (Alexander Dyce, 1902)
❖Well-to-do. (Thomas Sternberg, 1851)

**kink** Laughter. *To kink,* as spoken of children, when their breath is long stopped, through eager crying or laughing; hence, *kink-cough.* (Francis Grose, 1811)
❖A paroxysm of coughing or laughter. (William H. Patterson, 1880)
❖*Kinky,* lively, strong, energetic. (Harold Wentworth, 1944)
cf. *smirk, spleen*

**kittie** A name given to any kind of cow. (John Jamieson, 1879)
cf. *frog, hog*

**knack** To speak affectedly; to ape a style beyond the speaker's education. (John Brockett, 1825)
❖To speak finely; and it is used of such as do speak in the Southern [English] dialect. (John Ray, 1674–91)

**knave** How many serving lads must have been unfaithful and dishonest before *knave,* which meant at first no more than 'boy,' acquired the meaning which it has now! (Richard Chenevix Trench, 1859–60)
cf. *flunk, lackey, lout, slut, villain*

**knick-knacks** Castanets, pieces of wood or bone held between the fingers and struck together. (Joseph Wright, 1896–1905)

**knocked up** Fatigued. (Sylva Clapin, 1902)
❖To *knock up* is a familiar term, but is not unfrequently applied in the United States to a very curious purpose, characteristic of the false prudery of the people. An English traveller relates, with comic distress, how he inquired after a lady's health, and was told by her sister that she was *knocked up.* He insisted on knowing what had brought on the excessive fatigue—as he understood the term— and was only more embarrassed than the lady, by learning afterwards that the phrase was used in speaking of [pregnant] ladies. (M. Schele De Vere, 1872)
cf. *pregnant*

**knuckle** To submit. I suppose from an old custom of striking the under side of the table with the knuckles, in confession of an argumental defeat. (Samuel Johnson, 1755)
❖The German *knöchel* is any joint whatsoever. Nor was our *knuckle* limited formerly, as it well nigh exclusively is, at least in regard to the human body, to certain smaller joints of the hand. (Richard Chenevix Trench, 1859–60)

**label** A word now very rarely used, except as referring to heraldry or the medicine phial. Its origin is the Latin diminutive *labellum*, a little lip. . . . We see in the old caricatures, and indeed in their ruder kindred, the wall frescoes executed in chalk by satirical street-boys, a sort of balloon represented as hanging from the mouths of the figures, on which is written what the character represented is supposed to be saying. This method was formerly used in very much higher works of art, and there are few collections of good pictures in which specimens of its occurrence may not be found. . . . This appended *lip* it was which received the name of *labellum*, or *label*. The label used to be a piece of paper, broad at one end and narrow at the other, where it was tightly tied round the neck, and close to the *lip* of the phial. And, in point of fact, we see this practice still prevalent among apothecaries on the continent. The shape of this label far more resembles that of the lip-balloons than any of the rectangular slips pasted on phials in the present day. (W. L. Blackley, 1869)

**lace** That which now commonly bears this name has on it the score of its curiously woven threads. But *lace* . . . being the same word only differently spelt as *latch*, is commonly used by our earlier writers in the more proper sense of a noose. (Richard Chenevix Trench, 1859–60)
cf. *hemp*

**lackey** In the fifteenth century, a kind of foot soldier. (James Murray et al., 1888–1928)
❖A runner. To act as a footman; from Old French *laquet*, Old German *läcken*, to run. (James Donald, 1877)
❖ "*Lackeying* the varying tide," (*Antony and Cleopatra*) floating backwards and forwards with the variation of the tide, like a page or lackey at his master's heels. (Alexander Dyce, 1902)
cf. *caddy*, *flunk*, *knave*, *pioneer*, *slut*, *villain*

**lamb** The expression, "I'll *lamb* you," used as a threat, is often heard among the poorer classes. One might imagine that, like so many phrases, it was merely a corruption of something else, the *lamb* being an innocent creature with nothing threatening about it. But the verb *to lamb* is good Old English: "A fellow whom he *lambed* most horribly," says Misson in his *Travels*. (Basil Hargrave, 1925)

**lame duck** A name given to a member of the Stock Exchange who, because he cannot meet his liabilities on settling day, has been black-boarded and struck off the list of members. Wild ducks, when in flight, marshall themselves into battalions of triangular form, each individual with legs and head in a horizontal attitude. A duck which is lamed or disabled in any way cannot keep its place. (Basil Hargrave, 1925)
cf. *waddle*

**landowner** A dead man; from his occupation of his grave. A common colloquialism in the war for a man killed on the Western Front was, "a *landowner* in France." (Edward Fraser and John Gibbons, 1925)

**lantern** [Romeo:] "A *lanthorn*, slaughter'd youth, for here lies Juliet, and her beauty makes this vault a feasting presence full of light." A *lantern* may not, in this instance, signify an enclosure for a lighted candle, but a louvre, or what in ancient records is styled *lanternium*, a spacious round or octagonal turret full of windows, by means of which cathedrals, and sometimes halls, are illuminated. (Alexander Dyce, 1902)
cf. *gazebo*

**lard** To sweat; of a horse out of condition. . . . It is rare in literature, and only in the sense to ooze with fat. (Edward Gepp, 1923)
cf. *fresh liquor*

**last** Utmost; highest; greatest; extreme. "Principles of the *last* importance." [1600s–1700s]. (Joseph Worcester, 1881)

**lathe**  A division of the county of Kent, which is divided into five *lathes*, Sutton-at-Home, Aylesford, Scray, St. Augustine's, and Shepway. (Samuel Pegge, 1735–36)
cf. *hundred*

**lather**  To *lather* is used here, as well as some parts of England, in the sense of *to beat*. It was originally *to leather*, a term derived from the leather belt worn by soldiers and policemen, which was often used as a weapon in street-rows, when firearms were forbidden. (M. Schele De Vere, 1872)
cf. *dad, rib-roast, spank*

**laureate**  Crowned with laurel. (John Kersey, 1772)
❖The appellation *laureate* seems to have been derived, through the Italian, from Latin *laurus*, a bay [tree], in allusion to the ancient practice of crowning poets. Petrarch received the crown at Rome in 1341. The earliest mention of a *poet-laureate* in England, under that express title, is in the reign of Edward IV. (Joseph Worcester, 1881)
cf. *coroner, garland, insolent*

**lavatory**  A sort of stone table upon which, in the Middle Ages, dead bodies were washed before burial in monasteries, hospitals and elsewhere. (William Whitney, 1889)
❖A place where gold is obtained by washing. (Noah Webster, 1828)
cf. *morgue*

**lavender**  Old French [for] a washerwoman. (Thomas Tyrwhitt, 1871)
❖A laundress; from French *lavande*, lavender. So called because used in washing, or because laid in freshly washed linen. (William Whitney, 1889)
❖The name comes to us from the Low Latin *lavendula*, the root of which is the Latin *lavare*, to wash, and in which also our word *laundress* and the French *lavandière* both originate. (Basil Hargrave, 1925)

**lawn**  Fine linen. (Stephen Jones, 1818)
❖A white cambric handkerchief. (James H. Vaux, 1812)
❖A fine sieve, generally of silk, through which porcelain 'slip,' cement, etc., are strained to ensure uniform fineness. Short for *lawn sieve*. (James Murray et al., 1888–1928)
cf. *rudder*

**lax** Diarrhœa. (Robley Dunglison, 1844)
❖*Laxative*, having the power of relaxing. (James Murray et al., 1888–1928)
❖From Latin *laxativus, laxare*, to loosen. (Joseph Worcester, 1881)
cf. *excrement*

**leasing** The faculty of lying. *Twelfth Night*. (C. H. Herford, 1902)
❖*Leasing-maker*, a liar, a propagator of lies. (Joseph Wright, 1896–1905)

**lecture** Where words like *lecture* and *reading* exist side by side, it is very usual for one, after a while, to be appropriated to the doing of the thing and the other to the thing which is done. So it has been here, but they were once synonymous. (Richard Chenevix Trench, 1859–60)

**leech** A physician. Obsolete in this sense, except perhaps for compounds, as *horse-leech*. [From] Anglo-Saxon *læce*, a physician, a leech. (Hensleigh Wedgwood, 1878)
cf. *surgeon*

**left–handed** Unlucky; inauspicious; unseasonable. (Noah Webster, 1828)
❖Underhand, malicious. (Michael Traynor, 1953)
cf. *ambidextrous, dexterity, sinister*

**lewd** Originally 'illiterate, untaught,' as opposed to the educated clergy. (Hensleigh Wedgwood, 1878)
❖Useless. . . . In the remote parts of Yorkshire, a vicious horse is termed *lewd*. (James Halliwell, 1855)
❖In Anglo-Saxon, *læped* is almost equivalent to 'wicked,' except it includes no agency of infernal spirits. It means led astray, deluded, imposed upon, betrayed, into error; *lew'd* is the past participle. *Lewd*, in its modern application, is confined to those who are betrayed or misled by one particular passion. (John Horne Tooke, 1840)

**libation** The act of pouring wine on the ground in honour of some deity; the wine so poured. (William Grimshaw, 1854)

**liberal sciences** Grammar, logick, rhetorick, music, arithmetick, geometry, astronomy. (Elisha Coles, 1713)
cf. *trivial*

**liberty** *To give a woman her liberty* means to church her after childbirth. It is incorrect to go out till this is done. (Edward Gepp, 1923)

**libido** That irresistible passion of the soul which makes a man break apparently through the evidence of the senses and the laws of reason, and drives him by a power which nothing can control, to embrace some truth which alone can satisfy the natural cravings of his being. (Max Müller, 1863) cf. *incontinent, liver, spleen*

**life-preserver** The apparatus of Captain Manby to mitigate the horrors of shipwreck. . . . Rope is thrown by a shot from a mortar, with a line attached to it. For the night, a night-ball is provided with a hollow case of thick pasteboard, and a fuze and quick-match, and charged with fifty balls and a sufficiency of powder to inflame them. . . . The apparatus was brought into use in February, 1808. (Joseph Haydn, 1841)
❖A stick or bludgeon loaded with lead, intended for self-defence; often referred to as a frequent weapon of burglars. (James Murray et al., 1888–1928)
❖A weapon, as a pistol . . . used for defence against assailants. (William Whitney, 1889)

**light-fingered** Prompt at giving or returning a blow [1500s–1600s]. (James Murray et al., 1888–1928)

**lights** The organs of breathing; the lungs. We say *lights* of other animals and *lungs* of men. (William Grimshaw, 1854)
cf. *humble pie*

**likely** Such as may be liked; pleasing, as a *likely* man or woman. This use of *likely* is not obsolete, as Johnson affirms, nor is it vulgar. But the English and their descendants differ in their application. The English apply the word to external appearance, and with them *likely* is equivalent to 'handsome, well-formed,' as a *likely* man, a *likely* horse. In America, the word is usually applied to endowments of the mind, or to pleasing accomplishments. With us, a *likely* man is a man of good character and talents, or of good disposition or accomplishments that render him pleasing or respectable. (Noah Webster, 1828)

**linger** With *for* or *after*, to long, wish greatly. (Edward Gepp, 1923)

**lingerie** A linen warehouse; Latin *linum*, flax, linen; [from] French *linger*, a dealer in linen goods. (William Whitney, 1889)
cf. *warehouseman*

**linguist** An old word for an interpreter, formerly much used in the East. It survived long in China, and is there perhaps not yet obsolete. Probably adapted from the Portuguese *lingua,* used for an interpreter. (Henry Yule, 1886) cf. *master of ceremonies*

**lint** Flax; from Old English *linne,* whence also *linen.* (Charles Mackay, 1874) ❖A soft material for dressing wounds (formerly also to burn for tinder), prepared by ravelling or scraping linen cloth. In plural, pieces of this material [1400–1800s]. (James Murray et al., 1888–1928) cf. *tent*

**liquored** Oiled or greased to keep out water; said of boots. "Justice hath *liquor*ed her." *1 Henry IV.* (C. H. Herford, 1902)

**listerine** A solution containing the antiseptic constituents of thyme, eucalyptus, baptisea, gualtheria, and *mentha arvensis,* with two grains of benzo-boric acid in each drachm. (*Sydenham Society Lexicon,* 1889) ❖An antiseptic preparation consisting of a solution of benzoic acid, boric acid, thymol, etc. From Sir Joseph Lister [1827–1912] founder of the antiseptic surgery. (William Whitney, 1889)

**lithography** A description of stones or rocks. (James Murray et al., 1888–1928)

**litigious** This word has changed from an objective to a subjective sense. Things were *litigious* once which offered matter for going to law; persons are *litigious* now who are prone to going to the law. (Richard Chenevix Trench, 1859–60)

**liver** Anciently supposed to be the inspirer of amorous passion, and the seat of love. "I had rather heat my *liver* with drinking." *Antony and Cleopatra.* (Alexander Dyce, 1902) cf. *kidney, spleen, stomach*

**livid** Of a leaden colour, black and blue; discoloured, as the flesh by a blow; clouded with grayish, brownish, and blackish. From Latin *lividus,* to be bluish [1600s–1800s]. (Robert Hunter, 1894) cf. *carnation*

**living** A farm, [in] Leicestershire. (Joseph Wright, 1896–1905)
❖A London man might call a person's house and grounds a nice *place*, but a Norfolk man would use the word *living*. In this sense, too, it occurs in Ben Jonson: "I have a pretty *living* o' mine own." *Every Man in His Humour*. . . . I was once told that I seemed to have a nice *living*, *i.e.* a pleasantly situated house. (Walter Skeat, 1896)
❖*Livings*, possessions. *Merchant of Venice*. (C. H. Herford, 1902)
cf. *breadwinner, quality*

**local color** In painting, the colour which belongs to an object, irrespective of all accidental influences, as reflections, shadows, &c. (Joseph Worcester, 1881)
cf. *carnation*

**loiter** Whatever may be the derivation of *to loiter*, it is certain that it formerly implied a great deal more and worse than it implies now. The *loiterer* then was very much what the *tramp* is now. (Richard Chenevix Trench, 1859–60)
cf. *drawl*

**look-out** An attendant at the gaming-table who is supposed to see that matters are conducted fairly, that no mistakes are made, and that money won goes to the right person. (John Farmer, 1889)

**lottery** An allotment. "Octavia is a blessed *lottery* to him." *Antony and Cleopatra*. (Alexander Dyce, 1902)

**lousy** Swarming or overrun with lice. (Daniel Fenning, 1775)
cf. *midget, vermin*

**lout** A servant [1500s–1600s]. (James Murray et al., 1888–1928)
❖A boy belonging to the lower division of a school. (Joseph Wright, 1896–1905)
cf. *flunk, knave, lackey*

**lover** The word has undergone two restrictions, of which it formerly knew nothing. . . . An unwillingness to confound under a common name things essentially different, has caused *lover* to no longer be equivalent with *friend*, but always to imply a relation resting on the difference of sex, while further, and within these narrower limits, the *lover* is always the man, not as once the

man or woman indifferently. (Richard Chenevix Trench, 1859–60)
cf. *coquette, lust*

**loving-cup** A large cup formerly passed round the table after grace was said, and partaken of in token of love. (Joseph Worcester, 1881)

**ludicrous** Belonging to sport or pastime. (John Kersey, 1772)
❖From Latin *ludus*, play, sport. (Hensleigh Wedgwood, 1878)

**luggage** Any heavy weight or burden [introduced in *1 Henry IV*, 1596]. (John Kersey, 1772)
cf. *carriage*

**lumbago** In medicine, a rheumatic affection of the kidneys. (James Barclay, 1848)

**lumber** Rubbish, trash, trumpery. (B. E., Gent., c. 1690)
❖*Lumber*, in England only known as meaning useless and cumbersome things, literally and figuratively, denotes in America timber cut and sawed for use. (M. Schele De Vere, 1872)
❖The worst sort of household stuff. (John Kersey, 1772)
❖As the Lombards were the bankers, so also were they the pawnbrokers of the Middle Ages. Indeed, as they would often advance money upon pledges, the two businesses were very closely joined, would often run into one another. The *lumber room* was originally the "Lombard room," or room where the Lombard banker and broker stowed away his pledges, *lumber*, then the pawns and pledges themselves. As these would naturally often accumulate here till they became out of date and unserviceable, the steps are easy to be traced by which the word came to possess its present meaning. (Richard Chenevix Trench, 1859–60)

**lunch** Lunch, in Scottish phrase, a large piece of bread, cheese, beef, &c., whence the modern English word *lunch*. This meal in Scotland is called a *piece*, the two words being synonymous. (Charles Mackay, 1874)
❖As much food as one's hand can hold. (William Grimshaw, 1854)
❖A large piece of anything, especially which is edible, as bread, cheese, &c. (Joseph Wright, 1896–1905)
cf. *hunch, snack*

**lust** Friendly inclination to a person [1400s–1500s]. (James Murray et al., 1888–1928)

❖*Lusty*, pleasant, gay. *Lustiness*, jollity. (Alois Brandl and Otto Zippel, 1949)
cf. *lover, luxury*

**luxury** A disposition of mind addicted to pleasure, riot, and superfluities.
. . . *Luxury* may be further considered as consisting in . . . a splendour that does not agree with the public good. In order to avoid it, we should consider that it is ridiculous, troublesome, sinful, and ruinous. (Charles Buck, 1835)

❖Leacherie. *Old French*. (Thomas Tyrwhitt, 1871)
❖Excess in carnal pleasures. (Edward Phillips, 1706)
❖The word . . . is derived from the Latin *luxus*, excess. (Basil Hargrave, 1925)
❖*Luxurious*, lascivious; its only sense in Shakespeare. (Alexander Dyce, 1902)
cf. *lover, lust*

**macaroni** An exquisite of a class which arose in England about 1760, and consisted of young men who had travelled and affected the tastes and fashions prevalent in continental society; a fop, dandy. This seems to be from the name of the Macaroni Club, a designation probably adopted to indicate the preference of the members for foreign cookery, *macaroni* at that time little eaten in England. (James Murray et al., 1888–1928)

**madam** *Madam* is the title given in many parts of the country [America], where old English customs are still in remembrance, in New England and Virginia for instance, to married ladies who have married daughters of their own name. (M. Schele De Vere, 1872)
❖In Plymouth, Massachusetts, it has been, and is still the practice, to prefix to the name of a deceased female of some consideration, as the parson's, the deacon's, or the doctor's wife, the title of *Madam*. (James Bartlett, 1849)
cf. *ilk, mistress*

**mad-money** Return [cab] fare carried by a soldier's feminine acquaintance in case she "got mad" because of too-amorous attention. (Sydney J. Baker, 1941)

**maggoty** Irritable, peevish. (Edward Gepp, 1923)
❖Whimsical, full of whims and fancies. Fancy tunes used to be called *maggots*; hence, we have *Barker's maggots, Cary's maggots*, &c. (E. Cobham Brewer, 1887)
cf. *dump, melancholy, peevish*

**maid** A word which, in its highest sense as 'virgin,' might once be applied to either sex, to Sir Galahad as freely as to the Pucelle, but which is now restricted to one. (Richard Chenevix Trench, 1859–60)
cf. *girls, hag, street-walker, wench*

**maids of honor** Ladies of high birth in attendance on a queen, varying in number—Victoria has eight. (James Stormonth, 1884)
cf. *master of ceremonies*

**mail** To arm defensively; to cover, as with armour. (Samuel Johnson, 1755)
❖*Mail-box*, a box in which the mail-bags were placed on a mail-coach. (James Murray et al., 1888–1928)
❖*Mail-man*, a farmer; a rent-payer. (John Jamieson, 1879)

**manage** The age at which one becomes a man [1600s]. (James Murray et al., 1888–1928)

**mangle** To roll or smoothe clothes with a *mangle* . . . a machine in which damp clothes are smoothed by roller pressure. The old-fashioned *mangle* had a box, weighted with stones and reciprocating upon rollers, which ran to and fro upon the clothes spread upon a polished table beneath. (Edward Lloyd, 1895)

**mango** A musk-melon stuffed with various condiments and then pickled. (John Farmer, 1889)

**man-handle** To handle or wield a tool [1400s]. (James Murray et al., 1888–1928)

**mankind** Masculine, man-like, mannish, impudent, ferocious. "Twas a sound knock she gave me, a plaguy, *mankind* girl." Beaumont and Fletcher's *Monsieur Thomas*, 1619. (Robert Nares, 1859)
cf. *tomboy*

**mannequin** A little man; a dwarf; [from] German *klein*, little. (Samuel Johnson, 1755)
❖A pasteboard model, exhibiting the different parts and organs of the human body. (James Donald, 1877)
❖From Old Dutch *manneken*, a diminutive for 'man.' (Robert Hunter, 1894)

**manslaughter** The unlawful killing of a man upon a sudden quarrel, without foregoing malice. (John Kersey, 1772)
cf. *homicide*

**manure** To cultivate, train the mind or body [1500s–1700s]. (James Murray et al., 1888–1928)

❖ "*Manure* your heart with diligence, and in it sow good seed." (Zachary Boyd, *Zion Flowers*, 1645)
cf. *dungaree*

**marinated**  Transported into some foreign plantation. (B. E., Gent., c. 1690)
❖Pertaining to the sea, tasting of salt-water. (Elisha Coles, 1713)
cf. *plantation, transportation*

**marines**  Empty bottles. The *marines* are looked down upon by regular seamen, who consider them useless, like empty bottles. A marine officer was once dining at a mess-table when the Duke of York said to the man in waiting, "Here, take away these *marines.*" The officer demanded an explanation, when the colonel replied, "They have done their duty well, and are prepared to do it again." (E. Cobham Brewer, 1887)

**marksman**  A man who cannot sign his name and has therefore to make his *mark*. (Michael Traynor, 1953)
cf. *chris-cross, earmark*

**maroon**  It is extremely doubtful whether this term for a runaway negro can be classed as an Americanism. . . . *To go marooning*, however, picnicing for several days at a stretch, genuinely finds a place in these pages. *Marooning* is peculiar to the Southern States, and is very similar to what is known in England as "camping out." The sense is obviously an indirect derivative of the verb *to maroon*. (John Farmer, 1889)
❖*Marooning* differs from *picnicing* in this: the former continues several days, the other lasts but one. (Thomas Haliburton, 1855)
❖A person who is *marooned*. (James Murray et al., 1888–1928)
cf. *picnic*

**marrow**  One of a pair, a mate, a companion, an equal, a sweetheart; from the Gaelic *mar*, like, similar. This word is beautifully applied to a lover or wedding partner, as one whose mind is the exact counterpart of the object of his affection. It appears in early English literature, but now survives only in the poetry and daily speech of the Scottish and northern English people. (Charles Mackay, 1888)
❖An exact counterpart or likeness; a facsimile. (Joseph Wright, 1896–1905)

**master of ceremonies** The king's interpreter [who] introduces ambassadors, &c. (Elisha Coles, 1713)
cf. *linguist, maids of honor*

**matchmaker** One who makes matches for burning. (Noah Webster, 1828)

**mean** This word was originally used in the sense of 'common, lowly,' without the notion of moral baseness, which now attaches to it. (Richard Chenevix Trench, 1859–60)

**measles, measly** This has only been by later use restrained to one kind of spotted sickness, but *meazel*, spelt in innumerable ways, was once leprosy, or more often the leper himself, and the disease, *meselry*. (Richard Chenevix Trench, 1859–60)
❖The origin is the Old French word *meseau*, or *mesel*, a leper. Cotgrave has, "*meseau*, a meselled, scurvy, leaporous, lazarous person."(John Phin, 1902)
❖*Measly*, of or pertaining to *measles* [1700s–1800s]. (James Murray et al., 1888–1928)
cf. *mumps*

**meat** Originally food of all kinds . . . eaten by men or animals for nourishment. Horse-*meat* is still used locally for fodder, and green-*meat* is a term often applied to edible vegetables, such as lettuces, cresses, &c. (Edward Lloyd, 1895)
❖Food for animals. "After my breakfast I got the hens' *meat* ready." (Michael Traynor, 1953)
❖*White-meat*, food composed of milk, cheese, butter, eggs, and the like. (Robert Hunter, 1894)
❖*White-meat*, the flesh of the lamb, veal, and rabbits. (Edward Peacock, 1877)
❖*Milkmeat*, food made with or from milk. (James Murray et al., 1888–1928)
❖*Sweetmeat*, fruit preserved in sugar. (Daniel Fenning, 1775)
❖*Spoon-meat*, food that is, or must be, taken with a spoon; liquid food. *Bake-meats*, meats prepared for food in an oven. Noah Webster, 1828

**meddle** To mingle. (Samuel Johnson, 1755)
❖This had once no such offensive meaning of mixing oneself up in other people's business, as now it has. On the contrary, Barrow, in one of his sermons, draws expressly the distinction between *meddling* and being *meddlesome*, and only condemns the latter. (Richard Chenevix Trench, 1859–60)
cf. *officious*

**medicine** The alchemists call the matter, whatever it be, by which they perform transformation, a *medicine*. *Antony and Cleopatra*. (Alexander Dyce, 1902)

❖*Medicine-chest*, a chest in which medicines and drugs are kept, together with instruments and appliances necessary for surgery. (Robert Hunter, 1894)

cf. *alchemy, physics*

**mediocrity** A moderation of living, or the circumstances of those who are neither poor nor rich. (Thomas Dyche and William Pardon, 1740)

❖A *mediocrity* of condition is most favorable to morals and happiness. A *mediocrity* of talents well employed will generally ensure respectability. (Noah Webster, 1828)

**melancholy** A disease which proceeds from the overflowing of black choler. (John Kersey, 1772)

❖Used to describe every form of insanity. (Joseph Hunter, 1829)

❖The varieties are the gloomy, or *Melancholia attonita*, the restless, or *Melancholia errabunda*, the mischievous, or *Melancholia malevolens*, and the self-complacent, or *Melancholia complacens*. (Richard Hoblyn, 1859)

❖"I have neither the scholar's melancholy, which is emulation; nor the musician's, which is fantastical; nor the courtier's, which is proud; nor the lawyer's, which is politic; nor the lady's, which is nice; nor the lover's, which is all of these." (William Shakespeare, *As You Like It*)

cf. *giddy, hypochondria, incense, maggoty, spleen*

**memorize** To record. (Samuel Johnson, 1755)

❖To perpetuate the memory of in writing [late 1500s–1800s]. (James Murray et al., 1888–1928)

❖*Memorized*, made memorable. *Henry VIII*. (C. H. Herford, 1902)

**merchant** The term *merchant* was anciently used in contradistinction to *gentleman*. (Francis Douce, 1807)
❖A familiar and contemptuous term. "What saucy *merchant* was this . . . " *Romeo and Juliet*. (Alexander Dyce, 1902)

**mess** A party of four. At great dinners the company was usually arranged into fours, which were called *messes*. "Your *mess* of sons." *3 Henry VI*. (Alexander Dyce, 1902)
❖Probably in the distribution of food to large numbers, it was found most convenient to arrange them in fours, and hence this application of the word. A *mess* at the Inns of Court still consists of four. (Richard Chenevix Trench, 1859–60)
❖*Mess-making*, the act or practice of eating together. (Robert Hunter, 1894)

**meteors** Apparitions on high; vapours drawn up into the middle region of the air, and set out in divers[e] forms, as rain, hail, snow, thunder, &c. (John Kersey, 1772)
❖*Meteorology*, the doctrine of meteors. (William Grimshaw, 1854)
❖*Meteorologist*, one who studies the phenomena of meteors, or keeps a register of them. (Noah Webster, 1828)
cf. *climate, Noah's ark*

**methodist** Those philosophers who adopted a certain methodical manner in their speculations. One of a sect of ancient physicians who practised by theory or method. (Edward Lloyd, 1895)
cf. *leech, physiologist, surgeon*

**metropolis** The seat or see of a metropolitan bishop [1500s–1800s]. In Natural History, the district in which a species, group, etc. is most represented [1800s]. (James Murray et al., 1888–1928)

**middle-age** Belonging to the Middle Ages [1800s]. (James Murray, 1888–1928)
❖*Middle-aged*, having reached the middle age of life, generally taken as from thirty-five to forty-five years. (Edward Lloyd, 1895)

**middleman** A workman employed in some particular operation in the making of wire [1400s]. One of the soldiers in the fifth or sixth rank in a file of ten deep [1600s]. (James Murray et al., 1888–1928)
❖In negro minstrelsy, the man who sits in the middle of the semicircle of per-

formers during the opening part of the entertainment, and leads the dialogue between songs. A man of intermediate rank; a commoner. (William Whitney, 1889)

**midget** A little *midge* . . . a popular name for the gnat *(Culex pipiens)*, or any insect resembling that species. (Edward Lloyd, 1895)
cf. *lousy*

**mildew** A dew that falls upon wheat, hops, &c. (John Kersey, 1772)
cf. *aspersion*

**minister** *Minister* meant, etymologically, a small man, and it was used in opposition to *magister*, a big man. (Max Müller, 1863)
❖One is connected with the Latin *minus*, and the other with *magis*. (E. Cobham Brewer, 1887)
cf. *minuscule, minute, moment*

**minuscule** In printing, a small or 'lower case' letter, as opposed to a capital. (James Murray et al., 1888–1928)
❖*Minusculæ*, in printing, denotes the small or 'running' letters. (Ephraim Chambers, 1727–51)
cf. *minister, moment*

**minute** Minutes are now *minute* portions of time. They might once be *minute* portions of anything. (Richard Chenevix Trench, 1859–60)
❖The first draughts of any writings or orders. (John Kersey, 1772)
❖A sixtieth, or other definite part, of a unity [1300s–1800s]. (James Murray et al., 1888–1928)
cf. *farthing, minister, minuscule, moment*

**miser** We may notice a curious shifting of parts in *miser, misery,* [and] *miserable*. There was a time when the *miser* was the wretched man; he is now the covetous. At the same time *misery*, which is now wretchedness, and *miserable*, which is now wretched, were [respectively] *covetousness* and *covetous*. They have in fact exactly reversed their uses. (Richard Chenevix Trench, 1859–60)
❖*Misery*, in the South, means simply 'pain' . . . The word is a special favorite with the negroes, to whose mind it represents any feeling which they cannot definitely describe . . . [as] a *misery* in the leg, the chest, or the throat. (M. Schele De Vere, 1872)

**mistress** A title of address applied to a married lady, nearly equivalent to *madam*. Formerly, it was applied to married or unmarried women indiscriminately. It is now written in the abbreviated form *Mrs.* (Edward Lloyd, 1895)
cf. *madam*

**mittens** Gloves without fingers. (William Grimshaw, 1854)

**mixed-marriage** A marriage between persons of different religions. (James Murray et al., 1888–1928)
❖A marriage between a baptised and an unbaptised person is ecclesiastically invalid. . . . If a Roman Catholic and a Protestant desire to marry in England, they must promise that the children shall be brought up in the Roman communion. (Robert Hunter, 1894)

**moment** The smallest portion of time; an instant. (Edward Lloyd, 1895)
cf. *minuscule, minister, minute*

**money-makers** Counterfeiters of coins. (James Halliwell, 1855)

**mooch** To play the truant; *blackberry mooching*, to play the truant in order to gather blackberries. (Francis Grose, 1811)
❖In the fifteenth and seventeenth centuries, *mowche* and *mouche*, [with] senses similar to those of *miche*, (to play truant, to lurk out of sight) suggest that it was adopted from the source of that word, Old French *muchier*, to hide, skulk, etc. (James Murray et al., 1888–1928)
cf. *truant*

**moon** The chief of seven planets. (John Kersey, 1772)
cf. *galaxy, solarium*

**moonlighter** One who serenades by moonlight. (Harold Wentworth, 1944)

**moonlighting** The performance by night of an expedition or an illicit action. Specifically, in Ireland, the perpetration of outrages on the persons or property of tenants who incurred the hostility of the Land League [1800s]. (James Murray et al., 1888–1928)

**moonstruck** An epithet given to diseases which are supposed to appear at certain phases of the moon, or to those who are affected by them. (Robley Dunglison, 1844)

**morbid**  A term used of corpulence. (Edward Lloyd, 1895)
❖*Morbid*, in painting, is particularly applied to fat flesh very strongly
expressed. (Ephraim Chambers, 1727–51)
cf. *bald, carnation, crummy*

**morgue**  Though applied to a mortuary, this word really means the inner
wicket of a prison, where the identification marks of new arrivals are taken
before they have their cells and tasks assigned to them. (Basil Hargrave, 1925)
cf. *lavatory, mortuary*

**morose**  It is very curious that, while the classical *morosus* expressed one
given overmuch to his own manners, habits, ways *(mores)* the medieval *morosus* was commonly connected with *mora*, a delay. In treatises of Christian
ethics the technical word was to express the sin of *delaying* upon impure, wanton, or . . . malignant thoughts instead of rejecting them on the instant.
(Richard Chenevix Trench, 1859–60)

**mortify**  To kill. (John Bullokar, 1616)
✦To terrify. (Joseph Wright, 1896–1905)
❖*Mortified*, dead to the world; having the passions and appetites under con-
trol; ascetic. (Thomas Fuller, 1662)

**mortuary**  A payment due in some places for the buriall of the dead,
which is foure shillings and foure pence, where the goods of the deceased
party are above the value of twentie nobles, and under thirtie poundes; sixe
shillings and eight pence, where goods exceede thirtie poundes; and ten
shillings where goods amount above the value of three-score poundes. (John
Bullokar, 1616)
❖A gift left by a man at his death to the parson of the parish. (John Kersey,
1772)
❖A burial place; a gift left by a man at his death to his parish church for the
recompense of his personal tithes and offerings not duly paid in his lifetime.
(William Grimshaw, 1854)
cf. *morgue*

**mothering** It is still a custom on Mid-Lent Sunday in many parts of England, for servants . . . to carry cakes . . . as presents to their parents; and in other parts, to visit their mother for a meal of furmity, or to receive cakes . . . with her blessing. This is called *going a-mothering*. (William Hone, 1832)

**motley** Mixed, as a *motley* colour. (John Kersey, 1772)
❖Checquered, especially a fool's dress; hence a *motley fool* [late 1300s–1800s]. (James Murray, 1888–1928)

**muffler** A boxing glove [1700s]. A glove or mitten [1800s]. (James Murray et al., 1888–1928)
❖A kind of stuffed glove put on the hands of lunatics to prevent them from injuring themselves or others. (Edward Lloyd, 1895)

**mug** The rump of an animal. (James Halliwell, 1855)

**mugger** *Mugger*, originally, a travelling hawker of mugs and earthenware, but often applied to the whole tribe of itinerant hawkers indiscriminately. (R. O. Heslop, 1892–94)
❖In theatrical slang, a comedian who 'mugs' or grimaces. (James Murray et al., 1888–1928)

**multiplication** The art of making gold and silver. (Thomas Tyrwhitt, 1871) cf. *alchemy*

**mumble** To eat in a slow, ineffective manner; to chew or bite softly, as with toothless gums [1300s–1800s]. (James Murray et al., 1888–1928)

**mummy** Medical preparation originally extracted from the substance with which mummies were embalmed. (A. V. Judges, 1930)
❖A preparation for magical purposes made from dead bodies. "Witches' *mummy*." *Macbeth*. (Alexander Dyce, 1902)

**mumps**  A term of contempt or mock endearment for a woman [1500s–1600s]. (James Murray et al., 1888–1928)
cf. *crud, measles, wench, whiteboy*

**music**  Fun, frolic, amusement. Oliver Wendell Holmes uses the phrase, "I can't say it's *musical*," meaning amusing. This rendering is most frequently heard in New England, but is by no means confined to that part of the country. (John Farmer, 1889)
❖A friend informs me that in some towns in the interior of New England, this word [musical] is used in the extraordinary sense of *humorous*. (John Pickering, 1816)
❖A damsel will say to her lover, "Get away, you are so *musical*," when she thinks he is becoming too pressing. (M. Schele De Vere, 1872)
cf. *glee*

**myriad**  The number ten thousand. (Richard Coxe, 1813)
cf. *billion, century, trillion*

**napkin** A pocket handkerchief. Used by Shakespeare in several of his plays. (John Brockett, 1825)
❖A kerchief used to cover the head, or to tie around the neck. (Joseph Wright, 1896–1905)
❖From the French *nappe*, a cloth which appears to be a corruption of the Latin *mappa* . . . the original also of our *map*. (George Craik, 1886)

**nation** A vulgar term used in Kent, Sussex, and the adjacent countries, for very. (Francis Grose, 1796)
▪Extreme, as *nation strange, nation dark*; modified from an oath [damnation]. (William H. Cope, 1883)
❖Very, exceedingly; *nation foolish*. (John Brockett, 1825)

**natural** *Natural* is . . . derived from the association of what is natural with what is savage, belonging to a man's lower nature. . . . Hence, it means 'fierce, savage.' (M. Schele De Vere, 1872)
❖*Naturalist* [is] at present the student of natural history, but in the sixteenth and seventeenth centuries the name was often given to the deist, as one who denied any but a religion of Nature. *Natural religion men* such were sometimes called. (Richard Chenevix Trench, 1859–60)

**naughty** This is a word which has undergone more than one change in meaning. It is an extension of the English *naught*, which is derived from the Anglo-Saxon *naht*, meaning 'nothing,' and the primary meaning of *naughty* is good-for-nothing, worthless. In the Bible (Jeremiah 24:2) we find it used in that sense: "The other basket had very *naughty* figs." (Basil Hargrave, 1925)

**navigator** A labourer employed in the work of excavating and constructing a canal, or in later use, in any similar kind of earthwork [1700s–1800s]. (James Murray et al., 1888–1928)

**necklace** A lace or ribbon for the neck; a neck-tie. (Samuel Johnson, 1755)
cf. *negligee, tawdry*

**nectarine** Sweet as nectar. (Samuel Johnson, 1755)
cf. *tangerine*

**negligee** A necklace, usually of red coral; [from] *negliger*, to neglect.
(Daniel Lyons, 1897)
cf. *camisole, necklace, tawdry*

**nephew** Restrained at the present to the son of a brother or a sister, but
formerly of much laxer use, a grandson, or even a remoter lineal descendant.
*Nephew*, in fact, has undergone exactly the same change of meaning that
*nepos* in Latin underwent, which in the Augustan age meaning *grandson*, in
the post-Augustan acquired the signification of *nephew* in our present accepta-
tion of that word. (Richard Chenevix Trench, 1859–60)
❖Grandson. (Joseph Wright, 1896–1905)
❖"You'll have your *nephews* (grandsons) neigh to you." *Othello*. (Alexander
Dyce, 1902)
❖The illegitimate son of a priest. (John Farmer and W. E. Henley, 1890–1904)
cf. *aunt, brother-in-law, father-in-law, foster-child, nepotism, niece*

**nepotism** Fondness for nephews. Proneness on the part of the popes and
other ecclesiastics of the Church of Rome to heap wealth upon their nephews,
not having children of their own to inherit any property they may have
acquired. (Edward Lloyd, 1895)
❖From Latin *nepos, nepotis*, a nephew. (Joseph Worcester, 1881)
cf. *nephew*

**nervous** Muscles [in] "sinows." *Cymbeline* (C. H. Herford, 1902)
❖*Nervous*, a word which, till lately, when applied to a man, was expressive of
musculous strength, and a brawny make; and thence, metaphorically, a strong
and forcible style is called *nervous* and energetic, whereas now it is used only,
in a contrary sense, to express a man whose nerves are weak. . . . To preserve a
distinction when we speak of such a man, and of the disorder by which his
strength is impaired, we should rather say a *nervish* man, and a *nervish* disorder, which termination conforms with similar words, such as *waspish, devilish,
feverish, agueish*, all expressive of bad qualities or disordered habits. (Samuel
Pegge, 1844)
❖*Nervy*, robust, strong, vigorous. [Coined by Shakespeare.] A new form

derived from that sense of *nervous*, meaning pithy and spirited, as regards style in writing. (John Farmer, 1889)

**nest-egg** An egg left in the nest to induce the hen or other bird to lay more in the same. (James Halliwell, 1855)

**newfangled** Fond of a new thing. (Adam and Charles Black, 1851)
❖Desirous of new things. (Thomas Tyrwhitt, 1871)

**newspaper-man** A great reader of newspapers. (Alexander Warrack, 1911)

**nice** Curious, tender; pettish, scrupulous, exact. (John Kersey, 1772)
❖Trifling, unimportant, petty. "How *nice* the quarrel was." *Romeo and Juliet*. (Alexander Dyce, 1902)
❖From Anglo-Saxon *nesc*, soft, tender, effeminate. (Joseph Worcester, 1881)
❖When we speak of people being *nice*, we mean that they are agreeable, delightful. Yet the derivation of the word *nice* is the Latin *nescius*, ignorant . . . and the Old French *nice* meant 'foolish, simple.' (Basil Hargrave, 1925)
cf. *clever*

**nick** A cent piece. These coins are made of *nickel,* and the term has naturally been abbreviated to meet the inexorable demand for brevity in terms of popular use, and also to distinguish it from *nickel.* (John Farmer, 1889)
cf. *farthing, minute*

**niece** A priest's illegitimate daughter, or concubine; whence the expression, "No more character than a priest's *niece."* (John Farmer and W. E. Henley, 1890–1904)
❖A grand-daughter. (Edward Lloyd, 1895)
cf. *aunt, brother-in-law, father-in-law, foster-child, nephew*

**night-light** The faint light which is perceptible during the night [1600s–1800s]. (James Murray et al., 1888–1928)
❖Night-shine. (Henry Hexham, 1648)

**night-vision** A vision or dream that comes during the night [1300s–1700s]. (James Murray et al., 1888–1928)

**nil** Half; half profits, &c. (J. C. Hotten, 1887)

**Noah's ark** A cloud appearing when the sky is, for the most part, clear, much resembling a large boat turned bottom upwards, considered a sure prognostic of rain [in] Norfolk. (John Walker, 1835)
❖If it extends south to north, it is viewed as an indication of good weather; if from east to west, a squall of wind or rain is certainly looked for. (John Jamieson, 1879)
cf. *meteors, rack*

**nocturne** A part of a Roman church-service, said about midnight. (John Kersey, 1772)

**noise** An agreeable or melodious sound [1300s–1700s]. (James Murray et al., 1888–1928)

**nonconformist** One that does not conform to the discipline of the Church of England. (John Kersey, 1772)
❖They were of two kinds: first, those who, being religious, worshipped nowhere; second, those who attended the services of some other religious denomination than the established church. The name was first applied to those who declined to conform to the enactments of the Act of Uniformity, passed in 1549. (Edward Lloyd, 1895)

**nostalgia** An affliction produced by the desire of returning to one's country. It is commonly accompanied by slow wasting and . . . may speedily induce death. (Robley Dunglison, 1844)

**nourishment** Wine or spirits given medicinally. (Joseph Wright, 1896–1905)

**novel** Novels were once simply news, *nouvelles,* and the *novelist* not a writer of new tales, but an inventor, a bringer of new fashions into the Church or State. (Richard Chenevix Trench, 1859–60)

**nude**  Void, empty, destitute, poor. (Thomas Blount, 1656)
❖Devoid of furniture or decorations. (James Murray et al., 1888–1928)
❖Originally [a] sixteenth-century law term, later adopted as art euphemism for *naked*; [from] Latin *nudas*. (Ernest Weekley, 1921)

**nursery**  We have but one use of *nursery* at this present, namely as the place of nursing. But it was once applied as well to the person nursed, or the act of nursing. (Richard Chenevix Trench, 1859–60)
❖A college of young students designed for the priesthood. (John Kersey, 1772)

**oblivion** Forgetfulness. (John Kersey, 1772)
❖Perhaps from Latin *liveo, livesco,* to become dark. To forget is to have a thing become dark to one. (Hensleigh Wedgwood, 1878)
cf. *amnesty*

**obnoxious** This, in its present lax and slovenly use, a vague unserviceable synonym for 'offensive,' is properly applied to one who, on the ground[s] of a mischief or wrong committed by him, is justly liable to punishment (*obnoxam pœnæ obligatus*). . . . But there often falls out of the word the sense of a wrong committed, and that of liability to punishment, whether just or unjust. . . . We punish, or wish to punish, those whom we dislike, and thus *obnoxious* has obtained its present sense. (Richard Chenevix Trench, 1859–60)

**obsequious** Dutiful in manifesting regard for the dead. "So *obsequious* will thy father be." *3 Henry VI.* (C. T. Onions, 1911)
❖Of or pertaining to funerals, mourning. (Robert Hunter, 1894)

**occupy** To possess or enjoy. "These villains will make the word captain, as odious as the word occupy." *2 Henry IV.* (Robert Nares, 1859)
❖*Occupy* is called an odious word in Shakespeare's time, and *occupant* denoted a woman of the town, and *occupier,* a wencher. (Thomas Fosbroke, 1843)
❖"A bawdy or *occupying-house.*" Florio. (James Halliwell, 1855)

**octaves** Eight days next after some principal feasts of the year. (John Bullokar, 1616)

**odious** Exceedingly great. *Odious* . . . generally means everything inexpressible by the English language. (Michael Traynor, 1953)

**off color** Out of sorts. (Richard Thornton, 1912)

**off-hand**  Done promptly. (Joseph Worcester, 1881)
❖Of a farm, owned or held by a person who does not reside there. (James Murray et al., 1888–1928)

**officious**  Again and again, we light on words used once in a good, but now in an unfavourable, sense. An *officious* person is now a busy, uninvited meddler in matters which do not belong to him; so late as [the 1700s] he might be one prompt and forward in due *offices* of kindness. The more honourable use of *officious* now only survives in the distinction familiar to diplomacy between an *official* and *officious* communication. (Richard Chenevix Trench, 1859–60)
cf. *meddle*

**offing**  Implies to seaward, beyond anchoring ground. *To keep a good offing*, to keep well off the land while under sail. (William Smyth, 1867)

**ogle**  To cast side glances with a view to attract attention. (Edward Lloyd, 1895)
❖An ocular invitation to advances; from *ogle*, an eye [1500s–1800s]. (James Murray et al., 1888–1928)
❖"The gentry-mort has rum *ogles*," that lady has charming black eyes. B. E., Gent., c. 1690)

**oilman**  One who trades in oil and pickles. (Samuel Johnson, 1755)

**old-fashioned**  Having the ways of a grown-up person; hence, precocious, intelligent, knowing. "The pony was a bit *old-fashioned*, and could open the gate with his mouth." (R. E. G. Cole, 1886)

**operator**  [In] surgery, one who performs an operation upon the human body, either with the hand or by means of instruments. (Edward Lloyd, 1895)
cf. *surgeon*

**ordeal**  Saxon [for] *great judgement*, instituted long before the Conquest.
. . . *Ordeals* were of several kinds, but the most usual were by *wager of battle*, by hot or cold water, and by fire. (E. Cobham Brewer, 1887)
❖It was impiously supposed that God would, by mere contrivance of man, be called upon to exercise his power in favour of the innocent. (John Bouvier, 1843–56)
❖In the trial by cold water, the persons suspected were thrown naked into a pond or river; if they sank they were acquitted, but if they floated without

attempting to swim, it was taken for an evidence of guilt. (Joseph Worcester, 1881)
cf. *treadmill, whirligig*

**orgasm** Sudden motion. (Stephen Jones, 1818)
❖Immoderate excitement or action, as when accompanied by severe spasms. (James Stormonth, 1884)
❖A sudden violence, impulse, or appetite. (Daniel Fenning, 1775)
cf. *rape*

**ostracize** To banish by means of *ostracism*, a form of punishment which prevailed at Athens, and in some other democratic states, by which persons who, from their wealth or influence, were considered dangerous to the state, were banished for ten years, with leave to return and enjoy their estates after that period. (Joseph Worcester, 1881)
❖Each citizen wrote his vote on an oyster-shell, or *ostracon*, whence the term. (E. Cobham Brewer, 1887)
cf. *ballot*

**ouch** That part of a ring in which the jewel is set. A blow given by a boar's tusk. [From] French *oche*, a notch. (Joseph Worcester, 1881)

**ought** Owed; was bound to pay; have been indebted. This word the etymologists make the preterite of *owe*, but it has often a present signification. (Samuel Johnson, 1755)

**ounce** A measure of land [in the] Shetland and Orkney Islands. The sixteenth part of any property [in] Cornwall. (Joseph Wright, 1896–1905)
cf. *acre, minute*

**ouster** The act of bailing; the water bailed out of a boat. (Joseph Wright, 1896–1905)

**outbreak** When a vein of coal, &c. appears on the surface, it is called an out-breck, the same as a *crop-out*. (William Carr, 1828)
❖*Outbreak*, land that has only recently been cultivated. Outburst, an outcrop. (Joseph Wright, 1896–1905)

**out-cry** An auction. An auctioneer was called an *out-crier*. (James Halliwell, 1855)
❖Until recently, this old Saxon synonym for "public auction" was current in

some of the remoter districts. (Sylva Clapin, 1902)

❖*Outcry* is occasionally used in remote districts, instead of a similar old term, *at public cry*, meaning an auction. The word is Saxon, and found in almost all the North Country glossaries. (M. Schele De Vere, 1872)

**outfield** A name given to unenclosed farm lands at a distance from the farmstead. (William Whitney, 1889)

❖A term applied to arable land which is not manured, but cropped till it is worn out, so as to be unfit for bearing corn for some years. (John Jamieson, 1879)
cf. *infield, manure*

**outlandish** Not native; foreign. (Samuel Johnson, 1755)

❖*Outlandisher*, a foreigner. (William Whitney, 1889)
cf. *alien, barbaric, far-fetched, Frenchman, uncouth*

**outlaying** Of hens, laying eggs out of the regular nest. (John Jamieson, 1879)

**outrigger** An addition to a wagon to increase its carrying capacity [in] Wiltshire. (Joseph Wright, 1896–1905)

**overalls** The name was formerly applied to the boot pulled over the trousers, then to the trousers which were leathered at the foot, and up the inside of each leg to the knee, and lastly, when this was done away with, to the pantaloons only. (Edward Lloyd, 1895)
cf. *pantaloon, panties*

**overcast** A person or thing that is cast away, 'thrown over,' or rejected; an *outcast*. (James Murray et al., 1888–1928)

**overhand** The 'upper hand'; mastery, victory, superiority; usually the object of *to get, have*, and the like; properly two words, *over*, adjective, and *hand*, subject [1200s–1800s]. (James Murray et al., 1888–1928)

❖*To have the over-hand*, to obtain mastery. (William Carr, 1828)

❖Superiority. (Alois Brandl and Otto Zippel, 1949)
cf. *underhanded*

**overloaded** Intoxicated. (Joseph Wright, 1896–1905)
cf. *intoxicate, pot-shot*

**overlook** To bewitch with the "evil eye." This use has probably gone out with witches. (Edward Gepp, 1923)
cf. *fascination, glamour, overshadow*

**overshadow** To bewitch, overlook with the 'evil eye.' (Joseph Wright, 1896–1905)
cf. *fascination, glamour, overlook*

**overwhelming** Projecting. "In tattered weeds with *overwhelming* brows." *Romeo and Juliet*. (C. H. Herford, 1902)

**oxymoron** A smart saying which at first appears foolish; from Greek *oxys*, sharp, and *moros*, foolish. (Charles Annandale, 1897)

**pacific** [One] that tends to the making of peace. (John Kersey, 1772)

**painful** *Painful* is now feeling pain, or inflicting it; it was once *taking* pains. Many things would not be so painful, in the present sense of the word, if they had been more painful in the earlier, as perhaps some sermons. (Richard Chenevix Trench, 1859–60)

**panache** A plume or bunch of feathers upright upon the helmet; from Latin penna, a feather. (Edward Lloyd, 1895)
cf. *talk turkey*

**pandemonium** The abode of demons or evil spirits; hell; [from] Greek *pan*, all, and *daimonos*, demon. (Edward Lloyd, 1895)
✣A place represented by Milton [in *Paradise Lost*, 1667] as the capital of Hell. (James Murray et al., 1888–1928)

**panic** The word was originally used as an adjective, panic-fright being ascribed to the sudden appearance of Pan, the god of the country, as opposed to the town. He presided over the flocks and herds, but with his lower parts like the hind quarters of a goat. . . . The sudden fright or causeless dread which sometimes overtakes the lonely shepherd or the lost wanderer in the woods was ascribed to the unseen presence of Pan, and music was esteemed the most effectual means of preventing this panic. The "panpipe" was a simple musical instrument, the earliest form of a compound wind instrument. (Basil Hargrave, 1925)

**pantaloon** A man's garment, anciently worn, in which the breeches and stockings were all of one piece. (Samuel Johnson, 1755)
cf. *overalls, panties*

**panties** Trousers; the Americans never speak of this article of attire but as *pants* or *panties*. The term is an abbreviation of "pantaloons." (John Farmer, 1889)
cf. *overalls, pantaloon*

**pantomime** Now the mimic show itself, but at the first introduction of the word, the player who presented the show. (Richard Chenevix Trench, 1859–60)
cf. *antics, pedicure, rhetoric, zany*

**paraphernalia** This is a big-sounding word from the Greek, which some newspaper writers are constantly misusing. It is strictly a law-term, and means whatever the wife brings with her at a marriage, in addition to her dower. Her dress and ornaments are paraphernalia. To apply this term to an Irishman's sash on St. Patrick's day, or to a Freemason's hieroglyphic apron, it has been justly said, is not only an abuse of the language, but a clear invasion of women's rights. (William Mathews, 1884)
❖The word comes from the Greek *para*, beyond, and *pherein*, to bring. (Basil Hargrave, 1925)

**parlour** Properly, a thirteenth-century conversation-room in a monastery. (Edward Gepp, 1923)
❖In the cottages of poor people, if there are two rooms on the ground floor, the best room they live in is called the *house*; the other is called a *parlour*, though used as a bedroom. (James Halliwell, 1855)

**parole** A word of promise; a word of honour; from Low Latin *parabola*, a discourse, a parable. Specifically, a promise given by a prisoner, on his honour, that he will not attempt to escape if allowed his liberty. (Edward Lloyd, 1895)

**parquet** Few would recognize in this term an American equivalent for the "pit" of English playhouses; the usage is distinctly American. (John Farmer, 1889)
cf. *cockpit*

**passbook** A book in which a tradesman enters goods sold on credit to a customer. (Edward Lloyd, 1895)

**passengers** Passers-by. *King John.* (C. H. Herford, 1902)

**passionate**  Pathetic, sorrowful. Also a verb to express passion or sorrow. (James Halliwell, 1855)
cf. *pathetic, pity*

**pass-out**  A document giving permission to leave and re-enter a theater. (James Murray et al., 1888–1928)
cf. *permit*

**passport**  A licence for importing or exporting contraband goods or moveables without paying the usual duties. A certificate of character. (Edward Lloyd, 1895)
❖[From] French *passeport; passer,* to pass, and *porter,* to carry. (Noah Webster, 1828)

**patent**  Privilege, right. "My virgin *patent,*" my right to remain a virgin. *Midsummer-Night's Dream.* (John Phin, 1902)

**pathetic**  Expressive of, or showing passion; passionate. (Edward Lloyd, 1895)
cf. *passionate, pity*

**patron**  A name given in the Mediterranean to the person who commands the vessel and seamen; sometimes to the person who steers it [1300s–1700s]. (Ephraim Chambers, 1727–51)

**pecker**  Courage, confidence. "Keep your *pecker* up, lads." (John Wilkinson, 1924)
❖The human nose. *Down in the pecker,* in bad spirits. (Joseph Wright, 1896–1905)
❖"God bless you, my dearest, and as Papa [Prince Albert] says, 'Keep your pecker up,' meaning keep up your spirits." (Letter from Queen Victoria to her daughter Victoria, 1859)

**pedicure**  One whose business is the surgical care and treatment of the feet; a chiropodist [1800s]. (James Murray et al., 1888–1928)
cf. *homicide, pantomime, politics, rhetoric*

**peep-show**  A small picture made by children, who arrange flowers in a fanciful pattern behind a piece of glass. This is covered with a paper wrapper with a lift-up lid, in order that persons may inspect its beauties. (Francis Taylor, 1901)
cf. *puppet-show*

**peevish** By *peevishness*, we now understand a small but constantly fretting ill-temper. Yet no one can read our old authors with whom *peevish* and *peevishness* are of constant recurrence, without feeling that their use of them is different from ours, although precisely to determine what their use was is anything but easy. . . . *Peevish* is rather self-willed, obstinate. (Richard Chenevix Trench, 1859–60)
❖*Peevish* appears to have generally signified, during Shakespeare's days, 'silly, foolish, trifling.' "*Peevish* sheep." *Comedy of Errors*. (Alexander Dyce, 1902)
❖Of animals, fond of being petted. (Joseph Wright, 1896–1905)
cf. *maggoty*

**pee-wee** Pining, whining, whimpering. (Joseph Wright, 1896–1905)
❖From the sound uttered by a child when whimpering. (John Walker, 1835)

**pencil** The distinction between *pencil* and *paint-brush* is quite modern. The older use of *pencil* [from Latin] *pencillus*, or 'little tail,' was etymologically more correct than the modern, the brush being so called because it hung and drooped. (Richard Chenevix Trench, 1859–60)

**penitentiary** It is curious that this word has possessed three entirely independent meanings: a penitent, ordainer of penances in the Church, and place for penitents. Only the last is current now. (Richard Chenevix Trench, 1859–60)
❖A priest that imposes upon an offender what penance he thinks fit. (Edward Phillips, 1706)
❖A place in Rome where the priests hear confessions and enjoyn penance. (Elisha Coles, 1713)
❖Small square houses, in which the penitent shut himself up, sometimes in a grove, near a river, and at a distance from towns, were so called. (Thomas Fosbroke, 1843)
❖An institution for the reception and reformation of prostitutes. That part of the church to which penitents were restricted. (Edward Lloyd, 1895)

**penthouse** A shed hanging out aslope from the main wall. (Samuel Johnson, 1755)
❖A lean-to; [from] French *pente*, inclination, slope. (Hensleigh Wedgwood, 1878)
❖A porch or other projecting part of a building. *Merchant of Venice*. (C. H. Herford, 1902)

**periscope** A general view; a comprehensive summary. (Edward Lloyd, 1895)

**permit** Tickets of admission are called *permits*. (John Farmer, 1889)
cf. *pass-out*

**perspective** *Telescope* and *microscope* are both as old as Milton, but for a long while, *perspective* did the work of these. (Richard Chenevix Trench, 1859–60)
❖*Perspective* formerly meant a glass that assisted the sight in any way. Among these, that alluded to by the duke is thus described: "There be glasses also wherein one man may see another man's image, and not his own." *Twelfth Night*. (Francis Douce, 1807)
❖Delusion of the sight; commonly some delusive arrangement of mirrors or lenses. A glass producing optical illusion. *All's Well that Ends Well*. (C. H. Herford, 1902)

**pesky** Great, very, exceedingly. (James Bartlett, 1849)

**pestle** The leg of certain animals used for food, especially the ham or haunch of the pig; also the human leg. (James Murray et al., 1888–1928)

**petticoat** A wide outer garment made of oilskin or rough canvas, worn by fishermen in warm weather, and reaching below the knee, often undivided [1800s]. (James Murray et al., 1888–1928)
❖A man's waistcoat, by no means an inappropriate name. [From] French *petit*, small. (John Walker, 1835)
cf. *camisole, polka*

**pew** A wooden erection, in the shape of a square or parallelogram, used by lawyers, money-lenders, &c. (Edward Lloyd, 1895)
❖A box in a theater. Sir Christopher Wren is known to have objected to their introduction into his London churches. Milton uses the word *sheep-pen*, with contemptuous reference to those pews from which, "the hungry sheep look up, and are not fed." (T. Lewis Davies, 1881)
cf. *box-seat*

**pharmacologist** One who writes upon drugs. (Edward Lloyd, 1895)
cf. *physiologist, publicist, receipt*

**philander** To wander about. (Angelina Parker, 1881)
❖Used not only of young girls roaming in search of their sweethearts, but lads occupied in the same pursuit; real Greek. (W. T. Spurdens, 1840)
❖From Greek *phileo*, to love, and *andros*, a man. (Edward Lloyd, 1895)
❖Of a horse, to prance, caper. (Michael Traynor, 1953)
❖To ramble on incoherently; to write discursively and weakly. (J. C. Hotten, 1887)

**philology** The love of much babbling. (Henry Cockeram, 1623)

**photogenic** Produced by, or pertaining to, the chemical action of light on a sensitized surface; an earlier word for *photographic*. (James Murray et al., 1888–1928)

**physics** The science of, or a treatise on, medicine [1600s–1700s]. (James Murray et al., 1888–1928)
❖*Physical*, pertaining to *physic*; drugs, &c. (Joseph Wright, 1896–1905)
cf. *drench, medicine*

**physiologist** A writer on natural philosophy. (Noah Webster, 1806)
cf. *methodist, pharmacologist, publicist*

**picked** Sharp, pointed; sharp-featured; said of a person. It is never pronounced as a monosyllable. (William H. Cope, 1883)

**pickle** A small quantity; from Italian *piccolo*, small, akin to the Gaelic *peag*, little. *Pickle*, in familiar English, as applied to a small, unruly, and troublesome boy, is of the same origin. . . . *Pickle* is sometimes used for 'pilfer,' to steal small things. . . . A hen is said to *pickle up* when she searches for and feeds on grain. (Charles Mackay, 1888)

**pick-up** A *pick-up*, or a *pick-up dinner*, is a dinner made up of such fragments of cold meats as remain from former meals. (James Bartlett, 1849)

**picnic** An assembly where each person contributes provisions to the general entertainment. (William Grimshaw, 1854)
cf. *maroon, pot-luck*

**piddle** To eat here and there a bit; to do light and trifling work. The fundamental idea seems to be to pick, to use the tips of the fingers in doing. [Related to] German dialect *pitteln*, to meddle with anything by slightly plucking, picking, touching. (Hensleigh Wedgwood, 1878)

❖*Puddle*, the regular past tense of the verb *to piddle*. (John Horne Tooke, 1840)
cf. *pink*

**pie** Americans follow the old English usage and employ pie where we should now say "tart." In England, it is game or meat *pie*, and apple or fruit *tart*; in the States, *pie* is used in every instance. (John Farmer, 1889)

**pig** To bring forth pigs. (John Kersey, 1772)
cf. *slug*

**pigeon-toed** Putting the feet down straight, not turning out the toes. (T. Lewis Davies, 1881)

**pigskin** In sporting slang, a saddle. The skin of a hog used as a bottle [1800s]. (James Murray et al., 1888–1928)

**pimping** Little, petty; as a "*pimping* thing." Used in the interior of New England. (James Bartlett, 1849)

**ping-pong** A jewel fixed to a wire, with a long pin at the end, and worn in front of the cap [in] Scotland. (Joseph Wright, 1896–1905)

**pink** There seems no reason to believe that the name of this flower [the *carnation*] has anything to do with its colour. . . . In all probability, the flower takes its name from the cut or peaked edges of the petals, for the term *pink* [to cut a sawtooth edge] is still used in needlework. (Basil Hargrave, 1925)
cf. *carnation, piddle*

**pioneer** One whose business is to level the road, throw up works, or sink mines in military operations; from *pedito*, a foot soldier who was formerly employed in digging for the army. A pioneer is in Dutch *spagenier*, from *spage*, a spade; whence Junius imagines that the French borrowed *spagenier*, which was afterward called pioneer. (Samuel Johnson, 1755)
❖From Old French *peonier*, a pioneer, *peon*, a foot-soldier. (Edward Lloyd, 1895)
cf. *lackey*

**pipe down** The order to dismiss the men from the deck when a duty has been performed on ship board. (William Smyth, 1867)
❖"*Pipe-down* call is sounded at 9 p.m. on board ship." (*Dialect Notes*, 1913)

**pittance** The allowance of meat distributed in a monastery. (Robert Nares, 1859)

✣An allowance of victuals over and above bread and wine. The word originally comes from the people's piety in giving to poor mendicants food for their subsistence; [from] monkish Latin *pietancea*, Spanish *pitar*, to distribute a dole of food; *pitancero*, one who distributes the dole, or a begging friar who subsists by charity. (E. Cobham Brewer, 1887)

✣A *pittance* was an allowance [of food] in one plate between two [diners]. (Thomas Fosbroke, 1843)

✣Many etymologies have been proposed for this word. That of Vossius, preferred by Skinner, seems most deserving of adoption: "From Latin *pietas*, the dole of real or pretended piety." (Charles Richardson, 1837)

**pituitary** Of, pertaining to, or secreting *pituita*, or phlegm [1600s–1900s]. (James Murray et al., 1888–1928)

**pity** Love. "*Pity* is akin to love," says Shakespeare. (William H. Cope, 1883) ✣Probably the primary sense of the Latin *pius* and *pietas* may have been nothing more than emotion, or affection, generally. But the words have come to be confined to the expression of reverential affection towards a superior, such as the gods or a parent. . . . The French have moulded the word into two forms, which have been respectively appropriated to the two senses, and from their *piété* and *pitié* we have borrowed and applied in the same manner our *piety* and *pity*. *Pity*, which meant at one time 'reverence,' and afterwards 'compassion,' has come to suffer further degradation. By pitiful, Shakespeare [in "Our hearts . . . are *pitiful*," from *Julius Caesar*] means 'full of compassion.' (George Craik, 1886)
cf. *passionate*, *pathetic*

**placebo** |Literally| "I will please," an epithet given to any medicine adapted more to please than benefit the patient. (John Redman Coxe, 1817) ✣A flatterer, sycophant, parasite; adopted from Latin *placebo*, 'I shall be pleasing or acceptable,' and *placere*, to please; also used in Old French, Chaucer. (James Murray et al., 1888–1928)

**plagiarist** *Plagiarist* means strictly one who kidnaps a slave. Martial applies the word to the kidnappers of other men's brains. (E. Cobham Brewer, 1887)

**plaintiff** One who complains of illness. Generally, one who complains [1500s–1600s]. (James Murray et al., 1888–1928)

**plantation** A *plantation* is now of trees only, and not of men, as it was when "The Plantations" was the standing name by which our transatlantic colonies were known. (Richard Chenevix Trench, 1859–60)
cf. *bouquet, marinated*

**platitude** Flatness. (Daniel Lyons, 1897)

**plausible** That is *plausible* now which presents itself as worthy of *applause*, yet always with a subaudition, or at least a suggestion, that it is not so really. It was once that which obtained applause, with at least the *prima facie* likelihood that the applause which it obtained was deserved. (Richard Chenevix Trench, 1859–60)
❖Adaptation of Latin *plausibilis*, deserving applause [1500s–1700s]. (James Murray et al., 1888–1928)

**pluck** The heart, liver, lungs, etc. of a slaughtered animal. (Sylva Clapin, 1902)
cf. *gather, humble pie, lights*

**plum** All berries are called *plums* in New England. (John Farmer, 1889)
cf. *corn, rum*

**plumber** One who makes things of lead. (William Grimshaw, 1854)
❖French *plumbier*, from *plomb*, lead. (Edward Lloyd, 1895)
cf. *aplomb*

**plump** Suddenly, as with a heavy fall. (William Whitney, 1889)
❖To tell one something *plump* is to blurt it out, to tell it without circumlocution, like a mass of something wet flung down upon the ground, or a stone that sinks at once, without splash, into the water. And as it is only a compact and solid mass that makes a noise of the foregoing description, the term *plump* is applied to a compact mass. (Hensleigh Wedgwood, 1878)
❖Dry; a *plump whiting* [fish], a whiting dried. (Samuel Pegge, 1735–36)

**plunder** Personal luggage, baggage of travellers, goods, effects. A very common word throughout the southern and western [United] States. (James Bartlett, 1849)
❖Formerly *plunden*, rags, thence in a depreciatory manner, clothes of poor

people. (Hensleigh Wedgwood, 1878)
cf. *carriage, luggage*

**poach** To tread damp ground into holes and foot-prints, as by cattle. (William H. Cope, 1883)

**podium** A low wall, generally with a plinth and cornice, placed in front of a building. A projecting basement round the interior of the building, as a shelf or seat, and round the exterior for ornamental adjuncts, as statues. (Edward Lloyd, 1895)

**point-blank** Its literal meaning is a white spot, from the French *point blanc*, referring to the white spot in the centre of a target. (Basil Hargrave, 1925)

**policy** A conditional promissory note, depending on the result of a wager [1700s–1800s]. (James Murray et al., 1888–1928)
❖Of lottery tickets, to gamble with the numbers. (John Farmer, 1889)

**polite** Literally, polished; smooth and glossy; reflecting. Figuratively, polished or refined in manners or behavior; well-bred, courtly. From Latin *politus*, past participle of *polio*, to polish. (Edward Lloyd, 1895)

**politics** At the present, *politics* are always things, but they were sometimes persons as well in times past. (Richard Chenevix Trench, 1859–60)
cf. *homicide, pantomime, pedicure, rhetoric, zany*

**polka** A woman's tight-fitting jacket, usually knitted; more fully, *polka-jacket*; with reference to Polish *polka*, a polish woman [1800s]. (James Murray et al., 1888–1928)
cf. *camisole, petticoat, polonaise*

**pollen** A sort of fine bran. (William Grimshaw, 1854)

**pollution** The emission of semen at other times than during coition. (Edward Lloyd, 1895)
❖*Polluted*, puffed up with pride. (William H. Patterson, 1880)

**polonaise** A name applied, at various periods from *circa* 1770 onward, to an article of female dress, originally suggested by that of Polish women, being a dress or over-dress, consisting of a bodice, with a skirt open from the waist

downwards. (James Murray et al., 1888–1928)
cf. *petticoat, polka*

**polygraph**  An instrument for making a number of drawings or writings simultaneously. A copying machine. (Edward Lloyd, 1895)
❖One of the names given to the gelatine copying pad. (Edward Knight, 1884)

**pompous**  Full of *pomp;* stately. (John Kersey, 1772)
❖Splendid. (C. H. Herford, 1902)
❖Befitting a procession [late 1300s–1800s]. (Edward Lloyd, 1895)

**pond**  *Pond,* in England, is generally applied to small pieces of water by the roadside, in a field, or other restricted space. . . . An American pond is, in reality, a small lake. *To pond* is to accumulate water in a pond. (John Farmer, 1889)
cf. *server*

**pontificate**  To perform the functions of a pontiff, or bishop; to officiate as a bishop, especially at mass; adaptation of Latin *pontificatus,* the office or dignity of a pontifex. (James Murray et al., 1888–1928)
cf. *sanctimonious*

**poodle**  To hobble; to walk about slowly and feebly. (H. Harman, 1929)
❖From Dutch *poedele,* to paddle in the water. (Hensleigh Wedgwood, 1878)
❖A woolly sort of cloth; a garment of this cloth. (James Murray et al., 1888–1928)
❖"A short green cloak adorned with a collar of the woolly texture generally denominated *poodle.*" (George Sala, *Gaslight and Daylight,* 1859)

**poop**  A short blast in a hollow tube, as a wind instrument [1500s–1700s]. To make an abrupt sound, as by blowing a horn [1300s–1500s]. (James Murray et al., 1888–1928)
❖*Poops,* gulps in drinking. (John Ray, 1674–91)
❖*Pooping,* the shock of a high and heavy sea, upon the stern or quarter of a ship, when she scuds before the wind in a tempest. This circumstance is very dangerous to the vessel, which is thereby exposed to the risk of having her whole stern beat inwards, by which she would be immediately laid open to the entrance of the sea, and of course founder, or be torn to pieces. (William Falconer, 1769)

**popular** He was *popular* once who had not acquired, but who was laying himself out to acquire, the favour of the people. *Popularity* was the wooing, not, as now, the having won, that favour. The word, which is passive now, was active then. (Richard Chenevix Trench, 1859–60)

❖*Popular* has, in the New England states, the curious meaning of 'conceited.' Therefore, the Yankee phrase, "*Popular* as a hen with one chick." (M. Schele De Vere, 1872)

**pornography** A description of prostitutes, or of prostitution, as a matter of hygiene. (Robley Dunglison, 1857)

❖Licentious painting employed to decorate the walls of rooms sacred to bacchanalian orgies, examples of which exist in Pompeii. (Noah Webster, 1864)

❖From Greek *porne*, a harlot, and *grapho*, to write. (Edward Lloyd, 1895)

**porter-house** A *house* at which *porter*, ale, and other malt liquors are retailed; also, such a house at which steaks, chops, etc. are served up. *Porter-house* steak . . . is supposed to derive its name from a well known porter-house in New York, where this particular cut of the meat was first introduced. (William Whitney, 1889)

**porthole** A hole in a ship's side, where the guns are placed. (William Grimshaw, 1854)

**posthumous** Born after the father's death. (John Kersey, 1772)
cf. *abortion, afterbirth*

**posturing** The performance of acrobatic feats. (Joseph Wright, 1896–1905)

❖What is meant by *posturing* is the distortion of the limbs, such as doing 'splits.' (Henry Mayhew, 1861)

**pot-head** A blockhead; a stupid person. (Joseph Wright, 1896–1905)

❖One who habitually stupefies himself with drink; a fuddler; a soaker. (Edward Lloyd, 1895)

**pot-holes** Naturally formed depressions in rocks, thought at one time from being circular in shape to have been made by aborigines for grinding purposes. It is now certain, however, that the action of water and loose stones alone is the true explanation of the phenomenon. (John Farmer, 1889)

**pot-luck** In old days—and the practice is still in force in some few outlying villages—nothing came amiss to the great family cooking pot suspended from the familiar pot-hook. Anything edible was thrown in, and to "keep the pot boiling" the fire was seldom, if ever, let out. When meal-time came, persons fished for themselves, and what they might happen to get was "pot-luck." (Basil Hargrave, 1925)

❖*To take pot luck*, to accept an impromptu invitation to dinner where no special preparation for a guest has been made. (T. Lewis Davies, 1881)

cf. *picnic*

**pot-shot** A *shot* taken at game merely for the purpose of filling the *pot* for a meal, without regard to skill or rules of sport, and so from any position or point of advantage. 'Shot,' or overpowered by drink; intoxicated [1600s]. (James Murray et al., 1888–1928)

cf. *intoxicate, overloaded*

**pounce** To swoop down, as a bird of prey [1700s]. (James Murray et al., 1888–1928)

**precarious** Uncertain because depending on the will of another; [from] Latin *precor*, to beg. (Joseph Worcester, 1881)

**pregnant** Ready or apt to produce. The metaphorical senses of this word, by which it was applied to the productiveness of mind, genius, argument, &c. are now, in general, obsolete. The word was, however, used with great laxity, and sometimes abused, as fashionable terms are. (Robert Nares, 1859)

❖Ready to admit or receive; giving access; [from] French *pregnant*, participle of *prendre*, to take. (Edward Lloyd, 1895)

❖Prompt, facile. *Hamlet*. (C. H. Herford, 1902)

❖Dexterous, ready. "The pregnant instrument of wrath." *Pericles*. (Alexander Dyce, 1902)

❖*Pregnancy*, readiness of wit; from *pregnant*, intelligent, shrewd, artful. (James Halliwell, 1855)

cf. *knocked up*

**preposterous** A word nearly or quite unserviceable now, being merely an ungraceful and slipshod synonym for *absurd*. But restore and confine it to its old use, to one peculiar branch of absurdity, the reversing of the true order and method of things, the putting of the last first and the first last, and of what excellent service it would be! (Richard Chenevix Trench, 1859–60)

❖The derivation of this word is the Latin *pre*, before, and *posterous*, after. (Basil Hargrave, 1925)
cf. *puny*

**prestigious** Deceitful; blinding the sight. (John Bullokar, 1616)
❖Practising juggling or legerdemain; of the nature of or characterized by juggling or magic; cheating, deluding; deceptive, illusory [1500s–1900s]. (James Murray et al., 1888–1928)
cf. *hanky-panky, juggle*

**pristine** Of or belonging to an early period or state; Old French from Latin *pristinus*, ancient, former. (Edward Lloyd, 1895)

**privy** Of an animal, familiar with man; domesticated, tame [1300s–1400s]. (James Murray et al., 1888–1928)

**proctor** One who collected alms for lepers, or other persons unable to do it themselves. (James Halliwell, 1855)
❖An indulgence-seller. (A. V. Judges, 1930)
❖To hector, swagger, or bully. The corresponding [noun] appears to be out of use. If it were not, the greatest care must be taken not to confound those bullies and swaggerers with the officers in our universities, who bear the same title. (Robert Forby, 1830)

**professor** A person who lays claim to an uncommon amount of religious faith and fervour; a "professing Christian." (Joseph Wright, 1896–1905)

**prone** Language of mute and eager entreaty. *Prone* is used with a suggestion of its Latin sense, to convey not only the ardour, but the eager, bending-forward of an earnest supplicant. *Measure for Measure* (C. H. Herford, 1902)

**pronounce** To turn out. This curious usage is current in Nantucket; thus, a horse, when being put through his paces, is said to *pronounce well* or *ill*, as the case may be. (John Farmer, 1889)

**protocol** The first draught or copy of a document. . . . It meant, in Byzantine authors, originally the first leaf glued on to manuscripts, in order to register under whose administration, and by whom, the manuscript was written. It was afterwards particularly applied to documents drawn up by notaries because, by a decree of Justinian, such documents were always to be accompanied by a first leaf or fly-leaf. It means "first glued-on" [in] Greek. (Walter Skeat, 1879–82)

**prune** At present, we only *prune* trees, but our earlier authors use the word where we should use *preen*, which indeed is but another form of the word. . . . With us, only birds *preen* their feathers, while women . . . might *prune* themselves of old. (Richard Chenevix Trench, 1859–60)
❖To *prune* . . . is not confined to the case of the bird, but is extended to the notion of dressing or trimming in general. (James Donald, 1877)

**P's and Q's** *To mind one's P's and Q's*, a reference to the *pints* and *quarts* chalked up in country public-houses against credit customers. Originally a warning to the customer not to allow his account to mount too high. (Albert Hyamson, 1922)
❖Originating, according to some, from the similarity of *p's* and *q's* in the horn-book alphabet, and therefore the warning of an old dame to her pupils; according to others, of a French dancing-master to his pupils, to mind their *pieds* (feet) and *queues* (wigs) when bowing. (J. C. Hotten, 1887)

**publicist** A writer on the laws of Nature and nations; one who treats of the rights of nations. It is seldom used by English writers. (James Bartlett, 1849)
cf. *pharmacologist, physiologist*

**pucker** *Pucker*, in the sense of a state of apprehension, of anxiety, is familiarly used here, as in England. "I was in such a *pucker* I did not know what to do." Washington Irving's *Sketchbook* (M. Schele De Vere, 1872)

**puke** A dark color between russet and black; puce . . . reddish-brown. (William Whitney, 1889)
cf. *russet, vomit*

**punctual** Restricted now to the accurate observing of fixed points of time, it once had a wider use, a *punctual* narration being a narration which entered into minuter points of detail. (Richard Chenevix Trench, 1859–60)

**pundit** In Hindoostan, a learned Brahmin, one versed in the Sanskrit language, and in the science, laws and religion of the Hindoos. (John Ogilvie, 1865)
❖Within the last thirty years, the term has acquired in India a peculiar application to the natives trained in the use of instruments, who have been

employed beyond the British-Indian frontier in surveying regions inaccessible to Europeans. [From] Sanskrit *pandita*, a learned man. (Henry Yule, 1886)

**puny** The present use of *puny* as that which is at once weak and small is only secondary and inferential. *Puny*, or [French] *puis né*, is 'born after another,' therefore younger, and only by inference smaller and weaker. (Richard Chenevix Trench, 1859–60)
cf. *preposterous*

**pup** *Pup*, properly, means a little boy or girl; [related to] Latin *pupus*, French *poupée*, a doll, German *puppë*. (E. Cobham Brewer, 1887)
❖*Puppy*, a puppet. (Joseph Wright, 1896–1905)

**pupil** An orphan who is a minor, and hence a ward; in civil and Scottish law, a person below the age of puberty who is under the care of a guardian; adaptation of Latin *pupillus*, *pupilla*, orphan, ward, minor [1300s–1800s]. (James Murray et al., 1888–1928)

**puppet-show** A peep-show. (Joseph Wright, 1896–1905)
cf. *peep-show*

**purchase** Now always to acquire in exchange for money, to buy. But much oftener in our old writers simply to acquire, being properly 'to hunt' (pourchasser); and then to take in hunting; then to acquire; and then, as the commonest way of acquiring is by giving money in exchange, to buy. (Richard Chenevix Trench, 1859–60)
❖Gain, profit. *Pericles*. (C. H. Herford, 1902)
❖*Purchase*, ordinarily used only to denote a mechanical hold or advantage applied in raising or moving heavy bodies, is in America made to denote any good hold. (M. Schele De Vere, 1872)

**purple** To make red. *Purples*, spots of a vivid red, which break out in malignant fevers. (Samuel Johnson, 1755)

**puss** *Puss, pussey-cat*, a hare. (John Brockett, 1825)
cf. *frog, hog, kittie*

**pyjama** A kind of loose wide trousers or drawers supported by a cord drawn round the waist. They are worn in India, and are generally made of a light fabric, such as silk or cotton, and are sometimes made to cover the feet entirely. (Edward Lloyd, 1895)
❖Hindu *pae-jama*, literally 'leg-clothing.' (Henry Yule, 1886)
cf. *pantaloon, panties*

**quaint** Trim, precise. A *quaint phrase* is a phrase dressed or trimmed, and not expressed in the ordinary way; [from] Latin *comptus*, combed. (E. Cobham Brewer, 1887)
❖Ingenious, clever, artful. "How *quaint* an orator you are." *2 Henry VI.* (Alexander Dyce, 1902)
❖In *quaint*, there lies always now the notion of a certain curiosity and oddness, however these may be subordinated to ends of beauty and grace. . . . But all of this is of late introduction into the word, which had once simply the meaning of 'elegant, graceful, skillful, subtle.' (Richard Chenevix Trench, 1859–60)
❖Cunning, crafty, artful. Chaucer's *Canterbury Tales*. (Edward Lloyd, 1895)

**quality** A profession, a calling, an occupation, [especially] the profession of an actor. "Give us a taste of your *quality*." *Hamlet*. (Alexander Dyce, 1902)
cf. *breadwinner*

**qualm** A sudden fit of sickness or languor. (Hezekiah Burhans, 1833)
❖A pestilence, a plague; mortal illness. A sudden fit of illness; a sudden seizure of sickly languor; a throe or throb of pain. (Edward Lloyd, 1895)
❖A rising of the stomach, as it is commonly called; a fit of nausea. (John Ogilvie, 1865)
cf. *sick, stomach*

**quarantine** A terme in the common law, when a woman, after the death of her husband, remaineth fortie dayes in the chiefe mannor place, within which time her dower shall be assigned. (John Bullokar, 1616)
❖Adaptation of medieval Latin *quarentena*, forty. (James Murray et al., 1888–1928)
❖These forty days are called the widow's *quarantine*. (William Blackstone, 1765–69)
cf. *forty*

**quarrel**  A square of window glass, properly one placed diagonally; anciently, a diamond-shaped pane of glass. Hence the cant term, *quarrel-picker*, a glazier. (James Halliwell, 1855)

❖This old word is still sometimes heard in New England, but only among the illiterate. (John Pickering, 1816)

❖An old lady friend of mine, feeling a draught, said to her granddaughter, "Isn't there a *quarrel* out of the window?" The little girl looks out, expecting to see two boys fighting, and innocently says, "No, grandma dear, I don't see any." (Alfred Easther, 1883)

❖Adopted from Old French *quarrel*, medieval Latin *quadrus*, a square. (James Murray et al.,) 1888–1928

**queen**  *Queen* is a word which originally meant no more than 'woman' or 'wife,' though it early came to be used for the wife of a king. (Sidney Low and F. S. Pulling, 1904)
cf. *housewife*

**quibble**  To pun; to play on the sound of words. (Samuel Johnson, 1755)
cf. *conundrum*

**quid**  Something chewed or kept in the mouth, especially a piece of tobacco. A corruption of *cud*. (Daniel Lyons, 1897)
❖Derivation: Old French or Norman *quider*, to ruminate. (J. C. Hotten, 1887)

**quid pro quo**  A terme among all apothecaries when, instead of one thing, they use another of the same nature. (John Bullokar, 1616)

**quiz**  One who banters or chaffs another. Daly, manager of the Dublin theater, laid a wager that he would introduce into the language within twenty-four hours a new word of no meaning. Accordingly on every wall, or all places accessible, were chalked up the four mystic letters, and all Dublin was inquiring what they meant. The wager was won, and the word remains current in our language. Is it a corruption of *Quid est*, what is this? (E. Cobham Brewer, 1887)

**rack** *Rack*, says Mr. Malone, is generally used by our ancient writers for a body of clouds sailing along; or rather, for the course of the clouds when in motion. But no instance has yet been produced where it is used to signify a single small fleeting cloud, in which sense only it can be figurative here . . . [from] Dutch *racka*, a track. "But as we often see against some storme, a silence in the heavens, the *rack* stands still."
*Hamlet*. (John Horne Tooke, 1840)
cf. *meteors, Noah's ark*

**racket** A snow-shoe, formed of cords stretched across a long and narrow frame of light wood; used in Canada. (Edward Lloyd, 1895)

**racy** Having distinctive piquancy, as *racy wine*. It was first applied to wine and according to Cowley comes to us from the Spanish and Portuguese *raiz*, root, meaning "having a radical or distinct flavour," but it probably is a corruption of *relishy*, French *reléché*, flavourous. (E. Cobham Brewer, 1898)

**radical** Original; implanted by nature; serving to produce. *Radicle*, that part of the seed of a plant which becomes the root. (Daniel Fenning, 1775)

**ragged** A term applied to fruit trees when they have a good crop. Thus they say, "How full of fruit that tree is! It's as *ragged* as it can [be]." (James Halliwell, 1855)

**ramification** The production of figures resembling branches [1600s–1800s]. (Edward Lloyd, 1895)
❖We frequently find curious *ramifications*, as on glass-windows in winter. (Robert Plot, 1677)

**ramshackled** Confused and obstructed in motion. From *rams* being fastened, or *shackled*, by their heads to their forelegs. (John Walker, 1835)

**ranch** A hut or house in the country [1800s]. (James Murray et al., 1888–1928)

**ransack** To search a person for something stolen or missing; adopted from Old Norse *rannsaka*, from *rann*, house, and *saka*, to seek. (James Murray et al., 1888–1928)

**rant** Public meeting or fair; hence, *ranter*, a priest who preached on such occasions. (Charles Mackay, 1874)
❖To be jovial or jolly in a noisy way; to make noisy mirth. The act of frolicking or toying [1700s–1800s]. (John Jamieson, 1879)
❖"On the *rant*" means *on the spree*, or *on the booze*. (John Wilkinson, 1924)

**rape** Speed, hurry; chiefly in the phrases *to have rape*, and *in rape* [1300s–1400s]. The taking of anything by force; violent seizure of goods, robbery; adopted from Old Norse *hrapa*, to hasten [1400s–1700s]. (James Murray et al., 1888–1928)
❖To scratch with violence. (Joseph Wright, 1896–1905)
cf. *bribery, orgasm*

**rascal** A technical phrase for a lean and ill-conditioned deer [1300s–1600s]. (C. H. Herford, 1902)

**rather** Sooner; comparative of *rath*, soon, early. (William H. Cope, 1883)
❖Earlier, before; from Anglo-Saxon *hrœdh, hredh*, quick, swift [1300s–1400s]. (Edward Lloyd, 1895)

**razzle-dazzle** A spree . . . lasting perhaps a day. (John Wilkinson, 1924)

**real estate** This is a compound that has no proper place in the language of everyday life, where it is a mere pretentious intruder from the technical province of law. Law makes the distinction of *real* and *personal estate*, but a man does not, therefore, talk of drawing some "personal estate" from the bank . . . he draws *money*. . . . *Real estate*, as ordinarily used, is a mere big-sounding,

vulgar phrase for houses and land, and so used is a marked and unjustifiable Americanism. (John Farmer, 1889)

**rear up** To stand up straight, as plants do recovering after heat or transplanting. (Edward Gepp, 1923)

**recant** To sing again; to repeat in singing; to sing after another [1600s]. (James Murray et al., 1888–1928)

**receipt** A *receipt* is a written or printed direction for compounding or mixing together certain ingredients, and is also a written discharge to a debtor for payment of a debt. The word *recipe* is only properly used medically. It is Latin for "take" and, contracted into *Rx*, it is used as a prefix to doctors' prescriptions. (Basil Hargrave, 1925)
cf. *pharmacologist*

**red-handed** Murderous; applied to one who has shed blood. (Joseph Wright, 1896–1905)

**red neck** A name given to a Roman Catholic [in] Lancashire. (Joseph Wright, 1896–1905)

**red-tape** The red tape used in public and especially government offices for tying up documents, &c.; applied satirically to the intricate system of routine in vogue there. (James Donald, 1877)
✦Tape of a red colour, such as is commonly used in securing legal and official documents [1600s–1900s]. (James Murray et al., 1888–1928)
✦As far back as 1658, an advertisement in the *Public Intelligencer* offers a reward for the restoration of "a little bundle of papers tied with a *red tape*, which were lost on Friday last." (William Walsh, 1900)

**reduce** That which is *reduced* now is brought back to narrower limits or lower terms, or more subject conditions than those under which it subsisted before. But nothing of this lies of necessity in the word, nor yet in the early uses of it. According to these, that was *reduced* which was brought back to its former state, an estate that might be . . . an ampler, larger, or more prosperous one than that which it superseded. (Richard Chenevix Trench, 1859–60)

**reek** Smoke, vapor or exhalation; from *rauch*, smoke. (Charles Mackay, 1874)
✦*Reeky*, a name given to Edinburgh because of the cloud of smoke that overhangs the town. (Joseph Wright, 1896–1905)

**regurgitate**  To swallow again. (Thomas Blount, 1656)

**reign**  This is now in the abstract what *kingdom* is in the concrete, but there was no such distinction once between them. (Richard Chenevix Trench, 1859–60)

**remiss**  Weakened in consistency or colour [1400s–1600s]. Of sounds, weak, soft, low [1500s–1600s]. Of taste, faint, slight [1600s]. (James Murray et al., 1888–1928)
cf. *discolored, taste*

**remorse**  Pity. *Measure For Measure.* (C. H. Herford, 1902)
cf. *passionate, pathetic*

**rendition**  *Rendition* means surrender, giving up, relinquishing to another, as when we speak of the *rendition* of a beleaguered town to a besieger. (William Mathews, 1884)

**reprint**  *Reprint* is said to be an Americanism as far as it denotes the republication here of a work printed in a foreign country. It certainly used to be a charming euphemism in olden days, when the works of British authors were issued here without their sanction, and without giving them a fair compensation—a régime happily unknown in our day. (M. Schele De Vere, 1872)

**reptile**  An animal that creeps on many feet. (Hezekiah Burhans, 1833)
cf. *amphibious, antelope, caterpillar*

**resent**  When first introduced into the language [early 1600s] . . . to *resent* meant to have a sense or feeling of that which had been done to us. But whether a sense of gratitude for the good, or of enmity for the evil, the word itself said nothing, and was employed in both meanings. Must we gather from the fact that . . . our sense of injuries is much stronger and more lasting than our sense of benefits? It has fared with *retaliate* and *retaliation*, as it has with *resent* and *resentment*, that whereas men could once speak of the retaliation of benefits as well as of wrongs, they only retaliate injuries now. (Richard Chenevix Trench, 1859–60)

**restraining-order**  A temporary order to a bank or other public company not to permit the transfer of certain stock from one person to another, and not to pay dividends due upon it till permission is granted. (Edward Lloyd, 1895)

**rest room** A room in a public building, business establishment, etc. affording conveniences . . . for those desirous of rest and comfort. (Mitford Mathews, 1956)

**result** To decide or decree. Some of our writers on ecclesiastical affairs constantly use this verb in speaking of our own councils thus: "The council *resulted* that the parties should do certain things." (John Pickering, 1816)

**revamp** Originally a shoemaker's term exclusively, derived from "to wamp," meaning to put new upper leather to shoes. (Sylva Clapin, 1902) cf. *graft, translators*

**revenge** We might be staggered at finding *revenge* classed as good fruit of godly sorrow in 2 Corinthians 7.11, but the fact is worth noting that nearly every passion and senti-ment in our nature which can be expressed by words was implanted for a good and pure purpose . . . and only the perversion of that purpose which is bad and blameworthy. So, though such things as *just anger, proper pride*, and *holy jeal-ousy*, or *zeal*, exist, we cannot express them without a qualifying adjective before them, since anger, pride, and jealousy, without such qualification, bring only evil things before our minds. (W. L. Blackley, 1869) cf. *incense, jealous*

**reword** To repeat in the same words. "Bring me to the test, and I the matter will *reword*." *Hamlet*. (Edward Lloyd, 1895)

**rhapsody** Literally, dispersed pieces, or songs, loosely *sewed*, or strung together; [from] Greek *rhapsodia, rhapto*, to sew, and *ode*, a song. (James Donald, 1877)
❖A short epic poem, or a portion of a longer epic, recited by a rhapsodist. A confused or disconnected series of sentences or statements, composed under excitement, and without dependence or natural connection. (Edward Lloyd, 1895) cf. *dildo*

**rhetoric** A rhetorician [1300s–1400s]. (James Murray et al., 1888–1928)
cf. *pantomime, pedicure, politics*

**rib-roast** To beat. "I'll *ribroast* him to his heart's content." (Francis Grose, 1796)
cf. *dad, lather, spank*

**riddle** A hole made by a bullet [1800s]. (James Murray et al., 1888–1928)

**ridiculous** This is used in a very different sense in some counties from its original meaning. Something very indecent and improper is understood by it, as any violent attack upon a woman's chastity is called "very *ridiculous* behavior." A very disorderly and ill-conducted house is also called a *ridiculous* one. (James Halliwell, 1855)

**rifle** *Rifle* retains, in some parts of the Union, the meaning it has in old English, a whetstone for sharpening scythes, consisting either of the stone itself, or a strip of wood covered with emery. Its use is almost limited to the New England states and a few of the eastern counties of Virginia. (M. Schele De Vere, 1872)
❖This old English word is retained by farmers of New England [1400s–1800s]. (James Bartlett, 1849)

**rift** To belch; [from] Danish *ræver*. (John Brockett, 1825)
❖To break wind upwards in the stomach; also to utter words in a manner suggestive to this [1300s–1800s]. Figuratively, with *up*, to come back unpleasantly to the memory [1600s–1800s]. (James Murray et al., 1888–1928)

**rigging** In English, this word is seldom used except in reference to ships, and the arrangement of their masts, spars, ropes, &c. In the Scottish language, it is employed to signify the roof, cross-beams, &c. of a house. (Charles Mackay, 1888)
cf. *furniture*

**rigmarole** [From] Ragman's Roll, originally a collection of those deeds by which the nobility and gentry [including Ragimund, a legate] of Scotland were tyrannically constrained to subscribe allegiance to Edward I of England in 1296. (Robert Nares, 1859)
❖A confused, disconnected discourse or recital of circumstances. (James Halliwell, 1855)

❖The name [*Rigmarole*] was originally given to a game consisting in drawing characters from a roll by strings hanging out from the end, the amusement arising from the application or misapplication of the characters to the person by whom they were drawn. (Hensleigh Wedgwood, 1878)
cf. *charade*, *terrier*

**rival** A bank, shore, landing-place; adaptation of Latin *rivalis*, originally one living on the opposite bank of a stream from another, from Latin *rivus*, stream. (James Murray et al., 1888–1928)
❖An associate, a companion, a comrade. "If you do meet Horatio and Marcellus, the *rivals* of my watch, bid them make haste." *Hamlet*. (Edward Lloyd, 1895)

**road** Wharf, harbour. *Two Gentlemen of Verona*. (C. H. Herford, 1902)

**roadster** Applied chiefly to those [sailing] vessels which work by tides, and seek some known "road" to await turn of tide or change of wind. (William Smyth, 1867)
❖A vessel lying, or able to lie, at anchor in a *roadstead*. (James Murray et al., 1888–1928)
❖A horse fitted for the road, or fit for performing journeys. (Joseph Worcester, 1881)
cf. *tide over*

**rocket** Part of the dress of a bishop, and formerly of women; the diminutive of Anglo-Saxon *roc*, exterior vest[ments]. (John Horne Tooke, 1840)
❖A blunt-headed lance; a small rock [1500s]. (James Murray et al., 1888–1928)

**rollicking** A peculiar gait of a horse. (James Bartlett, 1849)
❖From *rollick*, to move about in a careless, merry fashion. (Edward Lloyd, 1895)

**rolling-pin** A cylindrical piece of wood round which a banner may be rolled to prevent creasing [1400s]. (James Murray et al., 1888–1928)

**romance**  To translate into a Romance language [1800s]. To compose in verse [1300s]. (James Murray et al., 1888–1928)
❖To tell a rouzing lie. (John Kersey, 1772)
❖*Romantic*, curious, out-of-the-way, unexpected. (Joseph Wright, 1896–1905)
❖*Romantically*: This is ridiculed in the *Monthly Anthology* as an "Indianism." It is not in use. I have, in one instance, met with the still more extraordinary word, *romanticity*. (John Pickering, 1816)
cf. *English, transfusion*

**rope-trick**  Probably [a corruption of] *rogues' tricks;* tricks that deserve the halter. (Samuel Johnson, 1755)

**rosary**  A bed of roses; a place where roses grow [1400s–1800s]. (Edward Lloyd, 1895)
cf. *seminary*

**roughness**  All over the [American] South they feed a horse *roughness* (any kind of fodder, as distinguished from grain) but in Texas they stake him out, and he gets nothing else but *roughness.* (John Farmer, 1889)

**roughshod**  Provided with shoes which are roughened to prevent slipping [1600s–1800s]. (James Murray et al., 1888–1928)

**roulette**  A device to keep the hair in curl; a light roller used in massage [1800s]. (James Murray et al., 1888–1928)

**roundabout**  A coat or jacket encircling the body. (Richard Thornton, 1912)
❖*Roundabout* is, in America, almost exclusively used for the short jacket of the English, as worn by boys, sailors, and others. (M. Schele De Vere, 1872)
❖A name given to [a] circular fort or encampment. (Alexander Warrack, 1911)
cf. *camisole, petticoat, polka*

**round-robin**  A petition remonstrance, or protest, signed in such a way that no name heads the list, the signatures being placed in a ring or circle. (Edward Lloyd, 1895)
❖The device is French, and the term is a corruption of *rond*, round, and *ruban*, a ribbon. It was first adopted by the officers of the government as a means of making known their grievances. (E. Cobham Brewer, 1887)
❖A blasphemous name given by some of the more disreputable of the reforming party to the sacramental wafer. (T. Lewis Davies, 1881)

**royalties** The royal rights or prerogatives of a king or queen. (John Kersey, 1772)
cf. *sacred*

**rub-a-dub** The imitative sound of a drum being beaten; so, *rub-a-dub-dub* [1700s–1800s]. (James Murray et al., 1888–1928)
cf. *tattoo*

**rudder** A sieve; [from] Anglo-Saxon *hrudrian*, to sift. (W. H. Long, 1886)
❖An instrument used for stirring the mash in brewing. (Joseph Wright, 1896–1905)
cf. *lawn*

**rude** The red taint in the complexion. (Adam and Charles Black, 1851)
cf. *complexion, yellow-belly*

**ruddy** To roar like thunder, or to rumble like wind in the stomach. Derivation uncertain, but possibly akin to *rowie* or *rowtin*, the bellowing of cattle. (Charles Mackay, 1888)
cf. *croon*

**rule-o'-thumb** No rule at all; guesswork. (John Brockett, 1825)

**rum** In some parts of the country [America], *rum* is a general name for all kinds of spirit—brandy, whisky, gin, and rum. (John Farmer, 1889)
cf. *corn, plum, sherbet, shrub*

**rummage** To remove lumber from one place to another. (John Kersey, 1772)
❖It is a sea-term, and signified at first to dispose with such orderly method, goods in the hold of a ship, that there should be the greatest possible room, or 'roomage.' The [following] quotation from Phillips shows the word in the act of transition from its former use to its present: "To remove any goods or luggage from one place to another especially to clear a ship's hold of any goods or lading in order to their being handsomely stowed and placed. The word is used upon other occasions for . . . 'to search narrowly.'" (Richard Chenevix Trench, 1859–60)

**rumour** A widespread report of a favourable or laudatory nature [in] Chaucer. Loud expression or manifestation of disapproval or protest [1400s–1500s]. (James Murray et al., 1888–1928)

**rump** To turn one's back upon a person, especially as a mode of snubbing [1700s–1800]. (James Murray et al., 1888–1928)
❖A still more decided cut than the "cold shoulder." (J. C. Hotten, 1887)

**rumple** To seduce. "He bin *rumplin'* that wench." (George Dartnell and Edward Goddard, 1893)

**rumpus** The rumbling noise heard in a rabbit's or fox's burrow when a terrier drives them out. (Joseph Wright, 1896–1905)

**run into the ground** A metaphor borrowed from forcing burrowing animals to seek refuge underground, and well expressive of constant and close persecution. (Sylva Clapin, 1902)

**running shoe** A strip of metal attached to a [sled] runner. (Walter S. Avis, 1967)
❖*Running-shoes*, pumps. (James Halliwell, 1855)

**russet** A coarse, homespun woolen cloth of a reddish brown, grey, or neutral colour, formerly used for the dress of peasants and country-folk; adapted from Old French *rousset, roset*, etc. diminutive of modern French *roux*, red [1200s–1800s]. (James Murray et al., 1888–1928)
cf. *puke*

**rustler** An active, busy individual. Formerly a rancher's term for a cook, and as it required considerable activity and energy to provide the whole army of cowboys and herders on a ranch with their three meals per diem, it was by no means a violent transition when the term got to mean any man peculiarly alert and energetic. By a still further amplification of its meaning, it signifies one who never succumbs to circumstances. This is about the highest compliment that can be paid to a man who, failing in one thing, finds something else available for his support. (John Farmer, 1889)

**sacred** Royal. *Cymbeline*. (C. H. Herford, 1902)
cf. *royalties*

**safe** *Safe*, a box or cupboard in which provisions are kept, has entirely superseded the English "larder," which is rarely used otherwise than figuratively. (M. Schele De Vere, 1872)
❖*Meat-safe*, a safe with perforated zinc or wire gauze front, in which to keep meat. (Edward Lloyd, 1895)

**safeguard** A riding-skirt; a large outer petticoat worn by females when riding to protect them from the dirt. (James Halliwell, 1855)
❖A kind of . . . attire reaching from the navill downe to the feete, [worn by] a baker. (Adrian Junius, 1585)
cf. *pantaloon, polka*

**salary** Salt rations. The Romans served out rations of salt and other necessaries to their soldiers and civil servants. The rations altogether were called by the general name of *salt*, and when money was substituted for the rations, the stipend went by the same name. (E. Cobham Brewer, 1887)

**salvage** A payment or compensation to which those persons are entitled who have, by their voluntary efforts, saved ships or goods from extraordinary danger, as from fire, the sea, an enemy, pirates, or the like. The amount of *salvage* to be paid is generally agreed on between the salvors and the owners of the property salved, but if they cannot agree, the sum to be paid [is] determined by the Admiralty Court. The crew of a ship are not entitled to any salvage for any extraordinary efforts they may make in saving their own vessel. (Edward Lloyd, 1895)

**sanctimonious** Possessing sanctity; holy; religious [1600s–1800s]. (Edward Lloyd, 1895)
cf. *pontificate*

**sandbagger** A robber who uses a sandbag to stun his victims. (Richard Thornton, 1912)
❖A sailboat upon which bags of sand are used as ballast. (Mitford Mathews, 1956)

**sarcasm** A flaying or plucking off of the skin. From Greek *sarkazo*, to flay. (E. Cobham Brewer, 1887)

**sash** At present, always a belt or girdle of the loins; not so, however, when introduced from the East. By the *sash*, or *shash*, as it was then always spelt, was understood the roll of silk, fine linen, or gauze, worn about the head—in fact, a turban. (Richard Chenevix Trench, 1859–60)
cf. *cummerbund*

**sauce** Vegetables, especially those eaten with flesh meat, are sometimes called *sauce* in New England. Also sometimes used in [the] sense of preserved or stewed fruits. This word is an undoubted survival of Old English usage, and is so quoted in Forby and other glossaries. . . . In the Southern states, *sauce*, for vegetables, is almost unknown, its place being supplied by *greens*. Beaumont and Fletcher use "green sauce" for vegetables. [Other phrases include] *long sauce*, carrots, parsnips, etc., *short sauce*, potatoes, turnips, *sauce man*, a green-grocer or other dealer in market produce. (Sylva Clapin, 1902)
❖Those farmers who supply the markets with vegetables are sometimes called *sauce-marketers*. (John Pickering, 1816)
❖To cut up, to carve; specially applied to a capon. "*Sauce* that capon." (Edward Lloyd, 1895)
❖The literal meaning of *sauce* is but *salted*, from the Latin *sal*, salt. (Basil Hargrave, 1925)
❖*Saucer*, a vessel to hold sauce. (Nathaniel Bailey, 1727)

**savagery** Wild vegetation. "Deracinate [uproot] such *savagery*." *Henry V.* (C. T. Onions, 1911)

**scallion** An onion in an advanced period of its growth, in which its flavour becomes coarse and rank, and its substance tough. (Robert Forby, 1830)

**scam** Of a shoe, to twist it out of shape by wearing wrongly, [in] Cornwall. (Joseph Wright, 1896–1905)

**scapegoat** In the Mosaic ritual of the Day of Atonement, the one of two goats that was chosen by lot to be sent alive into the wilderness, the sins of the people having been symbolically laid upon it, while the other was appointed to be sacrificed. Apparently invented by Tinsdale [in] 1530 to express what he believed to be the literal meaning of [the ritual] occurring only in Leviathan. (James Murray et al., 1888–1928)
❖"The goat, on which the lot fell to be the scapegoat, shall be presented alive before the Lord to make an atonement with him, and to let him go for a scapegoat into the wilderness." (Leviticus 16:10)

**scavenger** An officer well known in London that makes clean the streets by scraping up and carrying away the dust and dirt; from Teutonic schaben or Belgian *schaven*, to scrape or shave away. (Thomas Blount, 1656)
❖The *scavage* was originally a duty paid on the inspection of customable goods brought for sale within the city of London, from Anglo-Saxon *sceawian*, to view, inspect. The *scawengers* or *scavagers* were the inspectors to whom the goods were actually shown. Afterwards, the inspection of the streets seems to have been committed to the same officers, unless the name was used in the general sense of inspectors. (Hensleigh Wedgwood, 1878)

**scenic** Dramatic, theatrical. (Samuel Johnson, 1755)

**scoff** To eat greedily; [from] eighteenth-century *scauf*, food. (Edward Gepp, 1923)

**sconce** A seat at one side of the fire-place in the old large open chimney; a short partition near the fire upon which all the bright utensils in a cottage are suspended. (John Brockett, 1825)
❖A stone shelf. (William Dickinson, 1881)

**score** A notch, then from the custom of keeping count by cutting notches on a stick; account reckoning, the specific number of twenty being the number of notches it was convenient to make on a single stick. When that number was complete, the piece on which they were made was *cut off* [French, *taillée*] and called a tally. (Georgina Jackson, 1879)

**scot-free** Free from payment of *scot*, tavern "score." (James Murray et al., 1888–1928)
❖Untaxed, unhurt. [From] French *escot*, payment of one's share; Italian *scotto*, the reckoning at an inn; Anglo-Saxon *sceotan*, to shoot, throw down money. (James Donald, 1877)

**scram** To search about for what can be picked up; to search with slight hope of success. (Joseph Wright, 1896–1905)

**scrambled-eggs** Eggs, boiled and mixed up, in the shell, with vinegar, pepper, and salt. (Edward Lloyd, 1895)

**scribble** To sip. "*Scribblin'* tea from morning to night." (Michael Traynor, 1953)

**scrumptious** Particular, fastidious; probably a corruption of *scrupulous*. (James Bartlett, 1849)
❖First-class, capital; English slang. (Edward Lloyd, 1895)

**scrunch** To bite up quickly and noisily, as children do sweets. (Angelina Parker, 1881)

**scrupulous** Doubtful. (James Halliwell, 1855)

**scuff** Of dress, to make shabby by wearing at unseasonable times. (Joseph Wright, 1896–1905)

**scuttle-butt** A cask [or *butt*] having a square piece sawn out [*scuttled*] of its bilge and lashed upon the deck. It is used to contain the fresh water for daily use. (J. J. Moore, 1805)

**seaman** The male of the mermaid. (John Walker, 1835)

**secure** In our present English, the difference between *safe* and *secure* is hardly recognized, but once it was otherwise. *Secure* was subjective; it was a man's own sense, well-grounded or not, of the absence of danger. *Safe* was objective, the actual fact of such absence of danger. A man, therefore, might not be *safe* just because he was *secure*. (Richard Chenevix Trench, 1859–60)

**seedy** Applied to French brandy, having a particular flavour, supposed to be derived from the weeds growing among the vines. (Edward Lloyd, 1895)

**seep** Used in New England for the process of straining. Coffee is said to be *seeped* when run through muslin to clear it. (John Farmer, 1889)

**seminary** A seed plot or nursery of young plants. (John Kersey, 1772) ❖A plot of ground in which seeds are sown to be afterwards transplanted. (Edward Lloyd, 1895)
cf. *rosary*

**send-off** A journalistic Americanism for a notice; an item of news. Sometimes *send-off notice*. (John Farmer, 1889)

**senile** Belonging to old age; consequent on old age. (Samuel Johnson, 1755) ❖Now only of diseases. (James Murray et al., 1888–1928) ❖"A person in whom Nature, Education, and Time have happily match'd a *senile* maturity of judgment with a youthful vigour of fancy." (Boyle, *Style of Script*, 1661)

**serenade** Properly, music performed in a clear night; from Italian, Spanish, *serenata*, Latin *serenus*, clear, serene. (Noah Webster, 1828)

**servant** A wooer, follower, admirer, lover, not of necessity an accepted one, was a *servant* in the chivalrous language of two or three centuries ago. (Richard Chenevix Trench, 1859–60) ❖The [male] counterpart of *mistress*, used often for a recognised admirer, as well as for an accepted lover. (C. H. Herford, 1902)
cf. *dribble, go-between, lout, mistress*

**server** Where there are no wells, as in the Weald of Kent, the pond that serves the house is called the *server*, to distinguish it from the horse-pond; and from thence they take their water for boiling their meat, for their tea, &c. The etymon is clear, unless it be from a corruption of the French *reservoir*. (Samuel Pegge, 1735–36)
cf. *pond*

**session** The act of sitting; the state of being seated; from Latin *sessionem*, *sedio*, to sit. (Edward Lloyd, 1895)

**sewer** An officer whose duty it was to taste the dishes served at the king's table. (Charles Mackay, 1874)

**shabby** Of the weather, bad, inclement, without being violently stormy. (Joseph Wright, 1896–1905)
cf. *gruesome*

**shackle** The wrist; whence the verb, *to shackle*, to fetter. The modern *shackle* was formerly *schackle-lock* or *schacklock*, wrist lock. (Charles Mackay, 1874)

**shade** It has nothing in common with the shadows of the woods, but means either a pool or an open space of ground, generally on a hill-top, where the cattle in hot weather collect, or as the phrase is, *come to shade*, for the sake of water in the one, and the breeze in the other. (J. R. Wise, 1883)
❖*Shadow*, a shady place. *Twelfth Night*. (C. H. Herford, 1902)
cf. *glade*

**sham** False sleeves to put on over a dirty shirt, or false sleeves to put on over a plain one. (Francis Grose, 1796)

**shambles** The place where butchers kill or sell their meat; a butchery. (Samuel Johnson, 1755)
❖From Anglo-Saxon *scamel*, a bench; akin to Latin *scabellum*, diminutive of *scamnum*, a bench [1600s–1800s]. (James Donald, 1877)

**shampoo** To squeeze and rub the whole surface of the body after a hot bath, at the same time extending the limbs and wracking the joints for the purpose of restoring tone and vigour. It was introduced from the East. [From] Hindu *champná*, to thrust in, to press. (Edward Lloyd, 1895)
❖The word has now long been familiarly used in England. The process is described, though not named, by Terry in 1616: "Taking thus their ease, they often call [at] their barbers, who tenderly grip and smite their arms and other parts of their bodies . . . to stir the blood. It is a pleasing wantonness, and much valued in these hot climes." (Henry Yule, 1886)

**shank** The remainder, the rest. (John Farmer, 1889)
❖In some parts of Virginia, the word *shank* is quaintly used, and one friend will say to another, "Suppose you come in and spend the *shank* of the evening with me?" (M. Schele De Vere, 1872)

**shanty** Short for *shanty boat*, a river boat provided with living quarters similar to those of a shanty. The caboose of a train. (Mitford Mathews, 1956)
cf. *caboose*

**sheer** It is curious that Christopher Sly's declaration that he was 'fourteen pence on the score for sheer ale' [in] *Taming of the Shrew* should have given so much trouble to some of the early commentators upon Shakespeare. *Sheer,* which is 'pure, unmixed,' was used of things concrete once, although mostly of things abstract now. (Richard Chenevix Trench, 1859–60)

**sheik** An old man; [from] Arabic *sheikh,* to be old. (James Donald, 1877)

**sherbet** A compound drink lately introduced in England from Turkey and Persia, made of juice of lemons, sugar, and other ingredients. Another sort of it is made of violets, honey, juice of raisins, &c. *Sherbet,* in the Persian tongue, signifies pleasant liquor. (Thomas Blount, 1717)
❖Anything intoxicating. (Basil Hargrave, 1925)
❖A glass of any warm alcoholic liquor, as grog, &c. (Albert Barrère, 1911)
cf. *rum*

**shin-splints** Pieces of wood placed on the legs of persons who break stones for roads. (James Halliwell, 1855)

**shit-faced** Having a small face; [from] *shit,* a child; a puny, insignificant animal. (Alexander Warrack, 1911)

**shoddy** Woollen yarn obtained by tearing to shreds refuse woollen rags, which, with the addition of some new wool, is made into a kind of cloth. Of a person that pretends to a superiority to which he has had no just claim; said especially of those who claim, on the ground of wealth, a social status or a degree of influence to which they are entitled by . . . breeding. In the U.S. the word seems to have been first used with reference to those who made fortunes by army contracts at the time of the Civil War, it being alleged that the clothing supplied by the contractors consisted largely of *shoddy.* (James Murray et al., 1888–1928)

**shoot the moon** To remove furniture from a house in the night without paying the landlord. (J. C. Hotten, 1887)

**shortcoming** Failure to reach the required or expected amount [1600s–1800s]. (James Murray et al., 1888–1928)

**short-handed** Competent to write shorthand. Niggardly, mean; inefficient, ineffective [1600s]. (James Murray et al., 1888–1928)

**short-sighted** Having the focus of the eyes at less than the normal distance; unable to distinguish objects clearly at a distance; myopic [1600s–1800s]. (James Murray et al., 1888–1928)

**show off** To scold, to reprimand. (W. H. Long, 1886)

**shrew** There are at the present no *shrews*, save female ones. But the word, like so many others which we have met with now restrained to one sex, was formerly applied to both. It conveyed also of old a much deeper moral reprobation than now or in Middle English. Thus, Lucifer is a *shrew* in *Piers Ploughman*. (Richard Chenevix Trench, 1859–60)
❖*To shrewe*, to curse; Saxon. (Thomas Tyrwhitt, 1871)
❖*Shrewd*, shrewish, mischievous. *Merchant of Venice*. (C. H. Herford, 1902)
❖*Shrewd*, malicious; cursed. (Thomas Wright, 1857)
cf. *maid, wench*

**shroud** To gather together, as beasts do for warmth. (James Halliwell, 1855)

**shrub** To reduce to poverty by winning someone's property in gaming. (James Halliwell, 1855)
❖A prepared drink made with the juice of orange or lemon, or other acid fruit, sugar, and rum, or other spirit. Often, *rum-shrub*; also with other qualifying words indicating the ingredient which takes the place of the rum in drinks prepared in this way, to which the name shrub is extended [1700s–1800s]. (James Murray et al., 1888–1928)
cf. *half-and-half, rum, sherbet, sweepstake*

**shrug** A shake of the hand [1400s–1700s]. (James Murray et al., 1888–1928)

**shucks** The husks or shells of peas or beans, after the seeds have been taken out. (W. H. Long, 1886)

**sick** *Sick*, in England used only for sickness of the stomach, is in America applied to indisposition of any kind. . . . A Virginia lady in Europe, happening to be ill, sent for an English physician who, hearing from her servant that she was sick, soon made his appearance with a stomach pump. (M. Schele De Vere, 1872)

**side-dish** A person invited to an entertainment in order to make game of one or more of the guests. (Alexander Warrack, 1911)

**side-step** A false step which wrenches the limb. (Joseph Wright, 1896–1905)

**sightless** Invisible; unsightly; "sightless stains." *King John.* (Alexander Dyce, 1902)
cf. *speechless, timeless*

**sight-seeing** Seeing ghosts. (Joseph Wright, 1896–1905)

**silly** *Silly* is the German *selig*, blessed, whence the infant Jesus is termed the "harmless *silly* babe," and sheep are called *silly*, meaning harmless or innocent. As the holy are easily taken in by worldly cunning, the word came to signify gullible or foolish. (E. Cobham Brewer, 1887)
❖A deep conviction of men that he who departs from evil will make himself a prey . . . has brought to pass the fact that a number of words, signifying at first goodness, signify next well-meaning simplicity. The notions of goodness and foolishness, with a strong predominance of the last, for a while interpenetrat[ed] one another, till at length the latter quite expell[ed] the former. (Richard Chenevix Trench, 1859–60)
cf. *giddy*

**single men** Young men are called *single men* if their fathers are alive to advanced life. (Joseph Wright, 1896–1905)
cf. *posthumous*

**single woman** A "single woman," within the Bastardy Act, includes a widow, and also a married woman living apart from her husband, but not a woman single at the time of the birth of her child, who has since married and is living with her husband, even though she took out the summons before her marriage, and service of it was prevented by the putative father. (F. Stroud, 1890)

**sinister** Left[-handed]. *Midsummer-Night's Dream.* (C. H. Herford, 1902)
❖Situated on the left side of the body; lying on or towards the left hand; adapted from modern French *sinistre*, Latin *sinister*, left [1400s–1800s]. (James Murray et al., 1888–1928)
cf. *ambidextrous, dexterity, left-handed*

**siren** An acoustical instrument, invented . . . in 1819, for producing musical tones, and in numbering the vibrations in any note. (James Murray et al., 1888–1928)

❖It has been ascertained by means of the *siren* that the wings of the mosquito move at the rate of 15,000 times per second. (Edward Knight, 1874)

**sirs** This term could be used in the unceremonious sense, in addressing inferiors of both sexes, and even women alone. *Love's Labour's Lost*. (C. H. Herford, 1902)

**sixth sense** The female pudendum, and the penis. (John Farmer, 1896)

**sizzle** The half hiss, half sigh of an animal, of an owl, for instance. Also the effervescence of brisk beer, &c. through a cork; or the hissing of lightning very near one. Ray says that yeast is called *sizzling* from the sound of the beer working. (James Halliwell, 1855)

**skedaddle** The word is said to be still occasionally used in Dumfriesshire, and to be applied to the wasteful overflow of milk in the pails when the milk-maids do not balance them properly, when carrying them from the byre to the farm. It has been . . . derived from the two Gaelic words, *sguit*, to wander, to disperse, and *allta*, wild, irregular, ungovernable. (Charles Mackay, 1888)

**skillet** A small kettle. (Hezekiah Burhans, 1833)

**skirt** The border of a garment, or of a country. (John Kersey, 1772)

**sky-scraper** The light sails which some adventurous skippers set above the royals in calm latitudes are termed *sky-scrapers*. (J. C. Hotten, 1887)

**slang** A fetter worn by convicts, so called from being *slung* on their legs by a *sling* to prevent slipping down. (Robert Hunter, 1894)

**slaughter-house** A place where goods are bought from small makers at very low prices. (James Murray et al., 1888–1928)

**sleazy** Lacking firmness or consistence of texture or body; thin; flimsy; flaccid, as *sleazy* muslin. (A. Colange, 1871)
❖Of loose and open texture, easily torn, and soon worn out. (Robert Forby, 1830)
❖So call'd because brought from the province of Silesia, or as the Germans call it, Schlesia, where the capital city Breslaw is maintained by this manufacture. (White Kennett, c.1700)
❖From German *schleissen*, (the equivalent of English *slit*) to fray, wear out, tear. (Hensleigh Wedgwood, 1878)

**sleek** Slime, miry clay in the bed of a river or the seashore. (Joseph Wright, 1896–1905)

**sleep-over** Permission to sleep late on Sunday morning. (Harold Wentworth, 1944)

**sleeveless** In general use, paltry, petty, frivolous, vain or unprofitable. Of errands, ending in or leading to nothing. Sometimes used of pretended errands on which a person is sent merely to be out of the way for a time. Very common *circa* 1580–1700. (James Murray et al., 1888–1928)

**slim** Deceitful, crafty; a *slim* fellow, a rogue. (William H. Cope, 1883)
❖A word generally used in the same sense with *sly*. (John Ray, 1674–91)
❖*To slim o'er*, to do one's work in a careless and insufficient way. (John Jamieson, 1879)
❖Probably, the original meaning of the word may be 'flagging, flaccid,' then hanging down, sloping, leading to the idea of obliquity and depravity. (Hensleigh Wedgwood, 1878)

**slink** Of animals, especially cows, to bear or bring forth young prematurely [1600s–1800s]. (James Murray et al., 1888–1928)
❖The young of a beast, brought forth before its time. (Joseph Worcester, 1881)

**slipshod** Wearing shoes *slipped* on but not pulled up at the heels [1500s–1800s]. (Joseph Worcester, 1881)
❖Having shoes on the feet, but no stockings. (Joseph Wright, 1896–1905)

**slogan** The war cry or gathering word of a border clan, still traditionally remembered in Northumberland. (John Brockett, 1825)
❖Usually consisting of a personal surname or the name of a gathering-place. Adopted from Gaelic *sluagh-ghairm*, from *sluagh*, host, and *gairm*, cry, shout [1500s–1700s]. (James Murray et al., 1888–1928)

**slope** *To slope*, in the sense of disappearing from sight, as if gliding down a slope, and apparently connected in the minds of Americans with the idea underlying expressions like "going down South," is probably an Americanism. The term came first into use here, when the new state of Texas offered a ready asylum to unfortunate speculators, dishonest creditors, and even escaped criminals, so that the words, "Gone to Texas," meant to be gone to the American Alsatia, and the act of going so far "down South" became known as *sloping*.

It implied, virtually, that the *sloper* had cheated his creditors, plundered a bank, or robbed his employers. The precise meaning of the word has been elucidated in the statement, "a mean fellow does not *slope*, he sneaks." (M. Schele De Vere, 1872)

**slouch** To give oneself a vigorous douche. (John Mactaggart, 1824)

**slug** To hunt for slugs [1800s]. (James Murray et al., 1888–1928)
cf. *pig*

**slum** A room. (James H. Vaux, 1812)
❖To keep to back streets to avoid observation. (Albert Barrère, 1911)
❖A *slum*'s a paper fake. . . . Of these documents there are two sorts, "slums" (letters) and "fakements" (petitions). (Henry Mayhew, 1861)

**slumber** To sleep slightly or imper-fectly. (Daniel Fenning, 1775)
❖To doze, or take short naps. (Thomas Dyche and William Pardon, 1740)
cf. *snooze*

**slush-fund** In the Army and Navy, a fund derived from selling refuse fat, grease, etc. [called "slush," which is used for candle-making] and used to get small luxuries for the men. (Mitford Mathews, 1956)
❖It [the money] is to be used for . . . target firing, and not for ship's purposes. (*Naval Encyclopædia*, 1881)

**slut** A servant girl. A woman who is careless or negligent of cleanliness, and is dirty or untidy in dress, person, furniture, &c. The term was originally applied to males as well as to females. *Cover-slut*, an apron or pinafore; hence anything used as a cover for sluttishness [1400s–1800s]. (Edward Lloyd, 1895)
❖A female dog; from Frisian *slet*, a clout, Anglo-Saxon *sleac*, slack, slow. (Joseph Worcester, 1881)
❖An apron, [in] Lancashire. (James Halliwell, 1855)
❖A noise; chiefly in the phrase, a slut of thunder. (William H. Cope, 1883)
cf. *flunk, knave, lackey*

**smack** *Smack* divides its two principal meanings curiously between two different portions of the country. In New England, *to smack* a child means to cover it with kisses and caresses; in Pennsylvania, the same phrase means to punish the child by slapping it with the hand. The latter sense of the word is used throughout the South. (M. Schele De Vere, 1872)
cf. *smooch, spank*

**smart-money** Money required of a person so that he may *smart*, or be punished, by its loss. (Daniel Lyons, 1897)
❖Money paid by a person by way of indemnity, to release himself from embarrassing dilemma, awkward engagement, or humiliating or painful position. (A. Colange, 1871)
❖[Punitive] damages beyond the value of a thing sued for, given by a jury in cases of gross misconduct or cruelty on the part of the defendant. (Joseph Worcester, 1881)
❖A pension given to a wounded man, according to the extent of the injury and his rank. Thus, a lieutenant gets £91, five shillings for the loss of a leg, and a captain £300. (William Smyth, 1867)
cf. *guilt*

**smegma** Soap, or anything that scours; a wash-ball. (Edward Phillips, 1706)
❖*Smegmaticke*, any thing having the power to cleanse and scoure, as soap doth. (Henry Cockeram, 1623)

**smile** To laugh gently. (John Kersey, 1772)
cf. *kink, smirk, spleen*

**smirk** To smile pleasantly . . . but not satyrically; [from] Saxon *smercian*. (John Brockett, 1825)
cf. *smile*

**smock** The under linen of a female; [from] Saxon *smoc*. There used to be frequently, in my recollection, *smock races* among young country wenches in the North. The prize, a fine Holland chemise, was usually decorated with ribbons. The sport is still continued at Newborn, near Newcastle, on Ascension Day. (John Brockett, 1825)
❖*Smockster*, a go-between, a bawd [1600s]. (James Murray et al., 1888–1928)
cf. *camisole, go-between*

**smoke-shop** A tavern, public-house. (G. F. Northall, 1894)
cf. *tiddlywink*

**smooch** To sneak, creep; to wander or prowl round somewhere. Apparently an altered form of *mooch*. (James Murray et al., 1888–1928)
❖With *about*, to prowl about in a slovenly, furtive manner, generally with a view to mischief. (Joseph Wright, 1896–1905)
❖*Smouch*, obsolete in England, still survives in Pennsylvania, where it means to salute. (M. Schele De Vere, 1872)
cf. *smack, snoop*

**smudge** To burn without a flame, or any appearance of fire, except smoke. A sulphurous smell occasioned by smoke and dust; close, suffocating air. [From] German *schmutz*, smut, dirt. (John Brockett, 1825)
❖A heap of damp combustibles placed on the windward side of the house and partially ignited, that the inky steam may smother or drive away mosquitoes. (James Bartlett, 1849)
cf. *snuff*

**smug** Of male persons, trim, neat, spruce, smart; the word has been in very common use from the sixteenth century. *Merchant of Venice*. (James Murray et al., 1888–1928)

**smuggle** To hug violently; to smother with caresses, [from] Somerset, Devonshire. (Joseph Wright, 1896–1905)

**snack** Something *snatched*, taken hastily, *k* for *ch*; it is the past participle of the verb *to snatch* [1400s–1800s]. (John Horne Tooke, 1840)
❖Quick and active; whence a *snack*, a hasty meal. (Charles Mackay, 1874)
❖A small portion. (John Kersey, 1772)
❖A share. It is now chiefly or wholly used in the phrase, "to go *snacks* with one," that is, to have a share. (Noah Webster, 1828)
cf. *hunch, lunch*

**snail** An insect very hurtful to fruits and plants. (John Kersey, 1772)
❖It is curious what different objects men will be content for long to confuse under a common name. Thus, in some provincial dialects of Germany, they have only one name for frog and toad. So too, *snail* and *slug* with us were both, to a comparatively recent period, included under the former name. (Richard Chenevix Trench, 1859–60)
cf. *amphibious, antelope, reptile*

**sneaking notion** To have a *sneaking notion* for a lady is to have a timid or concealed affection for her. (James Bartlett, 1849)

**snob** The proper meaning of the word is simply a boy then, like German *knappe*, a journeyman or workman, servant. (Hensleigh Wedgwood, 1878)
❖In old dialect it means a cobbler's apprentice, perhaps from *snap*, a lad, Danish dialect *snopp*, silly. (Edward Gepp, 1923)
❖A cant name for a shoemaker . . . who is always pretending to be something better than he is; a vulgar person who apes gentility. (Charles Annandale, 1897)
❖A common name for a tailor. (John Brockett, 1825)
❖One who is not a gentleman, who overestimates wealth or rank. In some colleges, those who are not of noble birth are entered on the lists as "s. nob," that is, *sine nobilitate*. (Basil Hargrave, 1925)
❖The word *snobs* may be of classical origin, derived from *sine obola*, without a penny. It is not probable, however, that it was meant as a sneer at poverty only. A more ingenious suggestion is that, as the higher classes were called *nobs*, i.e. *nobilitas*, the nobility, the *s-nobs* were those *sine nobilitate*, without any blue blood in their veins, or aristocratic breeding. (William Mathews, 1884)

**snoop** Applied to children, servants, and others, who clandestinely consume dainties or other victuals which have been put aside, not for their use. A servant who goes slyly into a dairy-room and drinks milk from a pan would be said to be *snooping*. (James Bartlett, 1849)
cf. *smooch*

**snooze** A *snooze* sometimes means a lodging. (James H. Vaux, 1812)
❖*Snoozer*, a thief who follows the business of robbing the boarders at hotels. He takes board and lodgings, and endeavors to share a room and become familiar with some country merchant, after which, by various tricks, he succeeds in robbing him. (James Bartlett, 1849)
cf. *slumber*

**snore** Of animals, especially horses, to snort [1400s–1800s]. (James Murray et al., 1888–1928)

**snuff** The black carbonaceous deposit which gathers on the wick of an old-fashioned candle which, in the early part of the last century, was removed every little while by means of a pair of "snuffers." In these days of electricity, acetylene, gas, kerosene, and patent candles, which require no snuffing, the force of some of Shakespeare's expressions in which *snuff* is used is not evident. Thus, in *Cymbeline*, "To hide me from the radiant sun and solace i' the dungeon by a snuff," *snuff* means an unsnuffed candle, one . . . laden with snuff and which consequently gives a poor light. (John Phin, 1902)
cf. *smudge*

**soft money** Paper money was so called [circa 1870s, in America], whilst the term "hard money" was applied to the issues of gold and silver. (Sylva Clapin, 1902)
cf. *double-standard, sterling*

**solarium** A sun-dial; from Latin *solarium*. (James Murray et al., 1888–1928)
❖From *Sol*, the sun, one of the seven planets. (Thomas Blount, 1656)
cf. *moon, galaxy*

**soldier** *Soldier*, from the Latin *solidus*, the name of a coin, meant originally one who performed military service, not in fulfillment of the obligations of the feudal law, but upon contract, and for stipulated pay. *Soldier*, therefore, in its primary signification, is identical with *hireling* or *mercenary*. Since standing armies, composed of troops who serve for pay, have afforded to military men the means of a systematic professional training . . . we habitually ascribe to the soldier qualities precisely the reverse of those which we connect with the terms *hireling* and *mercenary*; and though the words are etymologically equivalents of each other, *soldier* has become a peculiarly honorable designation, while *hireling* and *mercenary* are employed only in an offensive sense. (George P. Marsh, 1863)

**solicit** *Solicit*, like so many other words derived from Latin, as *religion* for *worship* or *service*, had not lost its strict Latin meaning. The original signification of the Latin word seems to have been to move, and the various meanings attached to it by lexicographers are but modifications of this primary one. In the language of Shakespeare, "How he *solicits* heaven, himself best knows,"

Edward *solicited*, or *moved*, heaven by means known to himself. *Macbeth*. (Alexander Dyce, 1902)

**sonnet** A *sonnet* now must consist of fourteen lines, neither more nor less, and these with fixed arrangement, though admitting a certain relaxation of the lines. But *sonnet* used often to be applied to any shorter poem, especially of an amatory kind. (Richard Chenevix Trench, 1859–60)

**son of a gun** An epithet . . . originally applied to boys born afloat, when women were permitted to accompany their husbands to sea. One admiral declared he literally was thus cradled, under the 'breast' of a gun-carriage. (William Smyth, 1867)

**sophistication** A counterfeiting or debasing the purity of something by a foreign admixture; adulteration. (Noah Webster, 1828)
❖From Low Latin *sophisticatus*, past participle of *sophistico*, to corrupt. (Edward Lloyd, 1895)
cf. *adulterer*

**sounding-board** A board used to ascertain the depth of water [1700s]. (James Murray et al., 1888–1928)

**spank** To move rapidly; *spanker*, one who walks with a quick and lively step; *spanky*, frisky, lively, sprightly. The phrase, a *spanking tit*, is still employed by the sporting brotherhood of the lower classes to signify a fast horse. The English *spank*, to beat, to slap, seems to be derivable from the same idea of rapidity of motion which pertains to the Scottish word, and to be suggestive of the quick and oft-repeated motion of the hands in spanking or slapping the posterior. The word is derived by Jamieson from Teutonic *spannen*, to extend. (Charles Mackay, 1888)
cf. *dad, lather, rib-roast, smack*

**spay** To pierce or cut a deer, so as to kill; adaptation of Anglo-French *espeier*, Old French *espeer*, to cut with a sword, from modern French *épée*, sword. (James Murray et al., 1888–1928)

**speculate** To look out of the window, to spy about, [in] Latin. (E. Cobham Brewer, 1887)
❖*Speculation*, vision; faculty of sight. "Thou hast no *speculation* in those eyes which thou dost glare with." *Macbeth*. (Alexander Dyce, 1902)
❖*Spectacles*, organs of vision. *Cymbeline*. (C. H. Herford, 1902)

**speechless** Using few words; concise. The term constantly occurs in this sense in earlier writers, distinct from the modern synonym, *dumb*. (James Halliwell, 1855)
cf. *sightless, timeless*

**speed** Success, luck, fortune. "I wish you good *speed*." (Michael Traynor, 1953)

**spice** A general name for sweetmeats, such as peppermint, toffy, &c. Ray says, "Raisins, plums, figs, and such-like fruits, in which sense it seems to be used in spice-cake." In Chaucer, it seems to be all sorts of things in the way of spices, &c. A grocer was formerly a *spicer*, from French *épicier*. (Alfred Easther, 1883)

**spick-and-span** Bright as a spike just made, and a chip just split; from English *spike* and German *span*, a chip, a splinter. (James Stormonth, 1884)
❖Quite new. (John Walker, 1835)
❖*Spick* is from the root of the Italian *spicco*, brightness . . . *Span* is probably from the root of *spangle*, German *spiegel*, a mirror. (Noah Webster, 1828)

**spine** The hide of an animal; the fat on the surface of meat, [in] Devonshire. (James Halliwell, 1855)
cf. *hide*

**spinster** A name that was often applied to women of evil life, in that they were set to enforced labour of spinning in the house of correction [still called *The Spinning House* at Cambridge] and thus were *spinsters*. None of our dictionaries, so far as I have observed, take note of this use of the word. (Richard Chenevix Trench, 1859–60)
❖A woman employed in spinning. In law, a title given to all unmarried women, from the viscount's daughter downward. (John Kersey, 1772)

**spleen**  Haste in excess. "With swifter *spleen* than powder can enforce." *King John.* (Alexander Dyce, 1902)
❖As *spleen,* or anger, produces hasty movements, so Shakespeare has used it for hasty action of any kind. (Robert Nares, 1859)
❖Sudden outburst, as of passion. *Midsummer-Night's Dream.* The organ of laughter. *Troilus and Cressida.* (C. H. Herford, 1902)
❖Violent mirth. The spleen was supposed to be the cause of laughter. *Love's Labour's Lost.* (Alexander Dyce, 1902)
❖Ill-humour, a fit of anger, melancholy, hypochondriacal vapours, spite. (James Barclay, 1848)
❖Melancholy, hypochondria. (Edward Lloyd, 1895)
❖The teat of a cow. (Samuel Pegge, 1735–36)
cf. *hypochondria, kidney, liver, melancholy, stomach, wrangle*

**splurge**  A great effort; a struggle. (Joseph Worcester, 1881)
❖A noisy fuss. (Richard Thornton, 1912)
❖A splash; a word of imitative origin. (Edward Lloyd, 1895)
❖To make a blustering demonstration in order to produce an effect; a term in common use [in] the [American] South and West. (James Bartlett, 1849)
❖It referred originally to the floundering about of a great fish in the water, and the noise and splash it produced, and thence came to mean making a great swagger of wealth and importance. The word is apparently connected with the old English *splorage,* from Scottish *splore,* which means a merry, riotous meeting. (M. Schele De Vere, 1872)

**spouse**  An affianced suitor; one's fiancé [1500s]. Applied to . . . women of religion [1200s–1500s]. (James Murray et al., 1888–1928)

**sprawl**  To struggle in the convulsions of death. (John Walker, 1835)

**spread-eagle**  A slang term of various applications. At Cambridge University, England, it means a fowl opened down the back and grilled. (William Walsh, 1900)
❖A figure in fancy-skating. To cut 'spread eagles' in skating. As an adjective, pretentious, boastful, pompous, bombastic, as a *spread-eagle speech.* (James Murray et al., 1888–1928)
cf. *glorious*

**spring-garden**  A garden where concealed springs are made to spout jets of water upon visitors. (Robert Hunter, 1894)

**spunk** A spark; also an *ignis fatuus*, or will o' the wisp. The word is derived by Jamieson from Gaelic *spong*, rotten wood or tinder easily inflammable; but it is questionable whether the root is not the Teutonic *funk*, to sparkle of light, and *ausfunk*, to shine forth. *Ausfunk* is easily corrupted into *sfunk* and *spunk*. (Charles Mackay, 1888)
❖A match. (Adam and Charles Black, 1851)

**squab** A young rabbit, before it is covered with hair. (William Holloway, 1838)
❖The youngest or weakest . . . pig of a litter. (George Dartnell and Edward Goddard, 1893)
cf. *hog, stallion, viper*

**squabble** In printing, to disarrange or mix, as lines of type, by forcing them horizontally out of their place. (Joseph Worcester, 1881)

**squandering** Of plants, spreading about, growing untidily; irregularly shaped; too large for the purpose. (Joseph Wright, 1896–1905)

**squeal** In Shakespeare's time, still a dignified word [for the same sound as today]. (C. H. Herford, 1902)

**squeamish** Nice, to excess; scrupulous. (Robert Hunter, 1894)
cf. *nice*

**squelch** To squash to pieces, as a heavy stone would an egg. (George Dartnell and Edward Goddard, 1893)
❖The peculiar noise made when walking in boots which have taken in water. (B. Lowsley, 1888)
❖The sound produced by the fall of soft bodies. (Hensleigh Wedgwood, 1878)
❖A low, ludicrous word. (Samuel Johnson, 1755)

**stagger** One who hunts stags. (James Murray et al., 1888–1928)

**stale** Urine, now only of horses and cattle [1400s–early 1800s]. Of malt liquor, mead, wine, that has stood long enough to clear, freed from dregs or lees; hence, old and strong [1300s–1700s]. (James Murray et al., 1888–1928)
❖To void urine—of horses only. (Frederic T. Elworthy, 1888)
cf. *urinal*

**stallion** A male dog or sheep, with reference to its use for breeding. Applied to a person, a begettor [1300s–1600s]. (James Murray et al., 1888–1928)
cf. *chard, hog, squab*

**stanza** An apartment or division in a building; a room or chamber. (Edward Lloyd, 1895)

**starve** To perish or be destroyed with cold. (Joseph Worcester, 1881)
❖*To starve with cold,* to be extremely cold. (George Dartnell and Edward Goddard, 1893)
cf. *clumsy, dither*

**stationer** A bookseller; in a wider sense, one engaged in any of the trades connected with books. Adaptation of Latin *stationarius,* in medieval Latin used for a tradesman, chiefly a bookseller, who has a *station,* or shop, as distinguished from an itinerant vendor. (James Murray et al., 1888–1928)
❖There was a time when stationer, meaning properly no more than one who had his station, that is, in the market-place or elsewhere, included the bookseller and the publisher, as well as the dealer in the raw material of books. But when, in the division of labour, these became separate businesses, the name was restrained to him who dealt in the latter articles alone. (Richard Chenevix Trench, 1859–60)

**statue** Synonymous with "picture." *Two Gentlemen of Verona.* (Alexander Dyce, 1902)
cf. *counterfeit, facepainting*

**steeplechase** A footrace across country over a course furnished with hurdles, ditches, and other obstacles. *Steeplechaser,* one who runs in a steeplechase. (James Murray et al., 1888–1928)
❖The term arose from a party of fox-hunters on their return from an unsuccessful chase, who agreed to race to the village church, the steeple

of which was in sight. (E. Cobham Brewer, 1887)
cf. *wild-goose chase*

**stereotype** To prepare for printing by means of stereotype plates, as to *stereotype* a book. (Edward Lloyd, 1895)
❖*Stereo*, abbreviated from *stereotype*, one of the cheap-and-nasty manufactures in this country, the pages being usually left incorrect and blunderous, in pursuance of the saving plan which first suggested casting them in stereo. (Jon Bee, 1823)

**sterling** Genuine, applied to money. (Walter Skeat, 1879–82)
❖Originally a name of the English penny. . . . Some suppose it to be from the coin having had a star on the obverse, but the objection to which is that there is no evidence of any coin in which the star occupied a place sufficiently marked to give a name to the coin. There are indeed pennies of King John on which there is a star or sun . . . but it is a very inconspicuous object. Others suppose that the name was given to coins struck at Sterling, in Scotland. But the hypothesis most generally approved is that the coin is named from the Easterlings, or North Germans, who were the first moneyers in England. (Hensleigh Wedgwood, 1878)
cf. *double-standard, soft money*

**stethoscope** A tubular instrument for distinguishing diseases of the stomach. (Noah Webster, 1828)

**stew** The older sense was 'to bathe.' The verb was formed from the old subject *stew*, in the sense of bath or hot-house, which was chiefly used in the plural *stews*, with the low sense of 'brothel.' The corresponding English word is *stove*. (Walter Skeat, 1879–82)
cf. *stove*

**stickler** Now [one who] stand[s] with a certain pertinacity to one's point, refusing to renounce or go back from it, but formerly a word which the French language has now let go, [one who] interpose[d] between combatants and separate[d] them when they had sufficiently satisfied the laws of honour. (Richard Chenevix Trench, 1859–60)
❖A sidesman to fencers; a second to a duelist, one who stands to judge a combat. (Samuel Johnson, 1755)
❖A person who presides at backsword or singlestick, to regulate the game; an umpire, a person who settles disputes. (James Jennings, 1869)

❖It is supposed they bore sticks, wands, or sceptres as symbols of their authority. [From] Old English *stightle*, to rule. (Edward Lloyd, 1895)

**stick-up** To make the first tentative advances towards courtship. (George Dartnell and Edward Goddard, 1893)

**stilts** Crutches. A lame man is said to walk with *stilts*, which in the general sense of this word must be considered dreadfully dangerous, if it be at all practicable. (Robert Forby, 1830)

**stint** Grass for a season; a right of pasturage. From *stint*, to limit or restrain. (John Brockett, 1825)

**stipulate** In botany, having *stipules* . . . leafy appendages. (Edward Lloyd, 1895)

**stodgy** A thick, stiff substance. Clogging, sticky; muddy, clayey. Of food, causing a feeling of repletion. (George Dartnell and Edward Goddard, 1893)

**stomach** To resent; to bear an angry remembrance of. (Alexander Dyce, 1902)
❖Already in classical Latin, *stomachus* had all the uses (courage, pride, indignation, ill-will) which *stomach* may be seen in the following quotation to have once possessed, but which at this day have nearly or quite departed from it. "He was a man of an unbounded *stomach*, ever ranking himself with princes." *Henry VIII*. (Richard Chenevix Trench, 1859–60)
cf. *chubby, kidney, liver, spleen*

**stool-pigeon** The *stool-pigeon*, as familiar to English ears as to ours . . . [is] fastened on a stool, which can be moved up and down by hidden fowlers, an attraction which causes the bird to flutter anxiously. This attracts the passing flocks of wild pigeons, which alight and are caught by a net. (M. Schele De Vere, 1872)
❖*Stool-pigeoning* is for an officer to arrest a party of doubtful or perhaps decidedly bad reputation on "suspicion," and making him or her give up money or valuables to obtain liberty, when the officer would set the party free, and nothing would be heard by the public . . . of the arrest. (James Bartlett, 1849)

**stout** The temptation to the strong to be also the proud is so natural, so difficult to resist, and resisted by so few, that it is nothing wonderful when words, first meaning the one, pass over into the sense of the other. *Stout*, however,

has not retained, except in some provincial use, the sense of 'proud,' nor *stout-ness* of 'pride.' (Richard Chenevix Trench, 1859–60)
cf. *glorious*

**stove** This word has much narrowed its meaning. Bath, hothouse, any room where the air was artificially heated, was a *stove* once. (Richard Chenevix Trench, 1859–60)
cf. *caboose, stew*

**street-walker** A person of either sex, without reference to morals, who strolls about on Sunday instead of going to church or chapel. (Joseph Wright, 1896–1905)

**stretch a point** To walk quickly; to make haste in order to accomplish a purpose. (Joseph Wright, 1896–1905)

**stripper** *Stripper* is not only a person who strips, but in Pennsylvania also a cow which is nearly dry, and has to be *stripped* of the little milk she gives. (M. Schele De Vere, 1872)

**strum** To have carnal knowledge of a woman; also to play badly on the harpsichord. (Francis Grose, 1796)

**strumpet** A fat, hearty child, generally a baby, [in] Hampshire. (Joseph Wright, 1896–1905)

**sub-contracted** Betrothed for a second time. (C. T. Onions, 1911)

**subscribe** To write under. (John Bullokar, 1616)
cf. *carte blanche*

**subway** An accessible passage or tunnel beneath the street surface in which the gas and water pipes and sewers are lodged so that they can be examined, repaired, replaced, &c. without disturbing the pavement. (Edward Lloyd, 1895)
cf. *underground-railway*

**sucker** A sponger; one who lives on another. (John Farmer, 1889)

**suit** *Suit*, as applied to hair, is probably an Americanism. In the South, a lady is said to possess a wonderfully fine "*suit* of hair." (M. Schele De Vere, 1872)

**sunburnt** That *sun-burnt* had generally the plain, obvious meaning of "tanned by the sun" . . . and consequently connoted the destruction of beauty . . . is unquestionable. But it may also have had an idiomatic meaning. . . . This word, as it occurs in *Much Ado about Nothing*, "Thus goes every one to the world but I, and I am *sunburnt*," has received various explanations. Steevens says that *sunburnt* means, "I have lost my beauty and am consequently no longer such an object as can tempt a man to marry." [To] Hunter . . . *sunburnt* meant "destitute of family relations." (John Phin, 1902)

**surgeon** One whose duty is to act in external maladies by the direction of the physician; corrupted in conversation from *chirurgeon* . . . from *chiro*, the hand. (Samuel Johnson, 1755)
❖A *surgeon*, formerly, was a mere operator who joined his practice to that of a barber. In latter times, all that has been changed, and the profession has risen into great and deserved eminence. But the business of a surgeon is, properly speaking, with external ailments and injuries of the limbs. In strictness, to act as a surgeon, something must be done by the hand. Surgeons were formerly a sad lot. (F. Stroud, 1890)
cf. *chemist, leech, operator*

**swanky** Boggy. (James Halliwell, 1855)

**swan-song** There is an old superstition that the swan, which is voiceless through life, breaks out into song at the approach of death. (William Walsh, 1900)
❖"He makes a swan-like end, fading in music." (William Shakespeare, *The Merchant of Venice)*

**swarm** To climb a tree by the muscular action of the arms, legs, and thighs. (John Brockett, 1825)

**sweater** A street ruffian of the time of Queen Anne. The *sweaters* went about in small bands and, forming a circle around an inoffensive wayfarer, pricked him with their swords, and compelled him to "dance" till he perspired from the exhaustion. (Edward Lloyd, 1895)

**sweepstake** A gaming transaction in which a number of persons join in contributing a certain *stake*, which becomes the property of one or several of the contributors on certain conditions. (Edward Lloyd, 1895)
❖One who *sweeps*, or takes the whole of the *stake* in a game; from the fifteenth to seventeenth centuries, commonly used as a ship's name. The act of

sweeping everything away; a clean *sweep*; total removal or clearance; usually in the phrase *to make sweep-stake, to play at sweep-stake* [1500s–1600s]. (James Murray et al., 1888–1928)
cf. *shrub*

**sweet-tooth** The uncut tooth at the extremity of the jaw. (Joseph Wright, 1896–1905)

**swipe** To drink off the very bottom. (John Brockett, 1825)
❖To drink the whole at one draught; '*swipe* it off.' (Francis K. Robinson, 1876)

**symposium** A drinking together; a revel; a merrymaking; a banquet. A magazine article on some serious topic, in which several contributors express their views in succession, like the speakers in Plato's *Banquet*. From Greek *sumposion*, a drinking-party (*sum*, together, and *posis*, a drinking). (Robert Hunter, 1894)
cf. *banquet*

**syncopation** The contraction of a word by taking a letter, letters, or a syllable from the middle [*can't* for *cannot*]. (Noah Webster, 1828)

**tackle**  To *tackle* a horse is to harness him. (James Bartlett, 1849)
❖I never heard this word used in England, and it is not in Johnson's dictionary as a verb, in any sense. Ash calls it "a local word, from the substantive *tackle,*" and defines it, "To accoutre; to put the saddle and bridle on a horse." In England however, to harness is universally used, where in New England they say *to tackle*. (John Pickering, 1816)
❖*Tackled stair*, a rope ladder. *Romeo and Juliet*. (Alexander Dyce, 1902)

**talk turkey**  To say pleasant things. (John Farmer and W. E. Henley, 1890–1904)
❖To use high-sounding words. An allusion to the manner in which the male bird spreads and plumes himself. (Sylva Clapin, 1902)
cf. *panache*

**tall**  Our ancestors superintended on the primary meaning of *tall* a secondary, resting on the assumption that tall men would be also brave, and this often with a dropping of the notion of height altogether [1400–1800s]. (Richard Chenevix Trench, 1859–60)
❖Sturdy; lusty; bold; spirited; courageous. (Samuel Johnson, 1755)
❖In the United States, and especially in the South, the word is often used in the analogous sense of *great, excellent, fine*. (James Bartlett, 1849)

**tamper**  To work in clay, etc. so as to mix it thoroughly. *Tamper*, which appears in reference to clay in 1573, was probably a dialect or workman's pronunciation, which became at length established. (James Murray et al., 1888–1928)

**tangerine**  Of or pertaining to, or native of, Tangier, a seaport of Morocco, on the Strait of Gibraltar; [hence] *tangerine orange*. (James Murray et al., 1888–1928)
cf. *nectarine, plum*

**tantrum**  A foolish fancy; a whim; in plural form, high or affected airs. (Joseph Wright, 1896–1905)
❖This word [was] borrowed by the English from the Scotch. . . . The *English Slang Dictionary* derives it from a dance, called in Italy the *tarantula* because persons 'in the *tantrums*' dance and caper about. The word is composed of Gaelic *deanne*, haste, violence, hurry, and *trom*, heavy, whence violent and heavy, applied to a fit of sudden passion. (Charles Mackay, 1888)
cf. *rape, wrangle*

**target**  A shield or buckler of small size, circular in form, cut out of oxhide, mounted on light but strong wood, and strengthened by bosses, spikes, &c. often covered externally with a considerable amount of ornamental work. (Robert Hunter, 1894)
cf. *trophy*

**tariff**  A very familiar word in these days in connection with tariff reform. Yet it is really an Arabic word, *ta'rif*, meaning information, derived from *arafa*, 'to explain, to inform.' (Basil Hargrave, 1925)
❖*Tarif*, in Arithmeticke, is either a small table . . . to expedite multiplication, or else a proportional table contrived for the expediting [of] a question in the Rule of Fellowship (Nathaniel Bailey, 1727)
cf. *calculation*

**taste**  To smell. (John Ray, 1674–91)
cf. *flavour*

**tasteful**  Having many different *tastes* or hobbies. (Joseph Wright, 1896–1905)

**tattle**  To talk idly; to use many words with little meaning. (Samuel Johnson, 1755)
❖To speak hesitatingly, falter, stammer, especially to tattle as a young child; to utter baby-talk [1400s–early 1700s]. (James Murray et al., 1888–1928)

**tattoo**  The beat of the drum is represented by various combinations of the syllables *rap, tap, tat*, or the like; English *rubadub*. (Hensleigh Wedgwood, 1878)
❖A signal made by [the] beat of a drum or bugle-call in the evening by soldiers to repair to their quarters in garrison or tents in camp [1600s–1800s]. (James Murray et al., 1888–1928)
cf. *drummer, rub-a-dub*

**tawdry** *Tawdry laces* and such like were cheap and showy articles of finery bought at St. Etheldreda's, or *St. Awdrey's* fair. But it is only in later times that this cheapness, showiness, with a further suggestion of vulgarity, made themselves distinctly felt in the word. (Richard Chenevix Trench, 1859–60) ❖This fair was held in the Isle of Ely, and probably other places, on . . . the 17th of October. An old English historian makes Saint Audrey die of a swelling in her throat, which she considered a particular judgment for having been in her youth addicted to wearing fine necklaces. (Robert Nares, 1859) cf. *necklace, negligee*

**tee** A little earth on which gamesters at the gowf set their balls before they strike them. (Adam and Charles Black, 1851)

**teen** Angry. (John Ray, 1674–91) ❖Grief, trouble, vexation. (Alexander Dyce, 1902) ❖To trouble, to vex. (Robert Forby, 1830)

**temper** This word, when standing alone, has often a bad sense affixed to it in New England. Thus, "the book shows *temper*," means the book manifests warmth of temper. In England, it is invariably used in its original sense of coolness or moderation. (John Pickering, 1816)

**temperature** *Temperature*, a mean between opposites; a *tempered* or *temperate* condition of the weather or climate [1500s–1700s]. (James Murray et al., 1888–1928) cf. *climate*

**tent** A roll of lint put into a wound. (John Kersey, 1772) cf. *circus, lint*

**terrier** A register of landed property, formerly including lists of vassals and tenants, with particulars of their holdings, services, and rents; in later use, a book in which the lands of a private person, or of a civil or ecclesiastical corporation are described by their site, boundaries, acreage, etc. Also, in extended application, an inventory of property or goods [1400s–1800s]. The earth or burrow of a badger or fox; adaptation of late Latin *terrarium*, a mound of earth, hillock, burrow [1400s]. (James Murray et al., 1888–1928) ❖A keeper of terriers. Figuratively, a man of bad temper and character; a pugnacious fellow. (Joseph Wright, 1896–1905) cf. *rigmarole*

**testicle** The ovary in females [1500s–1600s]. (James Murray et al., 1888–1928)
❖Organs of seed in men and women. (John Kersey, 1772)
❖Literally, that which *testifies* or shews manhood . . . [from] Latin *testiculus*, diminutive of *testis*, a witness. (James Donald, 1877)
cf. *bisexual, cod, womb*

**thief** One who deprives another of property secretly, or without open force, as opposed to a robber, who uses open force or violence. In the times of Queen Elizabeth and James I, no such sharp distinction was made, as we now draw between a *robber* and a *thief* . . . The "penitent thief" crucified with Jesus should have been designated the "penitent *robber*." (Edward Lloyd, 1895)
cf. *bribery, hooker, jilt*

**thoroughbred** Thoroughly educated or accomplished; well-born, well-bred, sometimes implying characteristics of a thoroughbred horse, as gracefulness, energy, distinction, etc. Also, a first-rate motor-car, bicycle, or other vehicle. (James Murray et al., 1888–1928)

**thoroughfare** A town through which traffic passes; a town on a highway or line of traffic [1400s–1800s]. (James Murray et al., 1888–1928)

**three outs** When three persons go into a public-house, call for liquor generally considered only sufficient for two, and have a [third] glass which will divide it into three equal portions, they are said to drink *three outs*. (James Halliwell, 1855)

**thrifty** Thriving, flourishing; occasionally in the sense of being in good health. (William H. Cope, 1883)

**thrill** To pierce, bore, penetrate [1300s–1600s]. (James Murray et al., 1888–1928)

**thrilling** Piercingly cold. *Measure for Measure*. (C. H. Herford, 1902)

**thug** The Thugs were an Indian fraternity of hereditary assassins who subsisted on the plunder of the victims they strangled. They were bound to secrecy by oath, and had peculiar signs for recognising one another, and a slang language of their own. . . . [Until the 1830s] their victims were counted by thousands annually, and no district was free of their ravages. (Sidney Low and F. S. Pulling, 1904)
❖The Thugs were directed in all their proceedings by auguries supposed to be vouchsafed by their goddess Kali, and peculiar classes were altogether exempt from their attacks. (A. Colange, 1871)
❖From Hindu *thag*, Sanskrit *sthaga*, a cheat, a swindler. (Henry Yule, 1886)

**thunder** A most bright flame rising on a sudden, moving with great violence, and with a very rapid velocity through the air upwards from the earth horizontally, obliquely, downwards, in a right line, or in several right lines, and commonly ending with a loud noise or rattling. (Samuel Johnson, 1755)

**ticket** A mark stuck on the outside of anything to give notice of something concerning it. [From] French *étiquet*, a little note, especially such a one as is *stuck* up on the gate of a court. (Hensleigh Wedgwood, 1878)
cf. *etiquette*

**ticket-scalper** One who buys and sells unexpired or return railway tickets at less than the rates at which they are issued; so, *ticket-scalping*. (James Murray et al., 1888–1928)

**tiddlywink** A beer-shop licensed only to sell beer, cider, and tobacco; an unlicensed public-house. A small shed attached to a farm or cottage where beer is brewed. Hence, *tiddlywink*, drunk. (Joseph Wright, 1896–1905)
cf. *smoke-shop*

**tide over** Alternately sailing and anchoring, depending on the tide, in order to work a ship in or out of port. (William Falconer, 1769) cf. *roadster*

**tidy** Strangely enough, the term *tidy*, which strictly mean[t] only punctual to time, has become a perfect and comprehensible expression for . . . accuracy and neatness, and in fact expresses the widest extension of the word *punctual*, as applied alike to time and place and duty. (W. L. Blackley, 1869)

**timeless** Untimely. *Two Gentlemen of Verona.* (C. H. Herford, 1902)
❖Immature; done at an improper time. (Samuel Johnson, 1755)
cf. *sightless, speechless*

**time-table** A time-sheet on which a record is kept of the time worked by each employee. (James Murray et al., 1888–1928)

**tincture** An imperfect knowledge or smattering of an art or science. (Nathaniel Bailey, 1749)
❖A colouring matter, hue; a spiritual principle or immaterial substance whose character or quality may be infused into material things, which are then said to be *tinctured.* (Walter Skeat, 1914)

**tinsel** A stuff or cloth made partly of silk and partly of copper, so called because it glitters or sparkles like stars or fire, from French *estincelle,* a spark or sparkle of fire. (Thomas Blount, 1656)
❖Very thin plates of brass cut into small strips, and put on actors' cloaths, &c., to represent gold, silver, &c. (Thomas Dyche and William Pardon, 1740)
❖The true derivation is to be sought in the Anglo-Saxon *tyne,* to lose. . . .
In this sense, the small pieces and remnants thrown off in the manufacture of articles of gold, silver, and precious stones, originally called *tinsel,* and afterwards used up or applied to the ornamentations of cloths, silks, and velvets, may have led to the secondary meaning of the word, as signifying the appearance rather than the reality of gold. (Charles Mackay, 1874)

**tippler** The fact that the word *tippler*, from originally meaning a publican, now means any habitual sot, may teach us how universally, even in early ages, the tapster became the slave of his opportunities, and may justify the common saying, "He is his own best customer." (W. L. Blackley, 1869)
cf. *tobacconist*

**tobacconist** Now the seller, once the smoker, of tobacco. (Richard Chenevix Trench, 1859–60)
❖A person addicted to the use of tobacco [1500s–1800s]. (James Murray et al., 1888–1928)
cf. *smoke-shop*, *tippler*

**toddler** An infirm elderly person. (James H. Vaux, 1812)
cf. *unaccountable*

**toilet** A little cloth which ladies use for what purpose they think fit. (John Dunton, 1694)
❖Bag or cloth to put night clothes in. (Thomas Blount, 1656)

**toll-booth** The old Scotch name for a burgh gaol, so called because it was the name originally given to a temporary hut of boards erected in fairs and markets, and where such as did not pay, or were charged with some breach of the law in buying and selling, were confined till reparation was made; hence, any prison. The town prison of Cam-

bridge [England] was formerly known by this name. (Edward Lloyd, 1895)
❖*Toll*, originally a general term for a definite payment exacted by a king, ruler, or lord . . . in return for protection [since 1000]. (James Murray et al., 1888–1928)

**tomboy** A rude, rough, boisterous boy [1500s]. (Robert Hunter, 1894)
❖A worthless woman; a strumpet, a prostitute. (Edward Lloyd, 1895)
❖From the Saxon *tumbe*, to dance. (Thomas Blount, 1656)
cf. *bully*

**tongue**  To *tongue a person*, to answer again, as servants do sometimes to their masters or mistresses; to be saucy with the tongue in such case. (Samuel Pegge, 1735–36)
cf. *dumb-waiter, servant*

**tonight**  Last night. In literary use from the thirteenth to seventeenth centuries. "I dreamt a dreame *tonight.*" *Romeo and Juliet.* (Edward Gepp, 1923)

**topless**  Supreme, paramount [late 1500s–1900]. (James Murray et al., 1888–1928)
❖Having no superior. *Troilus and Cressida.* (Robert Hunter, 1894)

**topsy-turvy**  The expression is derived from the way in which turf for fuel is placed to dry on its being cut. The surface of the ground is pared off with the heath growing on it, and the heath is turned downward, and left some days in that state, that the earth may get dry before it is carried away. It means then *top-side-turf-way.* (Joseph Taylor, 1819)
❖Trench considers it a corruption of *topside the other way;* Fitzedward Hall prefers *top set turned;* and Skeat, *top side turfy,* the *top side* set on the turf, or ground. Others take it as top side turf-way, which has the same meaning. (Edward Lloyd, 1895)
cf. *divot*

**torpedo**  A species of eel having the power of giving an electric shock when touched, so as to produce *torpor,* or numbness. (Daniel Lyons, 1897)
❖Latin *torpeo,* to be benumbed, to be dull and drowsy. (Hensleigh Wedgwood, 1878)
❖*Submarine torpedo,* a torpedo placed beneath the surface of the water in a similar manner to a subterranean mine. (Edward Lloyd, 1895)

**touch-down**  [In American] foot-ball, the act of forcing the ball . . . through the goal-posts. (Robert Hunter, 1894)

**townhouse**  A town-hall; an hôtel de ville [city hall]. (Edward Lloyd, 1895)
❖This house has the same relation to a township as a *town hall* has to an English borough. (Sylva Clapin, 1902)

**toys**  Properly, a boy's books, paper, pens, &c., together with the cupboard which held them. In the process of time, the word came to mean the latter only. But the phrase *toy-time* shows the original meaning, when the toys were in use.

(William H. Cope, 1883)
❖A fantastic or trifling speech or piece of writing; a frivolous or mocking speech; a foolish or idle tale; a funny story or remark; a jest, pun [1500s–1800s]. (James Murray et al., 1888–1928)
cf. *travesty, trinket*

**tradesman**  A shopkeeper. (William Whitney, 1889)
❖"From a plain *tradesman* with a shop, he is now grown a very rich country gentleman." (John Arbuthnot, Law Is a Bottomless Pit, 1712)

**tradition**  The word *tradition* is now almost universally applied to oral, as opposed to written records . . . , an instance of the spontaneous tendency of language to let drop what is needless, while retaining what is useful. The word *tradition* is wanted in English to express oral, but not to express written records, and hence it is that Webster, in his dictionary, actually limits its sense to "oral communications without written memorials," a limitation which is, however, disproved by the very instance he quotes in its support: "Stand fast, and hold the *traditions* which ye have been taught, whether by word or our epistle." 2 Thessalonians 2:15. (W. L. Blackley, 1869)

**transfusion**  The act of pouring out of one vessel into another. "Something must be lost in all *transfusion*, that is, in all translations, but the sense will remain." Preface to Dryden's *Fables*, 1700. (Samuel Johnson, 1755)
cf. *English, romance*

**translators**  Sellers of old mended shoes and boots between cobblers and shoemakers. (Francis Grose, 1796)
❖Cobblers who buy old boots and shoes, and make them up anew for sale. (John Brockett, 1825)
cf. *revamp*

**transpire**  *Transpire* meant originally to emit insensible vapor through the pores of the skin. Afterwards it was used metaphorically in the sense of to become known, to pass from secrecy into publicity. But to say that a certain event *transpired* yesterday, meaning that it occurred then, is a gross vulgarism. (William Mathews, 1884)

**transportation**  Removal or banishment, as of a criminal to a penal settlement; deportation [1600s–1700s]. (James Murray et al., 1888–1928)
cf. *abandon, plantation*

**trappings** Those leathers that hang on horses' buttocks. (John Kersey, 1772) cf. *wallet*

**trash** To check the pace of a too forward hound by means of a *trash*, which—whether a strap, a rope dragging on the ground, or a weight—was fastened to his neck. *Othello*. (Alexander Dyce, 1902)

**travel** To take pains. (John Kersey, 1772) ❖Labour, toil; suffering, trouble; labour of child-birth; originally the same word as *travail*, in a specialized sense and form [1300s–1600s]. (James Murray et al., 1888–1928)

**travesty** A literary term used to denote a burlesque treatment of a subject which has been originally handled in a lofty or serious style. It differs from a *parody* in that in *travesty* the characters and the subject matter remain substantially the same, while the language becomes grotesque, frivolous, and absurd; whereas in a *parody*, the subject matter and characters are changed, and the language and style of the original humorously imitated. (Edward Lloyd, 1895)

**treadmill** A horizontal cylinder made to revolve by the weight of persons treading on boards arranged as equidistant steps around its periphery. Formerly in use as an instrument of prison discipline [c. 1822–1900]. (James Murray et al., 1888–1928) cf. *baffle*, *ordeal*, *whirligig*

**treasure trove** In Law, money which being found and not owned, belongs to the king. (Nathaniel Bailey, 1749) ❖When any money, gold, silver, plate or bullion, is found in any place, and no man knoweth to whom the property is, then the property thereof belongeth to the king, and that is called "treasure trove," that is to say, *treasure found.* (William Rastell, 1624)

❖In the United States, *treasure trove* usually belongs to the state in which it is found. . . . If it be found in the sea or *upon* the earth, it does not belong to the Crown, but to the finder, if no owner appears. Of Old French *trover,* to find. (Daniel Lyons, 1897)

cf. *waif*

**tremendous** Dreadful, horrible; astonishingly terrible. (Samuel Johnson, 1755)

cf. *awesome*

**trillion** 1,000,000,000,000,000,000. (Hezekiah Burhans, 1833)

cf. *billion, century, myriad*

**trinket** A knife, a tool, an implement. Skeat considers it to be the same as Middle English *trenket, trynket,* a knife, a toy knife; from French *trencher,* to cut. (Edward Lloyd, 1895)

cf. *toys*

**tripping** *Tripping,* in heraldry, is when a beast is drawn in a walking posture. (John Kersey, 1772)

**trivial** Well-trodden ('trite') or talked of at the corners of the roads, where three ways met. (Joseph Angus, 1870)

❖Such as may be picked up in the highway. (Samuel Johnson, 1755)

❖A *trivial* saying is at present a slight one. It was formerly a well-worn or often repeated one, or as we should now say, one that was *trite.* But this it might be on the grounds of the weight and wisdom it contained. . . . Gradually the notion of slightness was superadded to that of commonness, and thus an epithet once of honour has become one of dishonour rather. (Richard Chenevix Trench, 1859–60)

❖Initiatory, pedantically used in allusion to the *trivium,* or first three sciences taught in schools, grammar, rhetoric and logic. The higher set, consisting of astrology, geometry and music, constituted the *quadrivium.* (Robert Nares, 1859)

cf. *liberal sciences*

**trophy** Properly, a monument set up in a place where enemies were vanquished, with the ensigns, warlike harness, and other spoils hanging on it. (Nathaniel Bailey, 1749) ❖Any thing set up in token of victorie. This custome first began among the Greekes, who used in that place where enemies were vanquished, to cut downe the boughes of great trees, and in the stockes or bodies of them to hang up armour or other spoils taken from the enemies. (John Bullokar, 1616) cf. *target*

**trounce** To punish anyone by legal process. (W. H. Long, 1886)

**truant** A common beggar, a lazie rascal, a vagabond; a knave; a scoundrel [1200s–1600s]. (Thomas Blount, 1656) cf. *loiter, mooch*

**truce** The regular past tense and therefore past participle of the Anglo-Saxon *tripriam*, to pledge one's faith, to plight one's troth. The French *trêve* is the same word. (John Horne Tooke, 1840)

**truck** Exchange of commodities; to barter, to swap one thing for another. (John Kersey, 1772)

**trucker** A contemptuous term, always implying that the person to whom it is given has done something that is offensive. Often applied to a female in contempt, as equivalent to a worthless hussy. (John Jamieson, 1079)

**tryst** A fair for black cattle, horses, sheep, &c. (John Brockett, 1825)

**tuba** The straight, [three-foot] bronze, war-trumpet of the ancient Romans. (James Murray et al., 1888–1928) cf. *harmonica*

**tuition** One defends another most effectively who imparts to him those principles and that knowledge whereby he shall be able to defend himself;

and therefore our modern use of tuition as teaching is a deeper one than the earlier, which made it to mean external rather than internal protection. (Richard Chenevix Trench, 1859–60)

✦Protection. . . . It is derived from the Latin *tuitus*, past participle of *tueri*, to watch, protect. The word occurs only once in Shakespeare (*Much Ado*) but was in common use in this sense in his time. . . . Michael Drayton concludes a letter in 1619, "I commend you to God's *tuition*." (John Phin, 1902)

**tune up** [To] commence singing, or sing more loudly. (B. Lowsley, 1888)

**turn** A double of anything, as a *turn of water*, two buckets full, a *turn at the plough*, a furrow from one end of the field to the other, and back again. (W. H. Long, 1886)

**turn-off** A pretext, excuse. (Joseph Wright, 1896–1905)

**turn-out** A fine *turn-out*, meaning originally, as in England, only a handsome carriage with showy horses, has . . . come to be applied to any display; and even a man who builds a large house, or delivers an eloquent speech is, in the West, said to have made a fine *turn-out*. (M. Schele De Vere, 1872)

**turnpike** Originally meant what is now called a *turnstile*; that is, a post, with a moveable cross fixed at the top, to turn as the passengers went through. They seem originally to have belonged to fortifications, the points being made sharp to prevent the approach of horses; they were, therefore, *pikes* to *turn* back assailants. (Robert Nares, 1859)

✦In fortification, a spar of wood about fourteen foot long and about eight inches in diameter, cut in the form of a hexagon, every side being bored full of holes through which short pikes are run about six foot long, pointed with iron so that they stand out every way. (Nathaniel Bailey, 1749)

**turntable** A platform which rotates in a horizontal plane, and is used for shifting rolling-stock from one line of rails to another. (Edward Lloyd, 1895)

**tush** A tooth. (James Halliwell, 1855)

❖ *Tushes* of a wild boar, the great teeth that stand out. (John Kersey, 1772)

**tweezers** A surgeon's case of instruments. . . . *Tweesers* is thus for *tweeses*, a double plural from *twee*, from Old French *estuy*, a case of instruments, a sheath. The word does not now occur in the singular. (Edward Lloyd, 1895)

**twiddle** To turn about with the tongue. (Joseph Wright, 1896–1905)

**tyke** A rough, shaggy, mongrel dog. (Charles Mackay, 1874)

**typo** A printer's abbreviation of *typographer*. (Sylva Clapin, 1902)

**udder**  The breast of a female. (Noah Webster, 1828)

**unaccountable**  Said of persons, when advanced in years, if their memories fail. (Alfred Easther, 1883)
cf. *toddler*

**uncouth**  Now 'unformed in manner, ungraceful in behavior,' but once simply 'unknown.' The change in signification is to be traced to the same causes which made *barbarous*, meaning at first only 'foreign,' to have afterwards the sense of 'savage and wild.' Almost all nations regard with disfavour and dislike that [with] which . . . they are unacquainted, so that words which at first did but express this fact of strangeness easily acquire a further unfavourable sense. (Richard Chenevix Trench, 1859–60)
cf. *alien, barbaric, far-fetched, outlandish*

**underground-railway**  A railway wholly, or in large part, beneath the street surface of a city. (Edward Lloyd, 1895)
cf. *subway*

**underhanded**  Undersized in person. (C. Clough Robinson, 1876)
cf. *overhand*

**undertaker**  One who takes up a challenge; one who engages in serious study of a subject or science; a baptismal sponsor [1600s]. (James Murray et al., 1888–1928)
❖The *undertakers*, sometimes called *adventurers* [including Sir Walter Raleigh and Edmund Spenser], were English gentlemen, chiefly from Devonshire, who undertook to keep possession of the lands forfeited to the crown in Ireland. (Sidney Low and F. S. Pulling, 1904)
❖One who undertakes, or gives assurance, either for another or in regard to some special matter. The word occurs but twice in Shakespeare, and a great

deal of learning has been expended over the application of the term. . . . In *Twelfth Night*, Antonio has assumed responsibility for Viola; he *undertook* for her, and Toby tells him, "Nay, if you be an *undertaker*, I am for you." (John Phin, 1902)
cf. *applicant*

**unhappy** A very deep truth lies involved in the fact that so many words, and I suppose in all languages, unite the meanings of 'wicked' and 'miserable.' . . . So too it was with *unhappy*, although its use in the sense of 'wicked' has now passed away. (Richard Chenevix Trench, 1859–60)

**unmanned** This is a term in falconry. A hawk is said to be *unmanned* when she is not yet accustomed to her keeper. (John Phin, 1902)

**unthrifty** As the *thrifty* will probably be the thriving, so the *unthrifty* the unthriving. But the [pairs of] words are not synonymous any more, as they once were. (Richard Chenevix Trench, 1859–60)

**upright** Strait; "*upright* as a bolt," strait as an arrow. It is applied indifferently to persons lying as well as standing. (Thomas Tyrwhitt, 1871) ❖In architecture, a draught of the front of a building. (John Kersey, 1772)

**upshot** A metaphor from archery, where the final shot [that] decided a match, was so called [1500s–1600s]. *Twelfth Night*. (C. H. Herford, 1902)

**upstart** The deep impression of a horse's foot in a clayey soil, soon filled up with water, which, when another horse happens to tread in the very same place, starts upwards and plentifully bespatters the rider. (Robert Forby, 1830)

**upward** The wind is said to be *upward* when it is in the North, and *downward* when in the South. I think the North is generally esteemed the highest part of the world. (Samuel Pegge, 1735–36)

**urinal** A bottle in which urine is kept for inspections. (Stephen Jones, 1818)
❖In chemistry, an oblong glass vessel used in making solutions. (Noah Webster, 1828)
cf. *stale*

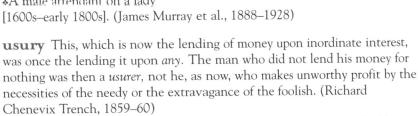

**usher** An assistant master in a boy's school. (B. Lowsley, 1888)
❖A male attendant on a lady [1600s–early 1800s]. (James Murray et al., 1888–1928)

**usury** This, which is now the lending of money upon inordinate interest, was once the lending it upon *any*. The man who did not lend his money for nothing was then a *usurer*, not he, as now, who makes unworthy profit by the necessities of the needy or the extravagance of the foolish. (Richard Chenevix Trench, 1859–60)
❖The fathers regarded interest as usury, and therefore as a species of robbery; this opinion prevailed in the Church till the sixteenth century, and numbered Luther among its defenders. (Edward Lloyd, 1895)
cf. *bribery*

**vacation** Freedom from trouble or perplexity. (Samuel Johnson, 1755)
❖The fact of a house being left unoccupied or untenanted; the loss of rent due
to this [1400s]. (James Murray et al., 1888–1928)

**vaccine** Of or pertaining to cows; from Latin *vacca*, a cow. (Edward Lloyd, 1895)
❖"We have milk . . . butter . . . cheese. All this is *vaccine* matter." (*Medical
Journal* XII, 1804)

**vagina** That long part between [a column's] base and the capital, found in
diverse manners, and with diverse ornaments. (Ephraim Chambers, 1727–51)
❖The upper part of the shaft of a terminus, from which the bust or figure
seems to issue or arise; [adopted from] Latin *vagina*, a sheath, a scabbard.
(Edward Lloyd, 1895)
cf. *flamboyant*

**vague** To roam, wander; to ramble idly, or as a *vagrant*; vagrant, vagabond.
(James Murray et al., 1888–1928)
❖It seems to have been first in use as a verb, parallel in use to *vagary* . . .
a whim, from Latin *vagari*, to wander. (Walter Skeat, 1879–82)

**valentines** Special saints chosen for a year . . . by an ancient custome
upon Saint Valentine's day, about which day birds choose their mates.
(Thomas Blount, 1656)

**vaudeville** A term originally applied to a country song of like kind with
those written by Oliver Basselin, of the valleys of Vaux de Vire, in Normandy,
in the fifteenth century. These songs, which were satirical, had for their subjects love, drinking, and passing events. They became very popular, and were
spread all over France under the name Lais des Vaux de Vire. The peculiarity

of their character lived after their origin was forgotten, and plays, interspersed with songs of this description, came to be called "Vaudevilles." (Edward Lloyd, 1895)

**vegetate** It is not uncommon to use this word in describing or complaining of a dull secluded life in the country. And yet the literal meaning of the word is exactly opposed to this signification, for it is derived from the Latin *vegetatus*, the past participle of *vegetare*, to enliven, to quicken. In the same way, the word *vegetable* is derived from the Latin *vegetabilis*, which means animating, full of life. (Basil Hargrave, 1925)

**venery** Hunting or chasing "beasts of venery," as the hart, the hind, the hare, boar, and wolf. (B. E., Gent., c. 1690)

**ventilate** Except in the application of this verb to persons, there is nothing specially American in the use of *ventilate*, meaning 'to make known.' (John Farmer, 1889)
❖*Ventilate*, as applied to persons, is a most objectionable abuse of the picturesque word, which has forced its way from the French into German and English. (M. Schele De Vere, 1872)

**ventriloquist** A person who speaks inwardly, or as it were, from the belly, as those who are possessed with an evil spirit. (Nathaniel Bailey, 1749)

**verbatim** Orally. "I . . . am not able verbatim to rehearse the method of my pen." *1 Henry VI*. (C. H. Herford, 1902)

**verge** The compass or extent of the king's court, formerly twelve miles extant, within the jurisdiction of the Lord High Stewart of the king's household, so called from the *verge*, or staff, which the marshall bears. (Nathaniel Bailey, 1749)
❖"A thousand flatterers sit within thy crown, whose compass is no bigger than thy head; and yet encaged in so small a *verge*." *Richard II*. (John Phin, 1902)

**vermin** Not always noxious, offensive animals of the smaller kind, but employed formerly with no such [size] limitation. (Richard Chenevix Trench, 1859–60)
❖Originally applied to reptiles, stealthy or slinking animals, and various wild beasts. (James Murray et al., 1888–1928)
❖"*Vermin* include kangaroos, wallabies, dingoes, stray dogs, foxes, and rabbits."

(Edward Jenks, *The Government of Victoria, Australia*, 1891)
cf. *lousy, reptile*

**veterinarian** He that lets horses or mules to hire; a muletor, a horse-courser, a hackney-man. It is also used adjectively. (Thomas Blount, 1656)
❖"Such were call'd at first . . . *Unguentatians, Emplastrists, Veterinarians, Hippo-Jatrists.*" (Myles Davies, *History of Oxford and Cambridge Writers*, 1716)

**vicarious** Belonging to a *vicar;* one in another's stead. (Elisha Coles, 1713)
cf. *attorney*

**vicious** Of the nature of *vice;* addicted to vice, or immorality; adaptation of Latin *vitiosus*, formed on *vitium*, fault, vice. (James Murray et al., 1888–1928)

**villain** *Villain* means simply one attached to a *villa* or farm. In feudal times, the lord was the great landowner, and under him were a host of tenants called *villains*. . . . The notion of wickedness and worthlessness associated with the word is simply the effect of aristocratic pride and exclusiveness. (E. Cobham Brewer, 1887)
cf. *bourgeois, heathen, knave, lackey*

**vinaigrette** A small, two-wheeled carriage drawn or pushed by persons, in use in France [late 1600s–1800s]. (James Murray et al., 1888–1928)
cf. *carriage, vis-à-vis*

**viper** The name is sometimes given to the lizard. (Edward Gepp, 1923)
cf. *hog, squab, stallion*

**virtuous** *Virtue* is still occasionally used as equivalent to 'might' or 'potency,' but *virtuous* has quite abdicated the meaning of 'valorous' or 'potent' which it once had, and which its etymology justified. (Richard Chenevix Trench, 1859–60)
❖*Virtuoso*, virtuous, honest. (Thomas Blount, 1656)

**virus** Venom such as is emitted by a poisonous animal; [from] Latin virus, slimy liquid, poison, offensive odour or taste. In Lefranc's *Cirurgy* (c.1400) the word [is] explained as "a thin, venomy quitter" [late 1500s–1800s]. (James Murray et al., 1888–1928)

**vis-à-vis** The French word is naturalized among us. It signifies a carriage to hold two persons, one opposite the other instead of side by side; also a person standing opposite another in a quadrille. (T. Lewis Davies, 1881) cf. *carriage, vinaigrette*

**vivacious** Remaining alive for a long time; long-lived. "Still grows the *vivacious* lilac a generation after the door and lintel and sill are gone." H. D. Thoreau's *Walden*, 1854. (James Murray et al., 1888–1928)
❖*Longevity*, as one might expect to find, is a comparatively modern word in the language. *Vivacity*, which has now acquired the mitigated sense of 'liveliness,' served instead of it. (Richard Chenevix Trench, 1859–60)

**volatile** That [which] can fly. (John Kersey, 1772)
❖A winged creature, a bird, butterfly, or the like; a fowl. Usually in the plural; formed on Latin *volat*, participle stem of *volare*, to fly [1300s–1800s]. (James Murray et al., 1888–1928)

**volume** Primarily a roll, as the ancients wrote on long strips of bark, parchment, or other material, which they formed into rolls or folds. From Latin *volumen*, a roll, *volvo*, to roll. (Noah Webster, 1828)

**vomit** A medicine or other preparation which causes the stomach to discharge its contents; an emetic. (Edward Lloyd, 1895)
❖"An excellent *vomit*." (Eliza Smith, *The Compleat Housewife*, 1758)
cf. *puke*

**vulcanize** To commit to the flames [early 1800s]. (James Murray et al., 1888–1928)

**waddle** To become a "lame duck," or defaulter. In full, to "waddle out." (James Murray et al., 1888–1928)
❖Jobbers, usually brokers, who cannot make good their engagements for the delivery of stock, or run short in funds to pay for what they have bought . . . become "lame ducks," and *waddle* out. (Jon Bee, 1823)
cf. *lame duck*

**waif** Such goods as a thief, when pursued, throws away to prevent being apprehended. They belong to the crown unless the owner takes the necessary steps for prosecuting and convicting the thief. (Edward Lloyd, 1895)
❖Anything found astray, without an owner. A Norman-French law term. (Walter Skeat, 1879–82)
cf. *treasure trove*

**wainscot** *Wainscot* [was] always, in the building trade, applied to oak only . . . and is used for *wainscoting*, or wood lining, of walls of houses. . . . It was never painted. In modern times, it was imitated, and was painted to represent real wainscot . . . while the name *wainscot* adhered to it, though the material was no longer wainscot. (Richard Chenevix Trench, 1859–60)
❖A superior quality of oak imported from Russia, Germany, and Holland [1300s–1800s]. Furniture made of wainscot [1500s]. (James Murray et al., 1888–1928)

**waitress** A waiting-maid, handmaid. A woman who waits upon the guests at a hotel. . . . One hired for a similar purpose or special occasions to supplement the staff of a private household. (James Murray et al., 1888–1928)

**wallet** A bag with two pouches in it. The *wallet* is used by cutlers, knife-grinders, &c., for carrying their work to and from the workshops. It is usual to put equal quantities in each pouch so that when slung over the shoulder, they

counterbalance each other [late 1300s–1800s]. (Sidney Addy, 1888)
cf. *trappings*

**wallop**  To bubble up in boiling [1500s–1900s]. (John Kersey, 1772)
❖To move as fast as possible, but not without much effort and agitation.
The gallop of a cow or cart-horse is a good specimen of *walloping*. (Robert
Forby, 1830)

**wardrobe**  A privy; a water-closet. (Edward Lloyd, 1895)

**warehouseman**  This is a term well understood in London, and means a
person who buys and sells linens, muslins, silks, and woollen goods by whole-
sale, and does not, it should seem, include in it every person who owns or
keeps a warehouse. (F. Stroud, 1890)
cf. *lingerie*

**water-bed**  A bed on board ship, as distinguished from one ashore [1600s].
A stratum through which water percolates [1700s]. (James Murray et al.,
1888–1928)

**water-colour**  The colour of water; blue; greyish-blue [1400s–1500s].
(James Murray et al., 1888–1928)

**water-wings**  Wings having a watered or wavy surface [1600s]. (James
Murray et al., 1888–1928)

**wealth**  Benefit, advantage. "I did once lend my body for his *wealth*."
*Merchant of Venice*. (Alexander Dyce, 1902)

**week**  A period of time indefinitely. (Alexander Dyce, 1902)
❖The six working days, as opposed to the Sunday; the period from Monday
to Saturday inclusive [1000-1800s]. (James Murray et al., 1888–1928)
❖*Weeks* of the eye or mouth signify, according to Jamieson, the *corners* of the
mouth or eyes. *To hang by the weeks of his mouth* is to keep hold of a thing or
purpose to the utmost, to the last gasp, an exaggerated phrase similar to that
in Holy Writ, "to escape by the skin of the teeth." *Week*, or *weik*, is a corruption of Gaelic *uig*, a corner. (Charles Mackay, 1888)
cf. *forty*

**weird** Most English dictionaries misdefine this word, which has two different significations, one as a noun, the other as an adjective. In English literature, from Shakespeare's time downwards, it exists as an adjective only, and is held to mean unearthly, ghastly, or witch-like. Before Shakespeare's time, and in Scottish poetry and parlance to the present day, the word is a noun, and signifies fate or destiny. Derived from the Teutonic *werden*, to become, or that which shall be. (Charles Mackay, 1888)

**weld** To pin two pieces of iron together by making them very hot, and beating them with a hammer. (Thomas Dyche and William Pardon, 1740)
✧Figuratively, to unite very closely. (Edward Lloyd, 1895)
✧*Welder*, a ruler; a governor. (Charles Mackay, 1874)

**wench** *Wench* is the Anglo-Saxon word, *wencle*, a child. In the Midland counties, when a peasant addresses his wife as "my *wench*," he expresses endearment. *Wench*, like *girl*, was at one time applied to either sex. . . . Similarly, *maid* is applied to both sexes. (E. Cobham Brewer, 1898)
✧In the United States, this word is only applied to black females. (James Bartlett, 1849)
cf. *crud, hag, maid, mumps, street-walker, whiteboy*

**went** A way, as *at the four wents*, at the meeting of four ways. . . . Just as *gate*, from the verb *go*, means 'a street' in Old English, so *went*, from the verb *wend*, means 'a lane or passage.' (Samuel Pegge, 1735–36)

**whirligig** An instrument for punishing petty offenders; a kind of wooden cage turning on a pivot, in which the offender was whirled round with great velocity. (William Whitney, 1889)
cf. *baffle, justify, treadmill*

**whiteboy** An old term of endearment applied to a favorite son, dependent, or the like; a darling. (Robert Hunter, 1894)
cf. *crud, mumps, wench*

**whitewash** A wash to make the skin seem fair. (Richard Coxe, 1813)

**wife** It is a very profound testimony yielded by language . . . that women are intended to be wives, and only find the true completion of their being when they are so, that in so many languages there is a word which, meaning first a woman, means afterward a wife. With us indeed, the secondary use of the

word has now overborne and swallowed up the first, which survives in a few such combinations as *midwife, fishwife, housewife*, and the like. In rural districts, a grown woman is a young *wife* though she be unmarried. (Richard Chenevix Trench, 1859–60)
cf. *housewife*

**wild-goose chase** One kind of horse-race, which resembled the flight of *wild geese*, was formerly known by this name. Two horses were started together, and whichever rider could get the lead, the other was obliged to follow him over whatever ground the foremost jockey chose to go. That horse which could distance the other won the race. . . . This barbarous sport is enumerated by Burton in his *Anatomy of Melancholy*, as a recreation much in vogue in his time among gentlemen. "If thy wits run the *wild-goose chase* . . . " *Romeo and Juliet*. (Alexander Dyce, 1902)
cf. *steeplechase*

**wild women** Those who go in for women's rights and general topsy-turvey-ism. Some smoke cigars in the streets, some wear knickerbockers, some stump the country as screaming orators. All try to be as much like men as possible. (E. Cobham Brewer, 1898)

**wind-breaker** A drug that expels flatulence; a carminative. "The sugared, oily carminative, or *wind-breaker*." *Bate's Dispensatory*, 1694. (James Murray et al., 1888–1928)
cf. *flatulent*

**windfall** Fruit blown off the tree. (John Kersey, 1772)
❖Wood fell[ed] by high winds. (B. E., Gent., c. 1690)

**wiseacre** A wise or learned person; a sage [1700s]. (James Murray et al., 1888–1928)
❖A wise or sententious man. It was antiently written *wisesegger*, as the Dutch *wisegger*, a soothsayer. (Samuel Johnson, 1755)

**witch-doctor** One who cures those bewitched [in] Scotland. (Joseph Wright, 1896–1905)

**womanize** To act or behave one's self like a woman. (John Kersey, 1772)
❖To emasculate; to effeminate; to soften. Proper, but not used [1500s–1800s]. (Samuel Johnson, 1755)

**womb** This . . . could once be ascribed to both sexes. "My *womb* undoes me." Falstaff, *2 Henry IV*. (Richard Chenevix Trench, 1859–60)
cf. *bisexual, concept, testicle*

**work** Manual labour only. (Angelina Parker, 1881)

**world** A long space of time; an age. Still retained in this sense in the last phrase of the general doxology, "world without end." (Thomas Sternberg, 1851)
cf. *age*

**worm** This, which designates at present only smaller and innoxious kinds of creeping and crawling things, once, as the German *wurm*, was employed of all the serpent kind; and indeed in some of our northern dialects, all snakes and serpents are *worms* to the present day. (Richard Chenevix Trench, 1859–60)
cf. *viper*

**worry** To tear, mangle, or shake, like beasts of prey. Figuratively, to harass or persecute brutally. (Daniel Fenning, 1775)
❖The word is derived from a representation of the gurgling sound made in the throat by a choking person. (Hensleigh Wedgwood, 1878)
cf. *annoy*

**worship** At present, we *worship* none but God. There was a time when the word was employed in so much more general a sense that it was not profane to say that God *worshipped*, that is honoured, man. (Richard Chenevix Trench, 1859–60)

**wrangle** To scream with passion. (Joseph Wright, 1896–1905)
cf. *incense, incontinent, liver, spleen, tantrum*

**wrangler** *Wrangler*, in Cambridge phrase, is one who has obtained a place in the highest mathematical tripos [examination]. The first man of this class is termed the *senior wrangler*; the rest are arranged according to merit, and are called *second, third, fourth, &c. wrangler*, as it may be. (E. Cobham Brewer, 1887)

**wretch** A term of endearment. "The pretty *wretch*." *Romeo and Juliet*. "Excellent *wretch!*" *Othello*. (Alexander Dyce, 1902)
cf. *crud, mumps, whiteboy*

**writer** An attorney; a solicitor licensed to conduct cases in the superior courts. (Charles Mackay, 1888)

**wrong** Past participle of *wring*. (Thomas Tyrwhitt, 1871)

**yard** *Yard of land*, a quantity of land which in some counties in England signifies fifteen acres, in some twenty, and in others twenty-four, thirty, and thirty-four acres. (Cuthbert Johnson, 1844)
cf. *acre*

**ycarn** To bark, as beagles at their prey. (Elisha Coles, 1713)
❖Properly, to shiver with desire or other emotion, as a dog may be seen to do when he is intently watching his master eating. (Hensleigh Wedgwood, 1878)

**yellow-belly** A person born in the fens of Lincolnshire, from the yellow, sickly complexion of persons residing in marshy situations. (William Holloway, 1838)
❖An allusion to the eels [or frogs] caught there. (Francis Grose, 1796)
cf. *complexion, rude*

**yelp** To squeak, as a mouse; to chirp, as a bird. (Joseph Wright, 1896–1905)

**zany** An imitator, mimic, especially a poor, bad, feeble, or ludicrous imitator. A comic performer attending on a clown, acrobat, or mountebank who imitates his master's acts in a ludicrous, awkward way. A fool, simpleton; adopted from French *zani*, or Italian *zanni*, name of servants who act in the Commedia dell'Arte. (James Murray et al., 1888–1928)
cf. *antics, pantomime*

**zig-zag** A road or path turning sharply at angles in alternate directions, especially
so as to reduce a gradient on a steep slope [from late 1720s]. (James Murray et al., 1888–1928)
❖Drunk; a French colloquial descriptive expression, used mostly among civilians in the war area in northern France. (Edward Fraser and John Gibbons, 1925)

# Bibliography

Adams, Ramon. *Western Words: A Dictionary of the Range, Cow Camp, and Trail*. Norman, Oklahoma, 1946.

Addy, Sidney. *Sheffield Glossary of Words*. London, 1888.

Angus, Joseph. *Hand-Book of the English Tongue*. London, 1870.

Annandale, Charles. *A Concise Dictionary of the English Language*. London, 1897.

Arnot, Hugo. *History of Edinburgh*. Edinburgh, 1779.

Avis, Walter S. *A Dictionary of Canadianisms on Historical Principles*. Toronto, 1967.

B. E., Gent. [pseud.]. *A New Dictionary of the Terms Ancient and Modern of the Canting Crew*. London, circa 1690.

Bailey, Nathaniel. *An Universal Etymological English Dictionary*. London, 1727, 1749 (later edition).

Baker, Anne E. *Glossary of Northamptonshire Words and Phrases*. London, 1854.

Baker, Sydney J. *New Zealand Slang: A Dictionary of Colloquialisms*. Christchurch, circa 1941.

Barclay, James. *A Complete and Universal Dictionary of the English Language*. London, 1848.

Barrère, Albert. *Argot and Slang: A New French and English Dictionary*. London, 1911.

Bartlett, James. *Dictionary of Americanisms*. New York, 1849.

Bee, Jon [John Badcock]. *Slang: A Dictionary of the Turf*. London, 1823.

Black, Adam and Charles. *Glossary to Allan Ramsay's The Gentle Shepherd* [1725]. London, 1851.

Blackley, W. L. *Word Gossip: Essays on Words and Their Peculiarities*. London, 1869.

Blackstone, William. *Commentaries on the Laws of England*. London, 1765–69.

Blount, Thomas. *Glossographia, or a Dictionary Interpreting All Such Hard Words . . . .* London, 1656.

Blount, Thomas. *A Law Dictionary*. London, 1717.

Booth, David. *An Analytical Dictionary of the English Language*. London, 1835.

Bouvier, John. *A Law Dictionary Adapted to the Laws of the United States of America*. Philadelphia, 1843–56.

Bowen, Frank C. *Sea Slang: A Dictionary of the Old-Timers' Expressions and Epithets*. London, 1929.

Brandl, Alois, and Zippel, Otto. *Glossary of Middle English Literature*. New York, 1949.

Brewer, E. Cobham. *Dictionary of Phrase and Fable*. London, 1887, 1898.

Brockett, John. *A Glossary of North Country Words*. Newcastle upon Tyne, 1825.

Browne, Thomas. *Union Dictionary*. London, 1810.

Buck, Charles. *A Theological Dictionary*. Philadelphia, 1835.

Bullokar, John. *An English Expositor of the Hardest Words Used in Our Language*. London, 1616.

Burhans, Hezekiah. *Nomenclature and Expositor*. London, 1833.

Carr, William. *The Dialect of Craven in the West-Riding of the County of York*. London, 1828.

Chambers, Ephraim. *Cyclopædia of Arts and Sciences*. London, 1727–51.

Chope, R. Pearse. *The West-Somerset Word-book*. London, 1891.

Clapin, Sylva. *A New Dictionary of Americanisms*. New York, 1902.

Cockeram, Henry. *Interpreter of Hard English Words*. London, 1623.

Colange, A. *A Universal Dictionary of English Language, Science, Literature, and Art*. Philadelphia, 1871.

Cole, R. E. G. *Glossary of the Words in Use in South-West Lincolnshire*. London, 1886.

Coles, Elisha. *An English Dictionary Explaining the Difficult Terms*. London, 1713.

Cope, William H. *A Glossary of Hampshire Words and Phrases*. London, 1883.

Cotgrave, Randle. *Dictionary of French and English*. London, 1611.

Coxe, John Redman. *The Philadelphia Medical Dictionary*. Philadelphia, 1817.

Coxe, Richard. *A Pronouncing Dictionary*. London, 1813.

Crabb, George. *A Dictionary of General Knowledge*. New York, 1830.

Craik, George. *The English of Shakespeare: A Philological Commentary*. Boston, 1886.

Dartnell, George, and Goddard, Edward. *A Glossary of Words Used in Wiltshire*. London, 1893.

Davies, T. Lewis. *A Supplemental English Glossary*. London, 1881.

De Vere, M. Schele. *Americanisms: The English of the New World*. New York, 1872.

Dickinson, William. *Additional Supplement to the Cumberland Glossary*. London, 1881.

Donald, James. *Chambers's Etymological Dictionary of the English Language*. London, 1877.

Douce, Francis. *Illustrations of Shakespeare and of Ancient Manners*. London, 1807.

Dunglison, Robley. *A Dictionary of Medical Science*. Philadelphia, 1844, 1857.

Dunton, John. *Dunton's Ladies' Dictionary, Being a General Entertainment for the Fair Sex*. London, 1694.

Dyce, Alexander. *A Glossary to the Works of Shakespeare*. London, 1902.

Dyche, Thomas, and Pardon, William. *A New General English Dictionary*. London, 1740.

Dyer, T. F. Thiselton. *Folk-Lore of Shakespeare*. New York, 1884.

Easther, Alfred. *A Glossary of the Dialect of Almondbury and Huddersfield*. London, 1883.

Elworthy, Frederic T. *The West Somerset Word-Book*. London, 1888.

Falconer, William. *An Universal Dictionary of the Marine*. London, 1769.

Farmer, John. *Americanisms—Old and New*. London, 1889.

Farmer, John. *Vocabula Amatoria: A French-English Dictionary of Erotica*. London, 1896.

Farmer, John, and Henley, W. E. *Slang and Its Analogues*. London, 1890–1904.

Fennell, Charles A. M. *The Stanford Dictionary of Anglicised Words and Phrases*. London, 1892.

Fenning, Daniel. *The Royal English Dictionary . . . of the English Language*. London, 1775.

Forby, Robert. *The Vocabulary of East Anglia*. London, 1830.

Fosbroke, Thomas. *The Encyclopædia of Antiquities and Elements of Archæology*. London, 1843.

Fraser, Edward, and Gibbons, John. *Soldier and Sailor Words and Phrases*. London, 1925.

Fuller, Thomas. *The Worthies of England*. London, 1662.

Gepp, Edward. *The Essex Dialect Dictionary*. London, 1923.

Graham, H. G. *Social Life in Scotland in the Eighteenth Century*. London, 1899.

Grant, William. *Scottish National Dictionary*. Edinburgh, 1941.

Grimshaw, William. *The Ladies' Lexicon and Parlour Companion, Containing Nearly Every Word in the English Language . . . .* Philadelphia, 1854.

Grose, Francis. *The Classical Dictionary of the Vulgar Tongue*. London, 1796.

Grose, Francis. *A Provincial Glossary*. London, 1811.

Grove, George. *A Dictionary of Music and Musicians*. London, 1902.

Haliburton, Thomas. *Nature and Human Nature*. London, 1855.

Halliwell, James. *Dictionary of Archaic and Provincial Words*. London, 1855.

Hargrave, Basil. *Origins and Meanings of Popular Phrases and Names*. London, 1925.

Harman, H. *The Buckinghamshire Dialect*. London, 1929.

Harman, Thomas. *A Caveat or Warening for Common Cursetors*. London, 1567.

Haydn, Joseph. *Dictionary of Dates and Universal Reference*. London, 1841.

Herford, C. H. *Notes on the Works of Shakespeare*. New York, 1902.

Heslop, R. O. *A Glossary of Words Used in the County of Northumberland*. London, 1892–94.

Hexham, Henry. *Groot-Worden-Boeck: A Large Netherdutch and English Dictionarie*. N.p.,1648.

Hoblyn, Richard. *A Dictionary of Terms Used in Medicine*. Philadelphia, 1859.

Holloway, William. *A General Dictionary of Provincialisms*. Lewes, Sussex, 1838.

Hone, William. *Year Book of Daily Recreation and Information*. London, 1832.

Hotten, John Camden. *The Slang Dictionary*. London, 1887.

Hunter, Joseph. *Hallamshire Glossary*. London, 1829.

Hunter, Robert. *The Encyclopædic Dictionary*. Philadelphia, 1894.

Hyamson, Albert. *A Dictionary of English Phrases*. London, 1922.

Jackson, Georgina. *Shropshire Word-Book*. London, 1879.

Jamieson, John. *An Etymological Dictionary of the Scottish Language*. Paisley, Scotland, 1879.

Jennings, James. *The Dialect of the West of England, Particularly Somersetshire*. London, 1869.

Johnson, Cuthbert. *The Farmer's Encyclopedia and Dictionary*. N.p., 1844.

Johnson, Samuel. *Dictionary of the English Language*. London, 1755.

Jones, Stephen. *A General Pronouncing and Explanatory Dictionary*. London, 1818.

Judges, A. V. *Glossary from the Elizabethan Underworld*. New York, 1930.

Junius, Adrian. *Nomenclator, translated by John Higgins*. London, 1585.

Kennett, White. "A Manuscript Collection of Provincial Words." N.p., circa 1700.

Kersey, John. *A New English Dictionary*. London, 1772.

Knight, Edward. *The Practical Dictionary of Mechanics*. London, 1874, 1884.

Lawson, Robert. *Upton-on-Severn Words and Phrases*. London, 1884.

Littré, Émile. *Dictionary of the French Language*. Paris, 1863–77.

Lloyd, Edward. *Encyclopædic Dictionary*. London, 1895.

Long, W. H. *A Dictionary of the Isle of Wight Dialect*. London, 1886.

Losh, James. *A Manuscript Collection of North Country Words*. London, 1783.

Low, Sidney, and Pulling, F. S. *The Dictionary of English History*. London,1904.

Lowsley, B. *A Glossary of Berkshire Words and Phrases*. London, 1888.

Lyons, Daniel. *The American Dictionary of the English Language*. New York, 1897.

Mackay, Charles. *A Dictionary of Lowland Scotch*. London, 1888.

Mackay, Charles. *Lost Beauties of the English Language*. London, 1874.

Mactaggart, John. *Scottish Gallovidian Encyclopedia*. London, 1824.

Marsh, George P. *Lectures on the English Language*. New York, 1863.

Mathews, Mitford. *Dictionary of Americanisms*. Chicago, 1956.

Mathews, William. *Words: Their Use and Abuse*. Chicago, 1884.

Mayhew, Henry. *London Labour and the London Poor*. London, 1861.

Minshew, John. *The Guide into Tongues*. London, 1627.

Moore, J. J. *British Mariner's Vocabulary*. London, 1805.

Morgan, W. E. T. *Radnorshire Words*. London, 1881.

Müller, Max. *The Science of Language*. New York, 1861, 1863.

Murray, James, et al. *A New English Dictionary on Historical Principles*. Oxford, 1888–1928.

Nares, Robert. *A Glossary [of] the Works of English Authors*. London, 1859.

*Naval Encyclopedia*. N.p., 1884.

Northall, G. F. *Folk-Phrases of Four Counties (Gloucestershire, Staffordshire, Warwickshire, and Worcestershire)*. London, 1894.

Ogilvie, John. *The Comprehensive English Dictionary*. London, 1865.

Onions, C. T. *A Shakespeare Glossary*. Oxford, 1911.

Parker, Angelina. *Supplement to the Glossary of Words Used in Oxfordshire*. London, 1881.

Parrish, W. D., and Shaw, W. F. *A Dictionary of the Kentish Dialect and Provincialisms*. London, 1887.

Patterson, William H. *A Glossary of Words in Use in the Counties of Antrim and Down*. London, 1880.

Peacock, Edward. *A Glossary of Words Used in the Wapentakes of Manley and Corringham, Lincolnshire*. London, 1877.

Pegge, Samuel the Elder. *An Alphabet of Kenticisms*. London, 1735–36.

Pegge, Samuel the Younger. *Anecdotes of the English Language*. London, 1844.

Pegge, Samuel the Younger. *Supplement to Grose's Provincial Glossary*. London, 1814.

*Penny Cyclopædia of the Society for the Diffusion of Useful Knowledge*. London, 1833–43.

Percy, Thomas. *Reliques of Ancient Poetry*. London, 1886.

Phillips, Edward. *The New World of English Words*. London, 1706.

Phin, John. *The Shakespeare Cyclopædia and New Glossary*. New York, 1902.

Pickering, John. *A Vocabulary Peculiar to the United States*. Boston, 1816.

Plot, Robert. *The Natural History of Oxfordshire*. London, 1677.

Rastell, William. *Exposicions of the Termes of the Lawes*. London, 1624, 1641.

Ray, John. *A Collection of English Words*. London, 1674–91.

Richardson, Charles. *A New Dictionary of the English Language*. London, 1837.

Robinson, C. Clough. *A Glossary of Mid-Yorkshire*. London, 1876.

Robinson, Francis K. *A Glossary of Words Used in Whitby*. London, 1876.

Scott, William. *A Dictionary of the English Language*. London, 1791.

Sheridan, Thomas. *Dictionary of the English Language*. London, 1789.

Shipley, Joseph. *Dictionary of Early English*. New York, 1955.

Simmonds, Peter. *A Dictionary of Trade Products*. London, 1858.

Skeat, Walter. *Etymological Dictionary*. Oxford, 1879–82.

Skeat, Walter. *Glossarial Index from Piers the Plowman*. Oxford, 1923.

Skeat, Walter. *A Glossary of Tudor and Stuart Words*. Oxford, 1914.

Skeat, Walter. *A Student's Pastime*. Oxford, 1896.

Smith, A. H. *Odhams Dictionary of the English Language*. London, 1946.

Smyth, William. *Sailor's Word-Book*. London, 1867.

Spurdens, W. T. *The Vocabulary of East Anglia*. London, 1840.

Sternberg, Thomas. *The Dialect and Folk-Lore of Northamptonshire*. London, 1851.

Stormonth, James. *Dictionary of the English Language*. Edinburgh, 1884.

Stow, John. *A Survay of London*. London, 1598.

Stroud, F. *The Judicial Dictionary of Words and Phrases*. London, 1890.

Sutton, Edward. *North Lincolnshire Words*. London, 1881.

*Sydenham Society Lexicon of Medicine and Allied Sciences*. London, 1889.

Taylor, Francis. *The Folk-Speech of South Lancashire*. London, 1901.

Taylor, Joseph. *Antiquitates Curiosae*. London, 1819.

Thoresby, Ralph. *A Glossary of Yorkshire Words*. London, 1718.

Thornton, Richard. *An American Glossary*. London, 1912.

Tooke, John Horne. *The Diversions of Purley*. London, 1840.

Traynor, Michael. *The English Dialect of Donegal: A Glossary*. Dublin, 1953.

Trench, Richard Chenevix. *A Select Glossary of English Words Used Formerly in Senses Different from Their Present*. London, 1859–60.

Tyrwhitt, Thomas. *The Poetical Works of Geoffrey Chaucer*. London, 1871.

Vaux, James H. *A New and Comprehensive Vocabulary of the Flash Language*. London, 1812.

Walker, John. *A Critical Pronouncing Dictionary and Expositor of the English Language*. Edinburgh, 1835.

Walsh, William. *Handy-Book of Literary Curiosities*. Philadelphia, 1900.

Warrack, Alexander. *A Scots Dialectic Dictionary*. London, 1911.

Webster, Noah. *An American Dictionary of the English Language*. New York, 1828; Springfield, Massachusetts, 1864.

Webster, Noah. *A Compendious Dictionary of the English Language*. Hartford, Connecticut, 1806.

Wedgwood, Hensleigh. *A Dictionary of English Etymology*. New York, 1878.

Weekley, Ernest. *An Etymological Dictionary of the English Language*. London, 1921.

Wentworth, Harold. *The American Dialect Dictionary*. New York, 1944.

Whitney, William. *The Century Dictionary*. New York, 1889.

Wilkinson, John. *Leeds Dialect Glossary and Lore*. London, 1924.

Wilson, A. J. *A Glossary of Terms of the Stock Exchange*. New York, 1895.

Wise, J. R. *The New Forest: Its History and Its Scenery*. London, 1883.

Worcester, Joseph. *A Dictionary of the English Language*. Boston, 1881.

Wright, Joseph. *The English Dialectic Dictionary*. London, 1896–1905.

Wright, Thomas. *Dictionary of Obsolete and Provincial English*. London, 1857.

Yule, Henry. *Hobson-Jobson: A Glossary of Colloquial Indian Words and Phrases*. London, 1886.

term signifying an order, decree. *Abandon* means properly to go away from your general

**rtion** The birth of a child before due time. (John Bullokar, 1616) ❖Miscarriage in women.

ealing off secretly. (E. Cobham Brewer, 1887) ❖To hide away; to conceal anything [1600s–early

21) **absurd** Musically, inharmonious, jarring, out-of-tune; adaptation of Latin *surdus*, inharm

*absurd* sound." (*Janua Linguarum*, 1617) cf. *tune up* **accolade** A ceremony used in conferrir

being the present method; hence, the blow itself. (William Whitney, 1889) ❖From Latin *ad*, to

e to mean a specific part, the measure still varied, until it was fixed by statute. (John Brockett,

**cture** The Eastern method of bleeding, by striking needles into any pained part. (John Red

'ly in poetry. (Edward Lloyd, 1895) ❖It is difficult to trace the exact motives which induced the

To wonder at; to be affected with slight surprise. In New England, particularly in Maine, this wo

dent." (M. Schele De Vere, 1872) **admittance** Of high fashion; admitted into the best co

m great freedom is allowed. The allusion is to an obsolete custom called *admission*, by which a

nited States, not solely applied to a violator of the marriage vows. It is also used, instead of *adulte*

**nturer** Originally all who belonged to a company of merchants united for the discovery ar

the *Merchant Adventurers*. (Edward Lloyd, 1895) **advertisement** Information. (John Phi

ander Dyce, 1902) **advice** Reflection. "My Lord Bassanio, upon more *advice*, hath sent you t

children. (James Murray et al., 1888–1928) cf. *abortion, posthumous* **after-life** The subsequen

Y *in Prelude*, c. 1805) **aftermath** That which comes and grows after mowing. (Samuel Pegg

space of time containing one hundred years. (John Kersey, 1772) cf. *century, world* **aim** Aim,

ure of the mind, which is very nearly its meaning [in] "I have some *aim*." *Julius Caesar*. (Georg

g all curves and windings. The term originated in the [American] West, where the surface of

o mean the most direct road from one point to another. (Sylva Clapin, 1902) ❖To take the air

grades that in the New World are rendered possible by the vast expanse of unbroken level. T

retended art of transmuting other metals into gold, but it was often used to express itself a certa

rne out by reality, frequently underlay the earlier uses of the word. (Richard Chenevix Trench,

**nate** To transfer one's title of property to another. . . . Whilst the feudal law existed in full fo

d tenements to another contrary to law, as a punishment, forfeited them altogether. (Edward L

Latin *amare*, to love. (James Murray et al., 1888–1928) ❖A man who makes a living by playing

g agreement with each of two antagonistic parties. (Edward Lloyd, 1895) cf. *dexterity, left-hand*

Rome, it was customary some time before an election came on for the candidates to go round t